Joyce!
What a long strange trip its been — yu frind, sister, comrade Ty

Sisters of Pain

An Ethnography of Young Women Living in Secure Care

Leon Fulcher and Aliese Moran

2015

The
CYC-Net
PRESS

Sisters of Pain

An Ethnography of Young Women Living in Secure Care

CYC-Net Press
An imprint of Pretext Publishing
P.O. Box 23199, Claremont 7735 SOUTH AFRICA
www.pretext.co.za • cycnetpress@pretext.co.za

Dedication

Aliese wishes to dedicate this work to her mother who has shared both wisdom and unconditional love; and to her children – Chelsea and Schuyler – who have always been precious angels.

Leon dedicates this work to his grandchildren – Jacob, Luke, Caitlin and Harley – for nurturing steep learning curves about the value of quality care with loving carers.

The Fox explained to The Little Prince,
"It is only with the heart that one can see rightly; what is essential is invisible to the eye".

Antoine de Saint-Exupery, 1943, Chapter 21, p.60

Contents

Preface

I hurt myself today
To see if I still feel
I focus on the pain
The only thing that's real

– from *Hurt* by Trent Reznor, sung by Johnny Cash
as one of his last recordings

This book is unique in my experience. The reader needs to be prepared for a psycho-emotional journey into self which will confront your beliefs, values and perceptions in personally and professionally challenging ways. The real authors of this text are the young women, many just girls, who give voice to their pain, often in a raw and disturbing manner. This is not a book for anyone who is not prepared to accompany these girls, their family members and their workers into the "heart of darkness". But it is also a book about hope, compassion and spiritual resilience.

The first story is written by Jenette, who sings the blues as eloquently as any jazz singer I have ever heard, and yet in a manner more gripping in its *a cappella* form, without the softening overlays of guitars and saxophones. Jenette gives the book its title – "Sisters of Pain"– and the pain of these young women flows through these pages as it does throughout their young lives.

My own experience of young people in the child welfare and juvenile corrections "systems" is that ALL of them suffer deep and profound pain, psycho-emotional pain which can become invisible to those around them. What family members, friends and child welfare workers observe is "acting out", "delinquent", "maladjusted" or "bad" behaviour, and we can become insensitive to what lies behind and underneath the surface. As a result of seeing too many workers "glossing over" the pain of the children and youths with whom they were working, and reading too many books on "troubled and troubling children" that left their pain hidden and largely unaddressed, I coined the term "pain-based behaviour" in an attempt to unveil this basic reality of the lives of young people in care (Anglin, 2002).

Young people in our "care systems" throughout the world have suffered unspeakable (or at least often unspoken) traumas, losses, violence and neglectfulness which interfere (sometimes in what seem to us as bizarre ways) with their growth into personhood and even the formation of healthy pathways in their brains. The central challenge of care work – which to be worthy of the name must involve at its core the formation of direct, emotional and reciprocally meaningful relationships – is to respond sensitively and effectively to pain and pain-based behaviour. To do this reasonably well, we need to be sufficiently healthy, self-aware and communicative with others (e.g. supervisors and co-workers), as this can be dangerous territory. These hurting young people are usually clever, sometimes seductive, often experienced and generally desperate enough to ensnare the naïve or unsuspecting "do-gooder" in their sticky webs.

At the same time, these are children of the Creator (however we may understand this great mystery), and as Aliese and these young women remind us, they too have souls which embody infinite potential. The stories told in this book are of "lost souls" who are desperate to discover their way (as we all are), to move from being victims of fate to becoming shapers of their own destinies. Leon and Aliese brilliantly connect their own personal and professional perspectives with these young women's accounts in a masterful feat of compassion and generosity, born of a committed and messy struggle to serve the best interests of these "sisters".

It is a paradox of group residential care that in an artificial and non-normative setting, young people can often develop a sense of belonging, perhaps for the first time. Being free, at least to some degree, of daily fear, abuse and demeaning reactions, young people can experience a sense of being respected, a sense of being cared for, a sense of self-worth, a sense of competence, and a sense of their own potential (amongst many other things) in a new way of living.

Several features make this text a compelling read and a powerful tool for learning. First, the stories and poems of the young women give voice to their deepest thoughts, emotions and aspirations. These are voices too often missing from the child welfare literature. In parallel, we can trace the struggles of the care workers, social worker and some of the parents and others who share in different ways some of the residents' life spaces. Then, following this "tango of perspectives", we get to hear the reflective voice of Aliese, one of the young residents herself, who speaks with the benefit of shared experience matured over four decades of subsequent learning and post-incarceration living. Finally, Leon offers a rich smorgasbord of ideas, strategies and tools that help youth workers and social workers develop their capacities to offer therapeutic support for young people struggling to find themselves – dazed and confused – in our child welfare, mental health and corrections systems.

I found I could not read this text from beginning to end in a single sitting. It would be like trying to eat an entire restaurant menu in one meal. This resource lends itself very well to inclusion in an educational course, or as the focus of a care work training program. It is perhaps the next best thing to actually working "on the floor" in an intensive residential setting, including having the benefit of good on-site supervision. Many core professional topics and issues such as children's rights, boundaries, routines, assessment, rhythms of care, developmental assets, self-awareness and corporate parenting are explored and clarified with the benefit of practice-based evidence. The rich and highly relevant reference list provides excellent direction for further study. I want to express my appreciation to Leon, Aliese, all of the young women and others who contributed to this amazing resource. I hope this book finds a place in every social work, youth work or child and youth care program on the planet.

Prof. James P. Anglin, PhD
School of Child and Youth Care
University of Victoria, BC, Canada

Leon's Foreword

This volume was written for young men and women seeking professional careers as social workers or youth workers in direct practice with children, young people and families involved with the Child Welfare and Youth Justice systems. It was written specifically for students engaged in the second half of their professional studies in colleges and universities, after completion of foundation level studies. The volume will also be of interest to recent graduates or new entrants without qualifications – including foster carers – who are already working with challenged and challenging young people in out-of-home care.

North America in the 1970s provided the historical, social and cultural context upon which this volume developed. Aliese provides a more detailed summary of such influences in her Introductory comments.

Readers will find this volume quite unlike most coursework texts. Some may find it a challenging read as it seeks to give voice to 16 young women in secure care at the 'end of the line' in the Child Welfare and Youth Justice systems. We believe those preparing to work with children and young people in out-of-home care need to enter the messy worlds as they exist for these youths and their families – moving beyond their own personal comfort zones and abstract theoretical models examined during college and university lectures.

A stimulus for this volume came whilst sorting through a box of old case notes gathered a lifetime ago during my employment as a Psychiatric Social Worker assigned to a state institution for teenage girls in the USA. With the enthusiasm of youth, a hand-picked team of carers, teachers and social workers back then were tasked with transforming part of the institution – an historic old youth justice secure unit – into a therapeutic community for 16 female residents. The girls had been assigned by Juvenile Courts to an Assessment Center. Then, after assessment and when sufficient 'progress' had been made, the girls were transferred to institutional campuses for younger and older teenagers, a variety of group homes and potential foster homes. The campus for older teenage girls where these 16 girls were placed included 2 secure units (populations separated on the basis of maturity), 7 open campus cottages, a high school, administration and professional support, as well as full recreational facilities.

The caseload of a Psychiatric Social Worker included 16 young women committed by the Juvenile Courts and assigned to one of the residential cottages in the institution, along with 2 or 3 additional cases involving young women either on extended furlough or AWOL status. In seeking to create an ethnography that shares something of the daily and weekly life in a secure unit for teenage girls some four decades ago, the reader is introduced to 16 young women whose stories are shared in the room-assigned chapters that follow. Three of the young women were of Native American ancestry, three were Afro-American, one was Hispanic and the rest were Caucasian.

The human ethics associated with fashioning this ethnography have received careful scrutiny since standard ethical protocols requiring informed consent and release of information within a formally recognised research project could not be followed in the decades since my professional notes were written. After graduating as an MSW qualified psychiatric social worker, and as part of my own professional development, I continued to use the technique of process recording in journals over the years to strengthen my recall and to prepare myself for on-going work with my clients. This was not a requirement of the job nor were these notes part of the official case records. I consider these notes to be part of the professional record of my experience. I have always been careful not to include in my journal anything that would reveal my clients' identity. My supervisors at the time knew of my personal professional record-keeping, and I shared notes with them from time to time as these were useful in our work together as a therapeutic team, though not part of the case recording system. These people agreed to my keeping a record of my professional experience in this way and accepted that my journaling did not jeopardize the confidence of the clients nor risk exposure of their identities. They also knew of my aspirations to one day share the stories of young women who experienced residential group care services 'at the end of the line'. Four decades on, we know of only one of those supervisors and managers who is still living, playing golf, far away from the events written about here.

Few of the services which featured in the lives of the *Sisters of Pain* now exist. The child welfare legislation and systems have been transformed into child protection and youth justice services. All cases are still processed through the Juvenile Courts which operate at County levels. Names of all who feature in the *Sisters of Pain* have been assigned pseudonyms and geographic locations have been altered. As participant observers in this ethnography, both authors share advocacy for ethical standards which honour the memory of the *Sisters of Pain*.

No claims are made – either by myself or our team of carers – about being infallible youth care experts with all the answers. Despite my co-author's more than flattering remarks about my abilities as a social worker, my own inexperience and naiveté are all too evident. However, it must be said that the team of men and women gathered together in this unit was highly gifted in many ways, and many of the carers were able to make closer connections with some of these young women than anyone in their past.

When reflecting back on that time, it is staggering to think of the complexity and trauma associated with placing 16 young women together – each with huge amounts of pain, challenge and distress – locked up in a secure unit. At the same time, I am reminded of the love, compassion and skills shown by the men and women who worked long hours, every day, trying to assist these young women create new lives for themselves through trying to make sense of lives they had lived.

New girls arrived at this institution from an Assessment Center on a Thursday afternoon. Diaries were cleared that afternoon each week so that new arrivals could receive as much time as they needed to talk about this life crisis of entering a lock-up facility. Life stories leading to placement in the secure unit were an essential starting point. 75 percent of girls entering this secure unit had spent time in other institutions, often moving around the Child Welfare System for up to 4-6 years until 'aging out' at age 18. Girls' progress was reviewed every week, with formal Review Boards at the start, and at three month intervals thereafter. Most young women would move from the secure unit into an open-cottage setting and attend campus school before returning to the community on parole.

Jenette's short story about life as a teenage prostitute reminded me of how rarely social workers or those entering the child and youth care field are provided with educational materials using the voices of young people, or voices of carers living most closely with challenging and challenged young people during significant times in their lives in out-of-home care. The book starts with Jenette because her verbal and writing skills are highly accessible, with many insights akin to those of a wise old woman. Like many of her peers who spent time in "The System", Jenette demonstrates an understanding and an awareness of how she has reached this place in her life.

The idea for this volume was further stimulated by old case notes written about other young women and their care workers during my involvement in their lives before moving overseas. Regardless of the passing of decades and regardless of the location of these incidents, the pain and events experienced by these sixteen young women are universal. Although some themes, such as HIV-Aids, "Crack" and "P" (methamphetamine) are missing from these historic narratives, other challenges for young women in most communities were highlighted, whether they be challenges with sexually-transmitted diseases or with substance abuse, through alcohol, tobacco, cannabis, psychedelics, amphetamines, barbiturates, cocaine or heroin.

The title – Sisters of Pain – was chosen out of respect for Jenette's story and stories of other young women whose childhoods ended prematurely. The Sisters of Pain narratives reinforce Anglin's (2002) claim that pain-based behaviour is central to the lives of most young people living in out-of-home care. Pain-based behaviour was especially prominent amongst these young women, living in secure care administered by the State Child Welfare System at 'the end of the line'. These young women stared at the prospect of an early death, or lengthy periods of their adult lives in the criminal justice or mental health systems. Relationships matter for all young people, but are especially important for those in out-of-home care.

The Sisters of Pain life stories reflect daily life events lived by adults and young people interacting together in and around one State-administered secure unit or life space environment during an intensive eighteen month period. Each young person's story is told – wherever possible – using historic narratives written in her own voice or in the voices of family members and friends. These accounts are supplemented with narratives written by carers and teachers.

Letters from family members and friends are also included where informative, and where disclosure resulted in no harm to either the young women or their family members. As indicated at the start, any identifying information has been removed and cities have been re-named. For ease of identification, the voices of the girls, family members and boyfriends are recorded in italics (with some of their spelling deliberately left intact). Carer and social work voices are located in shaded boxes.

As sadly so often happens, I – the social worker – left this particular employment after two years, and the girls were faced yet again with changes in the people who cared for them. Because I also left the area, my contact with people there almost ceased. However, contact has been maintained over the years with some of the girls and some of the staff. Facebook provided some up-to-date knowledge about outcomes based on fragments of information offered via a network of connections when available.

One major outcome involved the closure of this State institution for older girls. De-institutionalization policies resulted in institutional care provided by the State for non-delinquent girls being phased out, except for the most extreme cases. The authors know little about what happened to most of these young women so it is impossible to report on any "results" that might be attributed to any short-term interventions at the end of their many years of pain. That wasn't our purpose here. Our priority was to give voice to the life stories of young women in secure care, illuminating relationships and daily life events in one particular residential community with 16 young female residents and their out-of-home carers.

Reflections and Commentaries

The *Sisters of Pain* life stories are augmented by a voice rarely encountered in the child welfare literature. One of the young women who lived alongside Jenette and the other secure unit residents in this volume contributes her own reflections – using a contemporary voice – some four decades later. As the mother now of two successful young adult children, as a new grandmother, as an adult daughter caring for an elderly mother, as a Native American activist, as a legal aid professional, as a dog walker and as co-author of this volume, Aliese contributes a personal reflection in her Introduction, at the end of each chapter, and then again at the end of the book, after a short reflection at the end of the volume written by her mother. Aliese first saw these written materials more than forty years after they were written. She had seen some of the material written by and about herself, but nothing else. Her reflections are very enlightening.

In order to make the volume more useable for social workers and youth workers in training, each chapter has a sub-title and ends with a short professional commentary that draws together an eclectic selection of concepts and tools derived from contemporary information about evidence-based assessment and interventions with young people in out-of-home care.

Building on Anglin's (2002) notion of "pain-based behaviour" and Hewitt's (2003) autobiographical methods of a 'looked after kid', the sixteen commentaries have been crafted around the seminal writings of my mentor and friend, Henry Maier (1987) whose work was influential in our thinking then and is still highly relevant today; Trieschman, Whittaker & Brendtro (1969); Brendtro & du Toit (2005); research by the Search Institute about developmental assets (Benson et al, 2006; Fulcher, McGladdery & Vicary, 2011); and foundational work by Garfat (1998) and Garfat & Fulcher (2008; 2011; 2012); in collaboration with Ainsworth (2006); and with Smith & Doran (2013). At the end of each chapter, five questions are offered with the aim of facilitating discussion in staff training, group tutorials or cyber classrooms.

Most importantly, the narratives which follow give evidence for the importance of genuine, healthy, caring relationships, particularly when working with children or young people in out-of-home care. The fundamental need to develop relationships that matter is reinforced, not only by the young women themselves at the time, but also by my friend Aliese and her mother, forty years later.

Professional distance has its place in social work and youth work practice. However, ALL children NEED genuine, healthy, caring relationships with genuine, healthy, caring adults! The development of close, but professional, relationships strikes at the heart of therapeutic care-giving and relational caring.

Aliese's Introduction

My first thoughts are, "How sad that these were the options we had as young women". I have often thought about options, opportunities, consequences and how we perceive what those were yesterday, and what they are today.

For example, a child in any family might get into an argument with a parent and they would have a different set of immediate choices laid before them. That in part, is what defined us as juvenile delinquents, and later helped us to fulfil that destiny. I am not so sure that a child running away from something that is abusive and demeaning to a child, is being delinquent. In the past, I have remembered the stages of putting myself back together. I have forgotten these earlier years, as many years have rolled by since then. I have seen the aftermath of several generations in which to compare all the heart break, broken families, and lives, and finally the learning to forgive through understanding and compassion. I would never have become the woman I am today without the genuine care, love and trust so many people instilled into my life... Well that, and the tools I had earned and learned to use as the apprentice in my life.

Rebellion against identified authority figures in our lives is part of any normal growing-up process, and a daily feature of any family life. I think in part, this sort of division between youth and adults is universal and part of the grand scheme. Somehow in dysfunctional families, this course takes a twisting turn here that changes the lives of everyone involved, including the carers, the social workers and anyone else who touches their lives, as these young women were escorted from their homes and their lives and into institutional living.

Case studies and opinions are just that – but it is so very important to keep reminding one's self that the people in these case studies you will read about are human beings, young women who will be shaping their community, and their world, and have indeed done so. We had hearts that beat and break just like yours. Some would say we were born into this world cursed and at times we all felt that way. Now I perceive these experiences as gifts and challenges in life that we were given to overcome, so that in our turn, we would be able to help and guide those around us in this hurting world.

There were so many influences during those years, and the years to follow. Without going into great detail, or offering a guided tour through history, some of the more significant ideals, changes, and turbulence are highlighted since these affected us *Sisters of Pain* and the system in which we resided. Naturally, viewpoints and opinions about history depend upon our position on the fence.

The influence of music was as great then as it is today. There was a fresh newness to the music, and there was this huge awakening heralded through the music scene. Through the music we questioned everything from war and government brutality, to the existence and purpose of life. We listened to music that had meaning, whether it was the love melodies of the 40s, the Rock-n-Roll of the 50s, the British Invasion, Hard Rock, and Motown scene of the 60s. Those times musically energized our generation. Music has always been an escape for youth, (and very therapeutic too, as we have proven in later years). Music offered a way to ignore our surroundings, but the message was clear: we had a purpose, we had choices, and we were empowered. All we had to do was harness that energy and direct it towards a successful life. That was not an easy task for young people, adults, or the system struggling to cope with the challenges and changes of our turbulent times.

As a nation, the USA was dealing with the Vietnam War in which the "enemy" was never clearly defined. It seemed to be more about nationalism and neo-colonial economics than presenting any real national security threat. Watergate rattled the Nation's consciousness as did Nixon's presidency ending with impeachment. We were involved as youths and were front page, but most of us were a peaceful bunch seeking peace and freedom for our nation, intent on exposing the lies of those profiteering from war. We participated in peaceful protests and sit-in's, leaving school or our homes to attend these national events. There was also THE DRAFT and draft dodgers that divided the country and impacted on Canada. Such themes also divided families as we and our closest friends participated in these political movements and progress.

Later, the war brought the refugees and America was not ready. Many were still emotionally raw after the Japanese Internment. New lines were drawn and no one was really sure where they stood, or where they belonged. Racism was swept out from under the table to become a fundamental issue in law and in all community practices. Blacks were being beaten in the rural countryside, university students were shot on campus, Indian women were being raped, and young women on the run – including those whose cultural identity was not immediately apparent – were considered White trash by predatory males.

The times also brought an assortment of "Movements" that affected, influenced, got us thinking, and changed our lives in one way or another. There was some violence such as Kent State, and also very active were the Chicago Seven, the Black Panthers and AIM – American Indian Movement. Those of us who were of mixed blood and who had met other Native Americans in other foster homes, diagnostic centers and orphanages, really connected to Indian Rights. We were fighting for our fishing rights and Indian Child rights, so there was turmoil in Indian Country, as well as America.

Feminism was winking its eye and the birth of the ERA finally arrived. So here you had women involved, regardless of the political left or right, rich or poor, Black, White, Asian, Indian and Hispanic strongly united, probably for the first time in America as a powerful front. That brought on the "Contraceptive Liberation" and hand in hand with that came all the STD's because no one knew any better, and early teenage pregnancies. Later all the fallout helped to institute Women's Health.

Women were also united in that they could reach out for help against their abusers, be it physical or other. Prior to this time, there really was no safe outlet and medically speaking, a woman had no rights either. VAWA had not been born.

The Drug Scene was ON and had been for a solid couple of generations, in addition to the martini scene and happy hour crowd. It was a time when everyone was getting high on something, legal or illegal. I think the young people who are described in this book, including myself, were just along for the ride and were trying to escape all the chaos that adults had created. We were still just kids. I mean everybody was going through some kind of changes or awakening, struggle, involved in some aspect of the turmoil of the times. Everyone's world had been turned upside down or questioned, and the rules did not seem to apply any longer.

I am sure all of these evolving spins kept troubled youths in a whirlwind of exciting choices of mentors and superheroes, and gave us a real quick tour of reality as everyone tried on their grown up shoes. Those who were lucky enough to make it through to the other side alive are probably very strong and powerful women in their own right. I am sure they are probably better for their stay at this particular High-Security Unit, because of the type of structured program, care and communication that occurred there. I mean these folks stepped way out of their comfort zones, took tremendous risks, got somewhat personally involved, truly cared for and loved us girls. We knew it, we sensed it and we clung to it for our only salvation and escape from an otherwise condemned life. I know I was lucky, blessed, whatever one may call it, but I was also provided with powerful tools that taught me what the real values are in life.

Time and wisdom have surely given us all a different perspective now. Under today's circumstances, these opinions and evaluations of the carers would be different. As a people, they have evolved with the times too. Values, enmeshed cultural differences, tolerance, and a fuller understanding of people as a whole society have changed over these years. I think that it is important to re-evaluate the process and to take risks, and accept change because we are evolving as a species and we do not have all the answers, yet.

We were in the middle of it and it was an exciting time to be alive, and also to witness the progress and good changes that were coming about in the world. Up to this point many children had been failed by parents and family members, most adults, and certainly a system that didn't have all the right answers and often caused more damage than good to "troubled teens" over time. One would never think back NOW and make those same choices. I would hope not. The people we are now would not have made those choices. At that time, it was all we had.

To understand *Sisters of Pain*, you must read this with your heart, an open mind, and with the mind's eye of a child. We were tough, but still afraid of what we might do, in our fight for survival, identity, and search for love.

Room 1
Jenette – *Making Connections*

I was only fifteen at the time all this took place and I'm sixteen now, so I remember it all very well.

I'd had it up to my neck with my mother, the welfare people, the project I lived in and the constant demands for money from my Negro boyfriend. So I said "To hell with you all" and left one night with two of my girlfriends.

We walked down the main street to a chicken stand. We had knives concealed under our clothing, planning to rob someone. They went inside and me being my usual poor self couldn't buy anything, so I waited outside.

Ramona came back before Spanky did so we stood in the cold night air, laughing and talking. "Did you see the fine dudes that just went by?" Ramona asked me.

"No, where?"

"In a red car."

"Oh."

Finally Spanky came back and we stood talking about whether to go get high or not. If we didn't, that meant having to go back home and I didn't want to do that at all.

"Shit, let's just get a ride with some fine dudes so we can get high," I said, being my usual greedy self.

"What if they want to keep us though?" Spanky asked like an idiot.

"You're a chick shit, no one gon hurt you when we got knives!" Ramona declared looking evil.

A car full of dudes went by and honked their horn, so we waved at them. They made a screeching U-turn and came back. The driver was about twenty-three. He was also drunk and acting real crazy, so were the other dudes he had with him.

I backed away and so did Ramona and Spanky who were also scared and wishing they were at home. Even though we were on a busy street, that didn't help our fright.

"Say little mama, come and talk to me," the big one said to Ramona,

who looked like a scared rabbit.

"Say sugar, I like you, come talk to me," the driver said addressing me. I tried to play it cool and walked over slowly as possible, not knowing what to say now that I was confronted with the situation.

I leaned against the car and said rather dumbly, "Huh?" He eyed me sullenly and smiled slowly. "You sure looken fine baby, I want you for myself."

"Oh. Why?"

"Baby, we gon make us a palace in the sky, can you understand that?"

"I understand anything that needs to be understood," I answered dryly.

"Come on, get in," he said, giving me a look that made me very uncomfortable.

"No, that's okay, I'll walk."

"Shit woman, come on, I like you!"

"I can't leave my friends here."

"Tell them to get in, we can drop them off and then have a ball."

"Come on, let's get in," I said to Ramona and Spanky who were waiting patiently.

"No, we're walkin."

"Shit, come on!"

"Nope, we're walkin."

I couldn't decide what to do so I looked helplessly at the driver.

"Come on, get in, ain't no one gonna hurt you, pretty baby."

"Okay, you two tell Denny I said to fuck it, and don't be running your mouths off telling anybody any thing" I said to Ramona and Spanky, scared to death but trying to act as brave as I could.

"Sure Jenette, bye," they said, watching me get into the El Dorado and feeling rich already. "How old are you?" the driver asked, restarting the car and driving down the brightly lit Detroit streets at a higher speed than allowed.

"Seventeen and a half."

"You sure?"

"Of course," I answered, not feeling sure of anything except fear at the moment.

"What's your name?"

"Jenette. Who are you?"

"The one and only Ebony."

"Yeah baby, that is THE Ebony," a dude in the back seat said with a funny smile playing across his dark and handsome face. I look at Ebony. He was really kind of cute and the mink trim on his leather jacket proved he got his money from other sources than a square job.

"You gon stay with me?" he asked making it sound more like a statement than a question.

"Sure, but I have to get my clothes first."

"Okay, where do you live?"

"In the project down by the new school."

I gave him directions and he parked the car around the corner from my shabby house. I snuck inside and much to my feelings of relief, no one was home. I threw everything I owned into some suitcases and ran out the back door.

5 April: Care Worker Notes

Mrs F and I contacted Jenette in her room where she has been using her time away from the resident group to write her life story. As her new Keyworkers, we shared some ground rules which all the staff will abide by during the forthcoming days or weeks. Jenette showed little reaction other than twisting an empty cigarette packet in her hands throughout the entire period. I told her that she and I need a few days to get better acquainted before any heavy counselling would be attempted on my part. She could choose the topic for discussion — all I wanted to do was get some idea of how her mind worked before we could expect to accomplish very much.

We stressed that the time for game playing was behind us now and that we asked little more from her at this stage other than absolute honesty.

We were not interested in anything other than her true feelings and thoughts. Otherwise, it would be a complete waste of time. We were here to help her if she wanted help, would share the knowledge we had gained over many years of hard personal experience, and offer viewpoints which perhaps had not occurred to her.

It was all straight talk and Jenette accepted it as such. At the conclusion of our talk, Jenette gave us several pages of thoughts and feelings she had been writing down ...

"You got plenty of clothes," Ebony said, taking my suitcases and putting them into the trunk.

Once he had them lost in a pile in the trunk, he took me to a club and had me wait in the car while they went inside. A few minutes later a pretty Black girl came out and tapped on the car window. I pushed a button and the window rolled down.

"Hi, I'm your sister, welcome to the family," she said, leaning against the car and smiling sweetly.

"Oh, hi, ah, nice to meet you," I managed to mumble, all the while not sure of whether I wanted to get out and run or sit there and see what would happen next. She left and dear old Ebony came back, smiling and talking loudly with Marcus and Terry.

"Did you like her?" Ebony asked hopefully.

"Yeah, she seemed pretty nice."

"She's my other lady, her name's Anita."

"Oh, she is?" I asked, not knowing what he expected me to say.

"Yeah, you two will get along fine."

I didn't know what to say or do next, so I just sat there and played with my rings.

"You hungry?"

"No, I ate a little while ago."

"Pretty soon, Anita will be off work, oh, here she comes now," Ebony said. He seemed pretty nice, but Lord I was scared to death! Anita got into the car and sat next to me. The red haired girl – she came back and sat in the back and when I was introduced to her, I almost said "Nice meeting you, scare crow." She eyed me as the others had done and I took an immediate dislike to her.

Nobody did a thing or said a thing. Ebony drove with the radio blasting on the soul station and my ears felt like they would blow away any minute if he didn't turn it down. But he didn't and my ears continued hurting.

Finally, Ebony, Marcus and Monte started talking. I thought it was a bunch of jive but I didn't say so. We drove down a dark, bumpy road and Ebony started cursing the "White man" for not paving the roads. Since I was White, I gave him a dirty look and accidentally on purpose elbowed him.

"Oh, sorry," I said quickly, not wanting him to know I did it on purpose.

"It's alright, baby." He parked the car and we got out and went inside the house. The others went on to their own house which was about two feet away. The house was nice but slightly messy. It was then that I discovered Anita had four little kids. "Oh brother, just what I always wanted," I thought, getting slightly irked.

"Where can I sleep?" I asked, seeing only the couch was available.

"With us in the bed," Ebony said with that sly grin I was already used to. I almost choked. In a bed with him and another woman, is he crazy? I wondered.

I undressed quickly, not wanting him to see me naked. I put on a nightgown and robe and got into the double bed. Anita got in the middle between me and Ebony, which was fine with me. I didn't want him trying to do anything with her in the bed. I went straight to sleep and woke up to find Anita with her hand in my underwear. I was terrified, so I pretended to be asleep and turned over.

"She still asleep?" Ebony asked Anita.

"Yeah, I wanna fuck". I almost cried when I found that she was serious. Ebony got on top of her and away they went, moaning and groaning with me tryin to ignore them.

I felt a hand on my breast and one creeping into my underwear, so I did my fake sleep act again – my mistake. This time Ebony decided to have some fun with me, thinking I was asleep. He pulled off my underwear and away he went with me while Anita played with my hair.

I guess I felt like a corpse not doing anything back, so he left me alone and went back to Anita (bless her soul). I don't know how I did it but I finally went back to sleep and didn't wake up until noon.

I put on my bathrobe and asked Anita if I could use the iron. "Sure, you live here too," was her sweet reply. She was awfully pretty but I remembered the night before, so I didn't get too overjoyed.

I ironed my pants while she dressed and put on make-up while Ebony shaved. I didn't have a top to match the red platform shoes or white pants I had on so Anita gave me a real cute red shorty top with a sweater to match. I thanked her and she seemed real pleased with herself. "How you gonna fix your hair?" she asked in a real sweet voice that made me sick.

"I don't know, it's ugly anyway" I said looking at the dyed black mass of curls and friz that was a poor excuse for hair.

"Well, I have a blonde wig you can wear."

"You don't mind?" I asked, feeling real dumb.

"No, come on, I'll help you." She put the gypsy-styled wig on me and some false eye lashes. "There, you look real cute!" she said, making me feel two or three at the very oldest. I looked in the mirror and it did look good if I do say so myself. But I certainly did not look like the Jenette I had been the night before.

6 April: Care Worker Notes

Jenette has started a report to be presented at her Planning Board. There is some straight talk. Also more of her feelings are written down for Mrs F and me to read. While the others were watching the movie tonight, I spent about an hour and a half listening to a review of her life from the time she began getting into trouble (around age 9-10) up to the time she reached the age of 13. This was a non-stop, completely emotionless and confident recital. It was only interrupted at the movie intermission, and a couple of times when I needed some clarification on something I had not completely understood. The subject matter was entirely of her choosing. It's far too early to form any conclusions but already an interesting picture is beginning to take shape. Jenette is a much better talker than I had anticipated. She has no trouble communicating verbally or in writing. I'm already anxious to get going on the next instalment.

Then Anita insisted on putting on my make-up for me so I let her. When she was through at last, I looked in the mirror and I looked even more different. She is good at things like that, but every time she wanted to start in on something worthwhile, Ebony stepped in and wouldn't let her, or me for that matter, I soon found out.

"Thanks alot Anita, do you want to wear something of mine?"

"I'll let you wear my jacket if I can wear yours," she said looking at my white shorty jacket with the fake fur trim. I looked at her white leather midi coat with the real fur trim and decided she was nuts.

"Okay, but yours is a lot prettier though," I said.

"I think yours is," she said and we both laughed. Ebony came back into the bedroom and I tried to ignore him as he swung his penis around teasing Anita.

After a while I said "Where am I going?" I knew Anita hadn't dressed me up for nothing – and most of all I hated not knowing.

"Anita is going to work and I'm gonna buy you a purse and some make-up, maybe some new shoes; you only got two pair?" Ebony asked.

"Yeah."

Ebony dressed while Anita and I cleaned the house. After we were through, we got into the car and left. We dropped off Anita and went on our shopping trip. Everything was fine. He bought me a black leather shoulder purse, make-up, a wig and black leather platform boots.

He showed me off to all his friends and I went with him everywhere for a couple of days. Then he decided he wanted me to be a go-go girl. I knew he was nutty then. Fifteen, and I don't look seventeen, so how can I be lookin twenty-one? Well, he fixed that. He got me four pieces of I.D. including a driver's license, and I don't know how to drive. But they were all under the same name so he said not to worry.

So the next day I found myself in a skimpy royal blue costume, my new boots and a light brown wig styled in a shag, walking up to men in the plush club asking them what they wanted to drink. The men gave me a lot of tips; I probably reminded them of their daughters. Some were so old I might have been their grand-daughter.

Anyway I made good money, but I didn't like to get on a stage and dance like a sex pot with no top on, but those men sure enjoyed it!

Then I got word that my mom was getting Black FBI men to track me down since she knew a white one could not do it because I don't associate with White men unless it's to get their money, but that's as far as it goes.

12 April: Care Worker Notes

I've lost some continuity in working with Jenette since I was assigned security duties last Monday and then again last night, with two days off in between. It was good to see that Jenette remained cooperative and still a more than willing participant in our working relationship. I did think it went far better and smoother than anticipated. Her mother is not that tough when she does not have control of the situation. Jenette and I got together again tonight and covered the remainder of the historical material all the way up to her assignment to the secure unit. I think I am slowly gaining the trust and confidence of Jenette – as evidenced by the fact that she chose my side of the fence against Mama during our 3-way visit. That plus other signs I've picked up along the way. Putting her in the driver's seat and allowing her to steer and control the conversation was, I feel, a good manoeuvre. I have the feeling that the occasions where she was not almost exclusively on the receiving end of conversation-wise were few and far between. At any rate, she has gone almost non-stop during each session thus far. Tomorrow we begin communications which are more two-way, and some interesting pictures are emerging more clearly already.

Ebony found out I was only fifteen and cussed me out good and then he took me home. My mom had three fits when she saw how skinny I had gotten. Hell, what can you expect when the bum never feeds you?

I stayed home overnight, packed up the next day and went back to Ebony's. Anita was so happy she gave me a kiss. I thought she was "funny" myself. I went back to work at my hateful job and got more money than before.

I guess the old bastards missed me. Then I decided to go back to my ex-man Denny. Ebony had fifty fits and said "Go, and don't come back." I left and got to Denny's at midnight. "So Bitch, you decided to come back to your man?"

"Yeah, here I am," I said wearily.

"You wanna get drunk?" he asked eyeing me thoughtfully. I really had changed.

"Yeah, is it Mad Dog?" I asked knowing he had that raunchy wine prepared. I drank most of it and I was so drunk, I couldn't walk. He got crazy and took a stick and beat me with it for leaving him.

I just stumbled into the bedroom and took off my clothes, half crying because I knew my face would be black and blue the next day and so would my back. Denny came in and looked at me standing there naked and crying. "Come on, you know you want me," I said, looking dumb and ready to pass out. He undressed and so much for that, we stayed up half the night.

I was with him two days and he started jabbing needles full of speed into my arms. I lasted a week and then I went back to Ebony's. He had to buy me all new clothes because I had lost so much weight.

I got my job back and started working my ass off to make Ebony happy. Then Anita made a pass at me and I sat there and just laughed. I was wondering how two ladies are supposed to fuck.

Anyway I told Ebony I wanted to leave. "Bitch, are you crazy?" he roared and hit me so hard I fell out of my chair. I felt the throbbing in my eye and knew it was already getting way bigger than it should be.

"No."

"Bitch, do you know you're fuckin with a man?"

"Yes," I said helplessly. Then he took a stick and beat me in my face and back and stomach with it. I couldn't catch my breath long enough to scream or cry, but I knew it hurt like hell.

Don't say "How come the stupid bitch didn't hit him back" because hitting him back is really gonna make him kill you. He finally stopped and I lay on the floor bleeding and finally able to cry. Then he hog tied me and said "Bitch, I should kill you, but I like you."

"Thanks," I muttered. Then I said, "If you go to sleep, you dirty mother fuckin fuck up, you won't wake up ever again, you'll go straight to naughty pimps land".

"Why?" Ebony asked, getting very curious.

"Because I'm gonna kill you!" He laughed and went to bed and left me there on the floor. Anita came home and cussed him out and he told her to shut up and get in bed. I stayed on the floor like that all night, freezing and mad as hell.

Next day he untied me and things were fine until a couple weeks later. I went with his brother-in-law and sister to their house and got high. No fuckin him or even kissing him at all. His lady was there.

But Ebony thought different. He tried to chop my damn fingers off. I was so high, I laughed. Then he beat me worse than the last time. The next day he had the nerve to tell me to go to work. Two black eyes, a fat lip, bruises all over my body and almost unable to breathe through my nose because he had almost broken it and it hurt to just barely touch it.

And the inside of my ears were also black and blue. Ebony had done a good job; he hadn't missed a spot on my body.

I dressed up real nice, took all the extra money I could get and pretended to go to work. I got a twenty dollar loan from my boss and went to Nathan's house. I had a hell of a time getting there because I was so afraid Ebony or one of his goons would see me – then I would have really died.

I finally made it, but Nathan was not at home so I went to the next door neighbour's house. Dorothy opened the door and when a minute of staring at me passed, she screamed. I tried to laugh but it hurt too much.

After a few more minutes, she said "What the hell happened?"

"My ex so called man is crazy."

"Looks that way, you gonna press charges?"

13 April: Care Worker Notes

We talked for an hour tonight, during which time I shared some initial observations as the result of listening to Jenette and observing her for the past week. She was a bit dumbfounded that I had gotten to know her that well in such a short period of time merely by listening to her talk and watching her facial expressions. The areas covered were her views and/or feelings about specific people and also general groups. We have reached a position of trust and understanding now where the words flow easily back and forth during a free interchange of ideas.

I think it would be a good idea for all staff to read what Jenette has written while in her room, in chronological order. There was not a really significant change in what she wrote or how she wrote it until after our 3-way meeting with mother on Friday. Friday's effort is drastically different. Jenette has informed me that she feels her program will be loosened up this coming week. I asked her upon what she based that conclusion. She told me that another resident had told her that she had been told that she would be only staying in her room a half day after the Board meeting next week. I told Jenette that this was a very flimsy basis for her to accurately judge what action, if any, might be taken this coming week. I do feel that a more open life for Jenette is appropriate at this time in view of her positive and cooperative attitude. I do not desire to lose what I have gained thus far merely because Jenette becomes discouraged and figures 'What's the use of making any effort?' At the same time, I feel we need to move slowly – because we still have a lot of ground to cover and probably a good deal of it will be a lot rougher to traverse than what we've travelled until now.

"You's talkin crazy now," I said, sitting down and lighting a cigarette. Wish I felt "Kool" I thought, staring at the brand name of my cigarette.

"Nathan's home now, he's just walkin to the door," Dorothy called from the kitchen.

"Okay, bye," I said, glad to leave before her man came home and saw how ugly I was lookin.

"Bye," she called watching the face I made getting out of the chair. I walked down the steps wondering what Nathan's reaction would be.

"Nathan?" I said, not knowing what else to say.

He looked at me like I was a freak from outer space. "What the hell?" he finally said, not knowing who I was at first.

"It's me, Jenette," I said wishing he would hurry up and open the door.

"Sure and the fuck don't look like you!"

"Thanks a lot pal, can I stay here?"

"Yeah, come on in."

I went inside and plopped my sore butt into a chair. He wanted to know what had happened to me so I told him the story – especially how Anita was "funny".

"Shit, you picked a good pair – Gonna be my lady?" he said all in one breath.

"You know I am," I said thinking "Until I get the hell out of Detroit and get back on my feet". But of course I did not tell him this.

We stayed up all night long, doing the usual thing and the next day Nathan and some of his friends made some plans for us all to go to Chicago. I got some new clothes, since I'd left everything at Ebony's. I hope Anita is having fun wearing them.

Nathan's sister Melina was real sweet and we got along real good. She knew Ebony and hated him. It made me feel good to know that he really was a Bastard.

We left for Chicago on Friday. Lee, Delono, Gwen and her son Don – who was really a girl but she was making him into a punk and "it's real name was Donna".

We were riding in a Coup De Ville and even though it was big, we were all cramped up. We stopped to eat and pick up last minute things in Detroit before we left for good.

20 April: Care Worker Notes

I talked only briefly with Jenette last night and for the first time she showed some uptight, nervous and even despondent signs. Excited and a little nervous about our visit with mother and grandparents for one thing, but that was only a small part of it. Jenette has felt the previous 2 or 3 days gave her little feeling of accomplishment, and thought her progress had ground to a screeching halt. It was hard to believe Jenette showing concern about a 2 or 3 day lack of progress when she has gone months at a time not giving a damn about anything?!

It damn near blew my mind!! I assured Jenette that she had far surpassed anyone's expectations during her first two weeks on program and she could not hope to continue that sort of a spectacular pace continuously. I tried to explain that progress normally proceeds in spurts, with periods in between where gains are consolidated and reinforced. She was relieved but still had something eating on her. So I told her to spit it out and she did. Jenette has been thinking about where she will go after leaving the secure unit and at this point doesn't feel she is handling the uncertainty very well. I said it was too early to be discussing where she might go and that we would carefully consider where she could be most benefited. I would personally like Jenette herself to join with us in making this decision together. Jenette was reassured that careful thought would go in to any future placement and became less agitated. After some chit-chat, the session ended.

I went into a store and bought a gangster hat. While I was looking at the make-up (as if I needed any) someone said "Say, pretty baby, I like your ass".

I jumped, thinking it was Ebony or Denny. I turned around to look, holding my breath. It was not either of them.

As a matter of fact I had never seen this dude before. He sure is cute, I thought looking at him.

"You lookin nice baby, got a man?"

"Yeah," I said regretfully, and the dude knew it too.

"So come be with me, I know how to treat beautiful ladies like you."

Before I could say yes, like I wanted to, Nathan found me and gave me a murderous look. "Come on, Lee wants to go now." I followed him meekly still looking at the man that had spoken to me.

"He your friend?" Nathan asked when we were on the road heading for good old funky Chicago.

"Not really, he just told me I had a nice ass." Nathan gave me a dirty look and I smiled sweetly. I slept most of the way and so did Gwen and Nathan for that matter, but Lee stayed awake the whole time and so did Delono who was constantly telling Don to "Shut the fuck up and be good".

We stopped at a soul food restaurant and I ate nothing. I wasn't a bit hungry.

"Eat stupid!" Nathan growled.

"No."

"What?" he asked me, like I was nuts for not being hungry or telling him no.

I found out it was for telling him no. "I said no," I repeated calmly. Nathan was too scared of losing me to get too out of line.

"You eat!"

"No!"

"You crazy?"

"No, are you?"

"I'll beat your ass!"

"So, I ain't hungry."

"Go put this in the juke box and play 'For the Love of Money,' Nathan said handing me a quarter which I took but remained sitting.

"No, you got two feet to walk with!"

"Go!"

"No!"

"I swear I'll knock you out of your chair!"

"Ain't you got no manners?"

"What?"

"We're in a public place, eat with your mouth closed!" I said getting up and walking over to the juke box. I played 'Jungle Boogie' and 'Mighty Mighty' instead.

Nathan gave me a dirty look so I winked at one of the dudes that had just come in. He winked back and Nathan said, "I am gonna kick your sweet little ass as soon as we get to the motel!"

"Sure, Nathan, then what you gon do when I leave?" He didn't answer me and I smiled at him again.

We drove around Chicago for awhile with Lee and Delono telling Gwen and me what streets were good and what places to avoid.

We got to our motel room and Nathan and I took a bath together. It was hard because the tub was so small. But we did it. I got in bed first taking the best side. Nathan turned the television on and got in beside me.

"You happy, baby?" he asked, looking at me like I had to say yes or he'd cry.

"Yeah." He kissed me and said, "That's good because you're gon be happier tonight."

"What makes you think you can please me?" I asked cynically.

"You sayin I can't?"

"I'm sayin how do you know?"

"Well I'll find out," he said, turning me over.

We finally got to sleep at 4:30 and then woke up at 8:00, had another shower and dressed as fast as I could.

21 April: Care Worker Notes

Jenette's mother and grandparents arrived a minute or two before I arrived at work today, so we got right into our meeting. Grandparents, like Mother before them, were here to be convinced that what we were trying to accomplish with Jenette was more than mere lip-service and that we had their family member's best interests at heart. Suffice it to say that they came as doubters and departed as believers. I was completely open and honest with them, told it like it was and did not pull any punches. The clincher came when I told them that all questions and/or suggestions would be welcomed. The questions would be answered and if I felt the suggestions had merit, I would tell them so. If suggestions were out of line, involved an attempt to interfere, or were otherwise inappropriate, I would also tell them that too. I explained again the reasoning behind Jenette's program and what had been accomplished to date. Grandma wanted to know how come the Grandparents' visit was for one-time only. I explained that the visit would be evaluated and if it was beneficial to Jenette, they would be encouraged to keep visiting. However, if we considered that their visits were becoming a distraction for Jenette, we would discontinue their visits. Grandma didn't like this too well but accepted it gracefully enough. After all their questions were answered, I left the four of them to themselves then conferred with mother for about a half-hour just before they departed.

"Wear that pair of white pants," he said after I was fully dressed.

I would've argued but he had pimped before so I just put on the white pants.

"Now put on that baby blue shorty top," he said, so I put on the baby blue shorty top.

"Put on the white platform sandals."

"They ain't platforms, they're wedges."

"Well I ain't never seen a pair of wedges that big before."

"They're platform wedges."

"Shut up and put them on!" So I did.

"Now wear your baby blue shorty jacket."

"It's pink, white and yellow too".

"Shut the fuck up and put it on!" So I obeyed this command also.

"Now take your white purse." I picked up my black purse and emptied its contents into my white one.

Then he looked at my wig and said, "Wear the light brown wig." So I took off the one I had on and put on my light brown wig. I was mad because I still had to put on make-up so I had to hurry.

"You look good," Nathan said happily.

"Sure, thanks." We got back into Lee's car with all our luggage repacked and left the comfort of the motel.

"You two ladies put your money in the wigs you wearin, your underwear or any place but your purses," Nathan said. "And take your luggage and put it in a locker in the bus station," Delono said.

"Jenette you gon work right here on the strip. It's hot but there's only two other hoes so you gon make plenty green and stay around here so you don't get lost" Lee said, sounding like a police officer telling me my rights.

21 April: Care Worker Notes (cont)

Grandma asked whether I thought Jenette was gullible. I asked what she meant and she wondered whether I thought

Jenette was easily led. Maybe that was the reason she had gotten into so much trouble (implying that Jenette was merely a follower and not one to get into trouble on her own). I did not spare Jenette at all. I told them that Jenette was smart, an independent thinker, knew exactly what was going on and did not get into anything unless she wanted to. I could see Jenette out of the corner of my eye nodding in agreement.

I ignored him and waited patiently while he showed Gwen "her territory". Then we drove back to the strip and I got out with my luggage and put it in a locker at the bus station. I was scared as I walked down the street shaking my ass, but I held my head up high and smiled at all the passing men, even the men with their wives and girlfriends.

"Hey cutie, come with me," an ugly man said.

"No, you go to hell."

"Oh, you're real cute. I'm Bill, who are you?"

"Fawn."

"Oh, you're nice looking, I stay in the Hilton on the 17th floor, room 1716."

"What's your last name?"

"Zimmerman."

He walked away and a few minutes later I was in his room arguing over the price of my body. "Twenty dollars for an hour," he said like he was doing me a great favor.

I laughed hatefully and said, "Sixty or nothin!" I got the sixty, that's a dollar a minute, pretty good but not good enough. I checked him over and made him wash his self. It's terribly degrading to a woman's pride selling herself like that, the last thing I needed was a disease from some creep. He lay there panting over me and I lay there looking at my watch every five seconds and smoking. If I wouldn't have been breathing, they would have pronounced me dead – I wouldn't move an inch.

"Don't you like it?" he asked, trying to be sexy.

"Not hardly, get off, I have to go." He got off and I took a bath and dressed, putting the money in my underwear.

"Can I see you tomorrow night?" he asked, laying there like a king.

"If you have eighty dollars, and maybe even more ..." I left and got a ride from a dude because I wanted to see some more of Chicago. I got lost and had a hell of a time. It started to rain and I was glad I had stolen an umbrella. I had more money from a couple other tricks, well over a hundred dollars. Well over any amount I'd ever had at one time before.

I finally got a ride from another pimp that claimed his name was 'Money'. I snickered inwardly and wanted to tell him I was the great white hope.

"Who are you, Baby?" he asked, looking at his diamond rings.

"To you I am Jenette."

"What do you mean to me, is that your real name?"

"Yeah."

"You got a man?"

"No, I got lost and I don't know where he's at."

"Yeah?"

21 April: Care Worker Notes (cont)

Mother questioned whether Jenette was still communicating with "those people" – the ones she got into so much trouble with. I explained that I would have to check to be sure, but I knew that Jenette and her social worker had come to a mutual agreement that further correspondence with them could in no way aid in her progress. She had been corresponding with a boy she had known and associated with off and on since before she had gotten into trouble. This had our approval because we felt she needed a supportive source her own age in addition to family. Mother wanted to know if he was Black and I told her that he was. I asked if she had ever met him but she couldn't remember if she had or not.

"Show me a hundred dollars."

"I'll get it for you if that's what you mean," I said, not wanting him to know I had way more than that. I wanted to see just how serious he was.

"That's what I mean."

"Take me to the strip and I'll get it."

"You better be serious because I ain't got no time for free fuckin you."

"I know that, I don't have the time either."

He gave me a funny look and said, "I'll pick you up at three."

I started to get out and he said, "Can't you give your man a kiss?" I kissed him and got out. I liked him and I hoped he liked me but it's hard telling. He never came back at three and I was very glad I hadn't given him any money.

Anyway I wandered around mad as hell and tired beyond explanation. To add to the joy of my night I was followed by a pervert and the vice. I decided to just turn another trick but a vice car stopped and the finest looking dude I ever saw got out and walked up to me, leaving the funky looking White man in the car.

I was very suspicious. Why would a fine looking nigga like that be with a vice? One answer, he is a vice too.

"I know you think I'm a vice. I'm not, he is, but he's a crooked vice and he wants you to turn a trick with him."

"No."

"Come on baby, he got good money."

"No."

"You think I'm vice?"

"I don't know what you're talking about."

"Look sugar, just get in the car." I don't know why, but I got into the car and I'll be damned if the bastard wasn't a crooked vice. Just goes to show how 'straight' our police are.

"Hi there, I'm Steve, what's your name, Doll?" The way he said it made it sound like he thought it was Doll.

"It sure in the fuck ain't no Doll!"

"Well, what is it?"

"Fawn."

"Fawn what?"

"Fawn Brooks."

"Hey, those other vice are following us!" he said, speeding the car up. We went across the bridge and lost them and then we did a U turn on two wheels and went back. It was like a game of cops and robbers. I was scared shitless and I found myself clutching the fine dude's arm.

"Oh, I'm sorry," I said feeling real dumb.

"It's okay pretty baby, you're keeping me warm." I felt all fluttery inside and I gave him a cute look.

"You got some pretty blue eyes, they're nice," he said shyly.

"How come my heart keeps beating so fast?" I wondered getting mad at myself. We were back on the strip to get the fine dude's car. I still didn't know his name, so I decided to refer to him as Sweet Daddy.

The vice finally caught up to us and a man questioned Steve and my Sweet Daddy. Some bitch vice got me, "Name?"

"Fawn Brooks."

"Address?"

"None right now, I stay in a motel."

"Why are you down here?"

"I'm with my man."

"Okay, you can go now, but get some Chicago I.D."

"Sure," I muttered wanting to spit in her face. The vice left and Steve thought I was gonna be with him but I surprised him and said "Bye".

Sweet Daddy looked me and said "You're slick Baby, old punk thought he'd get you free."

"Shit, nobody gets me free, except for you." I don't know why I said it but I did.

He smiled and we walked to his car – a 'Runner'. It fit him somehow. He looked so young and shy. I wondered how he looked when he got mad, his face was too sweet and innocent-looking for me to imagine him ever being mad – upset but never mad.

We got in his car, only to find his gas tank was empty. "Shit, Baby, what we gon do?" he asked looking real helpless.

"Come on, let's catch a cab and go to a motel."

"I don't have any money," he said, looking even more helpless.

I felt like saying "I bet you don't", but I paid for the taxi and for the motel room. I knew the motel room lady remembered me from the night before with Nathan but she didn't say anything, just gave me the key to Room 16.

Sweet Daddy finally told me his name; it was Emerson. He looked more like a Johnny to me.

"How old are you?" he asked, sitting in a chair watching me take my coat off.

"Twenty."

"Your fake I.D. says you're twenty, but how old are you really?" he asked with a big grin on his face.

"Fifteen," I said, knowing he was going to think I was too young for him and a bunch of other shit.

"What?" he asked, not believing me.

"Fifteen." Now I was really worried.

"You know I could go to prison?"

"I could get into a lot of trouble too."

"Yeah, Baby, I know."

"How old are you?"

"Twenty-three."

"No, you're not."

"Nineteen."

"Age is just a number anyway," I said, feeling very close to him.

"I like you. Do you like me?" he asked, looking like a little boy that needs to be reassured.

"Yes."

"Go ahead and get in bed, I'm taking a shower."

Then I undressed and got into bed. I couldn't figure Emerson out. I knew he was a pimp, but he wasn't loud and jive-talking like the others I had met, and I really didn't know how to cope with someone like him after what the others had been like.

The others had been mean and sadistic and I knew what to expect. But Emerson was different, I felt like he was something special. He was like a little boy playin a man's role and I felt like I had to help him in any way I could.

"You look nice layin there with your big blue eyes," Emerson said, coming into the room with no shirt or shoes on.

21 April: Care Worker Notes (cont)

Mother then got into talking about Jenette's feelings in regard to Blacks and Whites.

I said that we had discussed this area in some length and her daughter held some strong feelings about it. Mother asked if Jenette was prejudiced against her own race. It was a tough question to answer truthfully because I am not honestly certain. I did say that Jenette was having some difficulties at the present time in trying to pin down how she really feels about many things. Jenette feels comfortable and understands Black people where she does not feel the same towards Whites. I asked Mother to forego any deep discussion about this area with Jenette until she got herself straightened out a little further. It is an area that certainly needs some resolution, but this is not the time for it. As Mother and I talked further, I finally realised that this Mother is looking for some guidance also. I'm not sure I'm up to that sort of thing, but am willing to give it a try. This session with family ended with me breaking a couple of old well-established secure unit rules by allowing Jenette to briefly see her little brother and sister at the front door. Though I may get myself into difficulty, being able to witness that short family reunion made it all worthwhile!

He was built strong and solid for his age. It showed he hadn't sat around on his ass all day like the others, while we prostitutes slaved our asses off for the lazy bums.

After he went into the bathroom and I took off my wig and brushed my own hair.

"You want some pop?" I asked.

"Yeah, you gon get some?"

"Yeah, what kind you want?"

"Whatever you like."

I went downstairs and bought two bottles of pop and hurried back inside. It was real cold and very dark.

"Here you go, I got grape."

"Thanks, come here, come here with me Sugar."

I put my pop down and got in bed and snuggled up against him. He was so strong and so sweet.

"You're soft baby, do you like to kiss?" he asked, looking at me and *pulling me closer. His big brown eyes so big and innocent-looking. I wondered if I loved him already.*

"Yeah, I guess so."

"I don't like to, it's nasty but I'll kiss you once to see if you're different." He kissed me gently and leaned back and looked at me.

"How come your lips are so soft?" he asked, looking at me like he really was bewildered.

"I don't know, maybe because yours are." At any rate we didn't get to sleep all that night. I really needed some sleep but he didn't want to, so I stayed awake too.

At seven in the morning he got up and said he'd be back at noon. He said he had to get his car and talk to his boss. He was the first man I'd met that had a job. I was surprised and he and I laughed, but then he got serious real fast, his little boy's face looking real anxious.

"What's wrong, Emerson?" I asked, getting real worried.

"You won't be here when I get back."

"Yes, I will Baby, I ain't gon run off and leave you alone."

He still didn't believe me but then I didn't believe he'd come back in the first place.

"You won't be coming back for me to be here," I said with my stupid voice shaking.

"Yes I will Sugar, yeah I'll be back but will you be here?" he asked, holding me close to him.

"Yes, I'll be here, I promise you. I won't leave you."

"Okay, I still don't believe you but I got to take that chance." He kissed me on the cheek and I watched him go, wanting to cry out for him to stay here with me.

I needed him by my side and he needed me. All he had to do was to look at me and I would do anything he wanted me to do. If he asked me for the moon, I would've gotten a ladder high enough to get it for him. I was sure he could feel the need in me. I needed him by my side and that's all there was to it.

I was running scared from Ebony, he'd kill me if he found me and I knew it. I was fifteen years old and I was doomed to die at any time if Ebony found me.

Without Emerson I felt helpless. I know he thought I was running a game on him. And that hurt because I wasn't. I really wanted that man.

And it scared me because I'd only been with him overnight but already I knew if I lost him, I'd probably get hurt.

I didn't need nobody but him and myself. That's so bad to want someone like I wanted him. I stayed in bed, thinking and I wished he would hurry back.

21 April: Care Worker Notes (cont)

Later when Jenette and I talked, she asked what her mother and I had talked about, so I told her. I mentioned that I might be available to sit in and try to help the two of them through some of the more hairy discussions which must take place before there can be any hope of a mutually good give-and-take relationship. Jenette almost leaped at the idea and remained enthusiastic even when I told her that I had to remain neutral out of necessity and that she must approach this with the knowledge that it could not go her way one hundred percent. I gotta say in all fairness that this kid generates one hell of a lot of enthusiasm on my part! I guess I had better save a few of these blank pages for someone else!

I hoped our relationship would last. But I knew no pimp and hoe could really have a relationship – it's a give and take game.

You give yourself and they give you money. Then you give your money to your man and he gives his self in the bed that's as far as it gets with the man, sex is all he can offer you. That's the only thing that keeps his woman with him. What else can? He doesn't make any money to support anyone. And half the time when you get put in jail, the bastards won't get you out.

And you get put in jail just because he wanted some money. We get all the pain, disrespect and vulgar acts. They get the money, diamond rings, Cadillacs and so on. Sure you get some of it, but if you leave the man you're with, he keeps everything. Even your clothes. That's so he can give them to the next lady that might and will come along sooner or later.

It's all you're doing. You do it all, without us women, those filthy pigs *would be out of business. And they are filthy pigs. Every single last one. Even Emerson who I wanted so much. It's bad to get yourself hooked on a pimp. Real bad, no matter what anyone may say. Because if he knows you are, then he'll use you more than you thought anyone could. And most of all, he can destroy you and your mind. He can rule you and make it so you couldn't get free even if you wanted to.*

I cry for all the sisters who have gotten their faces disfigured for life by these things that call their selves men. I don't mean sisters as Black sisters only. I mean every race of woman involved in this shit. Any woman who has been beaten by her so-called man is my sister. We are all sisters of pain. I cry for the sisters that have had their skulls smashed in by these cruel bastards. I cry for the sisters laying dead in the bottom of a lake and other places. I cry for Linda. They cut her up and stuffed her pieces of body in a sack and left her there to rot away with no feeling for her dead or alive.

Pimp is the ugliest word in the world. Think of all the pain, filth, disrespect, body and mind torture that goes with it, not to mention the diseases you can get, and the perverted tricks you might catch.

There are girls my age and younger in this and unable to get out because of the threats and beatings their pimps give them if they even THINK they're going to leave.

I can tell you that if I would've had a gun, I would've blown Ebony's brains out and laughed and then spat on him and walked away. He's the lowest pimp I ever met and he needs to be in prison or mental hospital because he's criminally insane.

You may ask how come we got involved in the first place. Right? Because we hear of all the furs, diamonds and other luxuries, and things like that are very appealing to any girl or woman living in poverty. Some of us have to do it to pay the rent and feed and clothe our children. Welfare does not give as much as it takes.

You never hear about the beatings, torture and killings. They only make it sound good, and it's not at all. But like I said before, they take everything if you decide to leave, sometimes your life – which happens more often than not.

Noon came and Emerson didn't come back and I was very mad. But mostly hurt. I took a shower and slept. When I woke up, he was back and banging on the door which I had locked and forgot to give him the key.

I let him in and we embraced like long lost lovers. Maybe we were, I still can't say.

"I'm sorry I'm so late. I had to do more than I thought I did," Emerson said still, holding me.

"Where are you going now?" I asked, noticing he hadn't taken his coat off or sat down.

"I got to do a few more things still."

"I'll get dressed and go with you."

"No, I'll be back in an hour or so."

I didn't like the idea of him leaving when he had just gotten back. I wanted to be with him all the time, but I didn't say so. I just said "Okay".

"Be ready to go when I came back," he said, knowing how I felt.

"I will." We kissed and he left. I took another shower for the hell of it and dressed, put on my make-up and a wig real slow with a lot of fussing, just to kill the time until Emerson came back.

25 April: Care Worker Notes

I was shocked and more than a little pissed off when I finally got around to my Keyworker session with Jenette tonight. When I left the secure unit on Monday night, I left a girl who was positive, enthusiastic, reasonably certain about where she was headed and why, and not only willing, but anxious to get everything together. Regrettably that was not the girl I talked with tonight upon my return after two days absence.

Let me tell you guys about the depth of Jenette's feelings. For the first time during our working relationship, and – believe me – we have had some rather heavy going at times, Jenette broke down and cried. Now some people might find it amusing that this sort of thing was upsetting to me. I finally got it out of her that she felt that some of the staff went out of their way to "treat me like shit and make me feel like I haven't done a damn thing!"

She followed this with "I know I'm supposed to be pleasant and respect all the staff here, but according to Mrs McG, I can't do anything right – and the way she talks to me, it's all I can do to remain civil!" There isn't any doubt that Jenette has some strong feelings about this and I must say that I share some of those feelings myself! We talked of the Board action of this past week and she said she was glad to have received the added lift to her program but was a bit mystified as to why the recommendations of her counsellors were not followed through. I had to confess that I wasn't too sure what rationale had been applied either. I intended to find out to satisfy my own curiosity and to gain some further understanding of the situation. I want to go on record folks – right now – that I don't expect to return again after two days off and pick up a whole bunch of pieces and try to fit a girl back together again. If you guys feel that I am totally over-involved with this girl and am concerned about her progress, then let me put your mind at ease: "You're damned right I am!"

I sat and watched TV and then I dozed off again and when I woke up, he was back again and I was happy. We had a lot of fun and I didn't go to work that night. We just rode around and I listened to my favourite tape and didn't sit still for a minute. Chicago was bit confusing and I had a lot of questions to ask about it.

The next day was sunny and real nice out. We went shopping and everything I said I liked, he told me to get, so of course I did. We were walking by a jewellery store and there was a diamond ring on display for $1000. I said "Oh, I like that!" and he started to tell me to get it, but then he saw the price and we both started laughing.

Everything was fine between us. Any time he wanted money, no matter how much, I got it. I had a gun he had gotten me and I robbed the tricks. Tricks are now low down bums. Quite a few of them stay in the Hilton or in the Waldorf. Others are not quite so fancy but they got money. They have to or they won't get anything except a bunch of dirty words thrown at them as far as I am concerned.

I also consider myself quite a bit higher than they are. After all, I don't have to buy anyone. Most of them also have wives and children. I could name some names if I wanted to but I wouldn't want to be the cause of a divorce.

Even though women hate to believe it, it's the truth. When your husband goes out of town, he is very seldom lonely. None of the men I met were. And, ladies, you can stop wondering where his money went to so fast.

Because us proud sisters got it and our pimps are paying off their Cadillac payments with it. I may sound mean to you but if it wasn't for your husbands and boyfriends, we would go out of business, just like our pimps would without us sisters.

Anyway, my little gun came in handy. I joined up with five Black girls I knew and we robbed those tricks blind. Money, checks, watches, rings, credit cards and even his clothes, if they were nice and would fit our man. We robbed men off ships too. But we gave it up awfully fast. They were too mean and would rather die than give up their money.

But Emerson and I were making it real good. With all the money and credit cards, etc. He got a $500 suit and felt real good, so did I.

But something happened. I didn't need him anymore. I didn't even want him. I just didn't care one way or the other and he knew something I felt for him was falling apart and drifting away. He tried to stop it as best as he could with little things like: "You don't need to work tonight" or "Why don't you buy something for yourself?"

None of it helped and it was not his fault. He had treated me better than any pimp I'd met and I loved him for that. Other than that I didn't give a damn, but I stayed with him. Something about him was changing too. He was sad a lot. And a lot of times he'd just sit and stare at me with neither one of us sayin a word.

I guess he knew he was going to lose me real soon and that there was nothing he could do to prevent it.

One night I went down on the strip to make a few dollars even though we really didn't need it.

26 April: Care Worker Notes

Personal involvement with a young person — while keeping your head on in the right direction — is tough and becomes even tougher when people start to question you about it, perhaps out of a different level of involvement on their part. For the record, let me say that a staff member's working relationship with a girl will become a mirror of how that staff member involves and invests herself in that relationship. For both teachers and care staff, if you're getting bad vibes from a kid fairly consistently, don't always blame the kid. Girls may be mirroring back the same bad vibes they are picking up from you. If there is a problem, let's remember that WE are getting paid to work past that problem, not hold the kid responsible for our inability to resolve differences. In short, if we tell the kid to handle herself responsibly when she has had difficulties doing so in the past, then, as care staff, teachers and adults we need to set the tone! I think it's time we review whether we knowingly, or without thinking, put thorns under a kid's saddle blanket instead of helping to soothe out the rough spots. We can be firm without being cold; purposely looking for the bad breath amidst the mouthwash; or roughing a kid's feathers when an alternative approach may in the long run be more productive. In short, when looking at treatment, we must consider what events lead to admission in a secure unit, and what we do here from point of entry to point of departure. What specific goals and daily objectives do we pursue? It is time we start talking more directly about these central issues in our work!

But I had to get out awhile. Emerson was so desperate-looking, I felt like I was killing him and it depressed me very much. I was thinking of a saying I had heard Cookie use once. It went like this: "When some women catch the blues, they tuck their heads and cry. But when this woman catches the blues, she grabs her shoes and slides."

That was my saying now and even though I had no place to go, I knew I was never going back to Emerson again. It made me sad, I had the blues, but it was time to slide and I knew it.

I got $100 real quick and just walked around. I was walking and I found myself crying – crying for my dead and beaten sisters. Crying for the love I lost for Emerson. And crying for the pain and torture I had gone through.

I stopped like a lost child and went inside a hotel. I had been in there often enough, so I went into the bar and got slightly drunk. I got my shoes shined from my dear friend 'Jimmy the shoe shine man'. He often caught tricks and brought them to me. Or let me know when a bust on us 'Sportin Ladies' was coming down, so I got away before they could mark me. Or in other words make me known as a prostitute.

"How come you look so sad tonight, Jenette?" he asked, knowing that I was in a terrible frame of mind.

"Shit, I feel dead baby, I think I'm a corpse."

"You look like one."

"Thanks a lot, how come you say that?"

"Because you're too skinny and you look like a ghost."

"Pale, you mean? I can't seem to get a feeling for anyone anymore."

"You need money?"

"Oh hell no, I've got money coming out my ears!"

"What's wrong then? You lose your man?"

"I lost the feeling for him, I lost the feeling for everything. I don't even care if I live or die."

"Yes you do."

"Maybe so, I think I'll catch a bus and go home."

"Where's home?"

"Detroit."

"Why don't you come go with me? I travel a lot."

"No, I can't. I'm sick of travelling and I'm sick of people."

"Thanks alot Jenette, you know how to make a guy feel good."

"It's not just you."

"Here, will you go across the street and buy me some milk?"

"Yeah." I took the money and bought his milk.

When I came back, I saw a cute dude standing in the lobby. I knew he was a pimp just by the way he was dressed. More so by the lion headed cane he was leaning on showing off his diamond rings.

I guessed he was about twenty-four. He was cute but too mean-looking. It was the way his eyes were so expressionless and his face looked like it was made out of black marble. No warmth came from him. You could feel his hate in your own blood. I ignored him and talked to Jimmy some more. I could feel the way old evil eyes was staring at me. It made me nervous and I started to stutter.

"Well, I'll see you later, I have to go and do something," I said to Jimmy. I felt wary and uncomfortable with evil eyes staring down my back.

I got halfway to the door and evil eyes said "Pssssst!" I felt like that's what he thought my name was so I ignored him and kept moving towards the door.

26 April: Social Worker Notes

I reviewed developments with Jenette this afternoon and explained why, as her social worker, I had opposed opening up her program more than what was done at the Board on Wednesday. She accepted this very well and was relieved that it was not because she was doing poorly. We talked about the writing she has been doing and I encouraged her to continue. Her writing offers a clear and gut honest portrayal of life as a teenage prostitute. It not only involves the reader in the innocence and pain of what happened, but also in the growth and optimism which builds to the end.

If this is seen as pornography (which I have heard some staff calling it already), then such attitudes are totally oblivious to the honesty and guts it took to write and share this story with us. I feel this kid has begun to trust, something which she never did before. Jenette has passed as a 21–23 year old quite successfully in the past, and is here today to share what she has learned from the pain of finding who she was. Jenette has lived around bullshit for so long that her first reaction is to be on guard.

It behoves us all to be looking at just how we come across to her, and if it ain't open, honest and caring, then we better start questioning our motives, not her.

Jenette admits that she is only beginning; so let's not be lax and purposely (or not so purposely) become millstones around her neck.

"Pssssst!" He did it again so I looked at him and he motioned for me to come over to him but I wouldn't so he came over to me instead.

He just stood there looking at me and all of a sudden he pulled out a card. I just stood there and stared at it with my mouth hanging open. It was a small black card and in gold letters it said "MAFIA". Now anyone should know that the real MAFIA does not go around flashing those cards, or even carrying them around with them. But since I was slightly dumb in a lot of ways, I believed him and I can tell you I was one terrified little girl. I looked around for a way to get out, but he had me by the arm leading me firmly but gently to a chair.

"What's your name, pretty lady?" he asked, looking me over as if to see if I was going to pull a gun on him. Although I had it with me, I was too scared to even reach for it, much less aim it or anything.

"Jenette," I finally said, not knowing who the hell he was.

"I'm the Villain," he said in answer to my thoughts.

I looked at him and I would've laughed but he really did look like a villain.

Then another dude came over. He looked good too, but he didn't look like he was too nice either, so I just sat and puffed on a cigarette. He looked me over real slow and I felt naked. I found myself wishing I was at home with Emerson.

"She a fine lady, ain't she?" the Villain said to the other man. Villain looked at me closely after he said this as if to see if I had any flaws or not. I passed his inspection much to my relief.

"She sure is, fine and young. What's your name, pretty lady?" I looked at him closely, feeling like I was up for auction and the highest bidder of compliments would get me.

"Jenette."

"I'm the Mack, International Mack." I still felt like laughing at them and telling them I was Peter Pan, but I didn't.

"You wanna get high, Sugar?" Villain asked me.

"On what?"

"Cocaine."

"Okay but where?" Cocaine was my favourite high, the rich man's high.

"Our house."

"I have a man," I said, deciding to use Emerson as an excuse.

"Most beautiful ladies like you do," was Mack's reply. I figures he picked that up from the movie called The Mack, but I wasn't about to ask him.

"We'll bring you back down here if you decide you don't want to stay."

"Okay," I said, getting up and walking beside the Villain to their car. I took one look at that car and thought, "Oh my god, that's Ebony's car!"

I looked at the license plates and it wasn't a Detroit licence plate thank God! Once at their house (which had girls' clothes scattered around, I told you they kept your things if you left), we sat down, snorted cocaine, drank wine and smoked weed. I was so high I couldn't make sense of anything. And of course I stayed but it took a lot of talking on their part to get me to make the final decision.

Much to my surprise, I was the Mack's lady and not the Villain's as I thought I would be.

Villain said he was from Detroit and Mack said he was from New York. I was surprised to hear that Villain was from Detroit's ghetto because I was too and I knew almost everyone there by name.

The next night I went to my so-called "work" and I saw Emerson. Unfortunately, he saw me too and he was madder than hell. Now I knew what he looked like when he was mad. His handsome boyish face was contorted into an ugly sneer and I felt uneasy.

First, he talked to me trying to get me to come back. Then he kind of yelled but it wasn't really a yell, more like a loud whine. I started crying and he held me close to him like the first time when he didn't believe I'd be at the motel when he got back. I wanted to go back "home" with him but I couldn't. It wouldn't be the same and the relationship would be strained and we both knew it.

After that I stayed downtown still trying to get more money for Mack and I was real sad because I did love Emerson in a way.

Anyway I caught a trick and he turned out to be a little nutty and beat me up and took all my money except for thirteen dollars. Thirteen lousy *dollars out of nearly $300.*

I knew Mack was going to be mad and I wished I had gone with Emerson.

27 April: Care Worker Notes

I only talked briefly with Jenette today but we did discuss how one's own attitude and manner could and did affect the attitudes of others in personal relationships. For example, if a person was sullen, uncommunicative and surly in manner, others were usually hesitant – certainly wary – in making an approach to them, if contact was even attempted at all. Also, a snotty, snarly and contemptuous attitude usually triggered a like response in others. Jenette quickly grasped what I was getting at but evinced surprise and shock when she was told that I had received at least one complaint personally about her being guilty of this sort of conduct, and similar complaints from second-hand sources. I had expected some denials to be provoked by my statement but this was not the case. Jenette asked for and was given some specifics.

She thought about it for a short time and then almost floored me with the statement: "I didn't realise that I had anything to do with the situation. I always had the feeling that they just didn't like me and thought I was some low down crummy person because of my past. So I ignored them whenever I could and stay away from them as much as possible. I guess I'll ask Mr T if he might talk it over with me so we can try to get things straightened out". When my eyeballs stopped flopping, I encouraged Jenette to do just that. Jenette is, however, dubious of having much success in working out any kind of resolution with Mrs McG. She has some extremely strong feelings about this, and refuses to accept that the causes could be mostly or even partly on her side. I would not push it at this point, but it will be discussed further and needs to be worked out eventually.

Mack was mad, but he didn't hit me, just cussed a little and then let it go like it never happened. After that I was real careful and I was doing real good. Satisfying Mack's need for money and also making enough to keep some without him knowing it. I just had to hope he wouldn't find out where I hid it.

Then one night when we were in bed, his "other lady" which was my stable sister came over. I had never met her before but Villain had told me she was a bitch, so I expected her to be terrible. Her name was Cameo and she was pretty enough to be a top fashion model. But she was just another prostitute, a simple sister of pain, so I really didn't care much about her one way or another.

She cried and cursed Mack for having me. I lay in bed, feeling pretty smug and giggling to myself feeling like I was a queen and knowing I would never cry because of another girl.

I could hear Villain in his own bedroom laughing so I went into his room where we sat on the bed and laughed together. He told me he hated Cameo and that she was always making a scene and throwing things at Mack when she got mad. I laughed even harder at this and especially when she said, "But Mack I love you!"

Every night she would call or come over. One night she came over and walked right in the house when Villain and I were playing a game of Tonk. Tonk is something like rummy.

Cameo gave me a dirty look and I returned it. After all, I paid for everything and she was just a lost soul in my book. Anyway she marched right into the bedroom I shared with Mack and shut the door.

"That dirty bitch!" I said loud and hoping she would hear it.

"She is a dirty bitch," Villain said a little louder.

"Take me out. I want to get away from here."

Cameo was laying on the bed and Mack jumped up and reached for his finger nail file, as if this was what he had been doing all along. His nails were long like daggers and he had a coat of clear nail polish all over them. Just goes to show how much work pimps do. "Okay sugar, go get dressed and we'll have a night on the town!" Villain said, getting extremely happy.

I got up and marched into the bedroom without knocking on the door. After all, it was mine. I paid for everything from cigarettes to car payments.

Jenette has been bright-eyed and smiling today and her positive cooperative attitude remains constant. Her Mother rang this afternoon explaining that she would not be able to visit this weekend, but that she would be down for sure next weekend. She asked if Jenette's Grandparents would also be allowed to visit. I said we would recommend this to the social worker and Planning Board since it was obvious that their visit affected Janette only in a positive way. She accepted that approval needed to be sought and asked that she be notified of the Board decision prior to next weekend.

Cameo lit a cigarette and I looked at her and snickered. I wanted to kill her, laying there on my bed like she owned it. As for Mack, I could've blown his brains out with a toothpick, that's how mad I was.

I jerked my red pants off a hanger as well as a white shorty top. Then I rummaged around on the floor of the closet for my brown platform shoes. I finally got them and walked out of the bedroom and put my things in Villain's room.

Then I waited a minute until I knew Mack and Cameo were relaxed again and barged into the bedroom. Mack jumped up again and I said "Baby, you don't have to get up just because a lady enters the room." He didn't say anything and went on filing his beloved fingernails.

I took my light frosted gypsy wig and a brown knit and leather shorty jacket and left, slamming the door behind me again. Villain was in the bathroom doing whatever it is men do to themselves so I dressed in his room and barged into my own room again.

I emptied the contents of my white purse into my brown one, stuffed my gun in the bottom drawer and put a pack of cigarettes in my purse along with all the other junk in there.

Since I had given all my money to Mack (except the secret money I was saving up) like all "nice little prostitutes" are supposed to, I said, "Give me some money."

"Where are you going?" Mack asked, looking me over like he could tell by the way I was dressed.

"To hell if I don't change my ways," I thought but didn't say it as usual.

"I'm going out, give me some money!" I repeated myself and that's one thing I hate to do.

He handed me five dollars and I laughed bitterly. "You can add a twenty to that any time now," I said, wanting to spit in his brown face. He handed me a twenty and I could tell he was embarrassed. I gave Cameo a dirty look and then I walked out of the room, slamming the door so hard the whole house rattled.

"You ready now, Jenette?" Villain asked me, putting on the tan suede midi coat with a brim to match.

"Yeah."

We went to five different clubs and we both got a little drunker in each one. We were having a lot of fun and everything that happened made us laugh. Even when the car wouldn't start, we laughed till we had tears streaming down our faces. By the time we got home we were laughing, singin and talking all at the same time.

We stumbled into the house with our arms around each other and drunker than skunks. Mack was up waiting for us and I smiled at Villain and then gave Mack a dirty look and walked into the bedroom and shut the door, simply ignoring the searching look he gave me. I undressed and got into bed and read a book called "The Happy Hooker".

Mack came in and apologized. I ignored him and turned away from him and went to sleep.

Cameo didn't come around anymore but her friend Mandy did, so that was just as bad, almost.

I ignored Mandy even when she spoke to me. I don't like girls at all, in my whole life there's only been a few that I halfway got along with.

Mandy really liked Villain and I would do things when Mack wasn't around just to make her mad. I thought it was funny and so did Villain. We would sit and get high, all the while we'd be laughing about Cameo and Mandy. Sometimes we'd laugh about Mack being so flipped over Cameo. I ignored Mack most of the time and treated him pretty cold, but I was still his lady, but no one knew it. They all thought I was with Villain because I spent nearly all my time with him and I didn't give Mack much money anymore. I kept it and added it to my "secret money". I had about $900 now and I was pretty pleased with myself about it.

One night on the strip I got into a Continental with two other pimps that I didn't know. I found out their names were Leeroy and Rufus. We were talking about Villain and Mack. I sure was surprised to find out what

27 April: Care Worker Notes (cont)

Jenette's mother asked for and received a brief report on her daughter's progress this past week. She had a lot of questions and these were answered. I must say there is still no detectable hint that she is in any way attempting to gain (or regain) control of the situation here. She is genuinely interested in her daughter, feels good about what is going on, and is cooperative to the extreme.

The feeling is strong that she is still a bit overwhelmed at our approach to both Jenette and herself, and certainly by Jenette's own present attitude, physical appearance and positive manner. She commented again today about all three items. Jenette was told about her mother's call and about not visiting this weekend. I didn't mention her grandparents since their visit is still undecided. I think that another visit by grandparents would be both timely and appropriate at this time since we want to ensure that Jenette is well stabilised prior to entering into the joint counselling with mother and herself. I'm itching to get started on this, but want to make certain that Jenette is ready for it when we do get started.

they told me, although I had a hunch about it all along.

"Villain's real name is Larry, he been born and raised right here," Rufus said with an amused grin on his face.

"Yeah, and when he was going to school with us, he was a cry baby," Leeroy said and I laughed.

"How about Mack?" I asked, wanting to know it all.

"His real name is Alonzo, he ain't from here, but he been around here the past five years with that bitch he has."

"Who? Cameo?"

"Yeah."

"What about Cameo?"

"She from here I think. I'm not sure but she been around a lot last few years off and on with old Alonzo. She leaves him a lot, her real name is Janet and she's twenty."

I laughed and said, "Big time losers, all three of them." They agreed with me and we drove around and got high. This is what I did most of the time instead of 'working'.

I would have Villain or Mack drive me downtown around 6pm and make a few quick dollars and then find a fine dude in a nice car, get in and talk awhile, then we'd get high and he'd want me to be his lady, but I always talked my way out of it. After we got good and high, I'd have him drive around until midnight. Then he would let me out where he found me and I would go and meet Villain or Mack who thought I had been working all this time.

After I got home on this particular night I said, "Hi Alonzo, Hi Larry, where's Janet?"

They looked at me real funny and I laughed and said, "When some women catch the blues, they tuck their heads and cry but when this woman catches the blues, she grabs her shoes and slides."

"Who you been with tonight?" Alonzo asked.

"Me and the breeze, like the song say – whatever way the wind blows is cool with me."

19 May: Care Worker Notes

We had our initial family group meeting this afternoon. Both Mrs F and I attended and I gotta say at the outset, that it went so well, it's a little hard to believe. There were some items which came out in our joint discussion that neither Mrs F nor I even suspected. Jenette's Mother claims she has never discussed these things in any of your conversations.

These items only concern Jenette indirectly, but certainly offer some insights into Mother's character. We're left

"You high?"

"Nope, are you?" I said lying.

"How come you're acting all crazy then?" Alonzo asked, looking at me like I was nuts.

"Because your game gone funky like a skunk!"

"You look at me and don't be itty bitty!"

"You think I'm itty bitty?"

"What the fuck you care what I think?" Alonzo asked, getting ready to lose his temper. I had not seen him mad before and I didn't care to see him mad now. He looked mean when he was normal and even happy.

"You're repulsive! Good night," I said, going into the bedroom. I went to bed and slept soundly. Funky like a skunk, I thought over and over again. Time for a change of scene, I got the blues, I thought wearily.

I woke up late, about 3:30pm. I cleaned the house good because I knew I was not coming back. Except to try and get my clothes. I knew Alonzo would give them to me. He was weak-minded as far as I was concerned.

I dressed in all green, money green. I felt rich but I wanted to stand out in the crowd downtown so I wore a white leather waist jacket with fur sleeves and collar. I'd only bought it a few days before. I put on a frosted gypsy wig and some make-up, picked up my white purse and called my cousin Tammi.

"Hello," she said after the phone had rung a couple times.

"This is Jenette, you get that twenty dollars I sent?"

"No."

"What?" I asked, not believing her.

"No."

19 May: Care Worker Notes (cont)

I was not surprised to have a suspicion confirmed that Jenette had been engaged in a bit of playing us against Mother, and vice-versa. Jenette freely admits that she looks for the side of the bread covered with butter before she makes any choice between available options. We covered a lot of ground today and really made far better progress than we had anticipated. At the very beginning, even though both Jenette and her Mother were anxious to continue what had begun last Saturday, (yes, despite what Jenette had reported, they had made a pretty good start on their own), I took a few moments to clarify what were our common goals. I reinforced the message that none of the four of us should ever for a moment lose sight of the fact that our primary goal is to do what is best for Jenette.

"I sent twenty last week!"

"It ain't here."

"You sure?"

"Yeah cousin dear, I know for sure, because without that money I can't buy any acid."

"Okay, hold on, I'll send twenty more tonight."

"Okay, I'll wait, I have to."

"I'm leavin Alonzo."

"Oh? How come?" She wasn't surprised. I never stayed with any man very long. I didn't want to be mixed up and tied down, so I kept moving all the time. Emerson had come pretty close to keeping me for good, but I broke free before he could snap the trap. I was what the pimps called an "outlaw hoe".

"Because ain't no man gonna snap the trap on me!" I said. 'Snap the trap' was another one of my favourite sayings.

"Yeah, old Jeffy baby thought he was gonna pull that one on me too."

"No one, remember our plans?"

"Yeah". We had all planned to send her some money to come on a bus and be Larry's lady. She had never been a prostitute or been with Blacks

41

before so she was scared. She was supposed to be here tomorrow and she would work with me. I knew it would be fun because we had always gotten along good. But I felt guilty having her run away to be a hoe. She would go through all the pain and suffering I had, and it would be my fault for talking her into it and lying to her and telling her how "fun" it was. I did not mention the beatings, etc. No one ever does when they're trying to get someone new into the game.

"You still coming even though I'm leaving?"

"If you tell me where you'll be," she said faithfully.

"Don't come then."

"Why?"

"Because I don't know where I'm going."

"You don't?"

"No, I'm on my own, the police aren't looking for me, even if they were, they wouldn't know I am me, I don't look the same."

"I know."

"Anyway, I'm free to do what I want to. Tonight I'll stay in a motel and maybe see Emerson, then I'm leaving Chicago".

"By yourself?"

"I got money up the ass, and I'm hip. I know how to get more if I want it. I'm leaving tomorrow."

"You got money for a bus ticket?"

"I just told you I got all the money I need. If I knew how to drive, I could buy a car with the money I have."

"You saved some?"

"Some ain't the word, try hundreds and then aim for the thousands."

"Really?"

"Yes, Tammi dear, and more too. I held back on all those bastards for this 'Great Escape' ".

"Where are you catching a bus to Jenette?"

"Shit, Tammi! I said I don't know yet."

"Just gonna wander?"

"Right, I'm tired and I feel fifty instead of fifteen."

"What you gonna do?"

"Get an apartment, work the first week and then be as lazy as those dirty dogs I been supporting."

"Okay, it sounds fun, but you sound real lonely."

"I am. I ain't got nobody but myself and I really don't know what to do. After a month I might get a square job and trick on the side."

"Sounds good but you still don't".

"I ain't tryin to."

"I know."

"Let me tell you something."

"Go ahead, cousin dear."

"I work my ass off (among other things). I get sore feet from too much standin and walkin down those damn streets. I get a sore back from too much layin down. I get cold standin out there. I lose my self respect. I lose my pride. I get funky from too much fuckin. I get worn out. I get busted and do all the fuckin time. I buy everything and make all the ends do more than meet. I work so hard the ends overlap each other, and all along they beat me and take the money I fucked to death for."

"And all they do is lay around and spend it."

"Right, and beat you if they feel like it. I'm leaving and I'm never comin back. I'll call you when I can, bye."

"Bye Jenette, take care."

"I will."

I hung up and Alonzo came home a little while later and drove me down to the strip. I got out of the car and walked around. I had all that money hidden safe and I could leave any time I wanted to. Going home entered my mind. I shrugged it off. I'm old before my time, I thought wearily. These streets have rung me dry of every feeling and emotion I have ever had.

I saw the police car cruising slowly and watching me as I entered a hotel lobby. Then I knew where I was going. Back to jail, then to an institution, to do time for a filthy fuckin pimp.

I could go to the bus station right now and get a bus ticket and leave for New York tonight. Or better yet, I could get a plane ticket. I didn't know if they had buses going to New York.

But I couldn't. Something had me trapped and I couldn't get away even though I knew just what to do. I could get away clean. "God, Jenette, run! You can get away easy as the breeze! Come on, you ass, you got the blues and you got your shoes, you got to slide now, it's time to run!" I said that to myself but I knew I wouldn't do it. I was going to let them get me, but why?

I met another pimp I knew named Johnny and he took me up to his apartment and we got high. He started the same old thing about wanting to take me to San Francisco with him and I had a hard time talking my way out of it and I finally ended up almost having to fuck my way out of it. But I got to talkin to him real sweet and he let me go on account my business, whatever the hell that was.

I could stay with Johnny and be safe from the police or I could catch that bus. "Catch that bus girl, are you crazy? Catch that bus, these blues got you and it's time to move!" I let those thoughts run through my mind and I knew

19 May: Care Worker Notes (cont)

Discussion between Jenette and her Mother kicked off by bringing up the letters Jenette had written which were so upsetting to her mother. We talked about Evan Richards and other "friends" that Jenette had been clinging to, as well as members of Jenette's family. It was really neat to observe how each of these two women were willing to give some ground and not demand everything going 100 percent their way. Jenette talked of her fears about going back home again. She volunteered that she expected and needed some limits placed upon her. She further admitted to her mother that Evan was not the big overwhelming love-flame in her life. Jenette put forth the possibility that she may eventually marry a Mexican, a White or an Indian. Or it may be a Black guy. ... This kid has really got her shit together and knows it is possible to be successful at almost anything if she is but willing to make the effort.

I would never run again. Something had me in a death grip and I was fighting to get free. And finally I knew what it was. I was fighting for survival!

I knew I wouldn't be doing time for some nasty pimp. I'd be doing it for myself. If I had the idea that the time I would be doing was for a pimp, then I would be on that bus already. If I did time, I would change and never get involved in prostitution again. But if I did catch that bus, I knew I would keep on going until someone killed me or I went crazy.

So with those thoughts I left Johnny with a kiss and walked down the strip, shaking my ass and half dancing. I sang a song called 'Slick' from the movie 'The Mack'. 'If he don't get you today, he'll get you tomorrow, talkin about Slick, yeah they call him Slick'. I sang it loud and clear and laughed occasionally at the funny looks I received. "Can we talk to you, miss?" I turned and saw the big red neck officer in his old funky police car.

"For what?" I asked. My voice was filled with hate and it felt like it was twisting my vocal cords. I was gonna play it slick just like I would any other time.

"What's your name?"

"Fawn Brooks."

"And just how old are you?" he asked getting a little mean look in his ugly pig eyes.

"I just happen to be twenty-three," I said equally mean, if not meaner.

"And what is the address of your place?"

"I don't have a place. I'm staying in a motel at the moment."

"Phone number listed?"

"I think you might find out if you looked in a phone book."

"Where are you from?"

"My mother's stomach."

"I mean what town or whatever."

"Detroit."

It went on and on and finally they told me I was under arrest. At the jail house I called them every dirty word I could think of and they cussed right back. What the hell, no one has got a perfect cure for a dirty mouth, or do they? I was thinking my own little thoughts and not giving a damn about how mad they were just because I wouldn't tell them my real name.

"Okay Fawn, what's your real name?"

"Fuck you."

"We're going to keep you here till you tell me your real name."

"Your daddy is my pimp, your mother is my stable sister, your wife sells it for a dollar down the corner from me. I just turned a trick with your grandfather and I am teaching your red neck son the facts of life."

"You're a nasty little bitch."

"And your mother-fuckin fucked up, fucker."

"Is that your favorite word?"

"Kiss my ass, you dog fucker!" They finally took me to the youth center and after a full night of pleading with me to tell them my name, I finally did. They had me on a prostitution charge and for forgery.

26 May: Care Worker Notes

Jenette's Grandparents attended our family session today, and while their contribution was not great, it was positive in all respects. We briefly reviewed what had been covered previously and after some questions were answered, both Jenette and her mother ran out of any additional differences which they felt needed resolving. A lot of warmth was demonstrated between Jenette and her mother, and this extended to and included grandparents. I tossed out the suggestion that it was maybe time for both Jenette and her mother to start talking about what limitations and expectations – or house rules – Jenette might be expected to operate under were she to return home. This question caught both of them by surprise and neither was certain about how to start. I explained that we all – including Jenette – recognised the need for some limitations in our daily living. The two of them would need to work out a mutually satisfactory agreement around ground rules. We could offer suggestions but the nuts and bolts of an agreement had to be theirs since they were the ones who would be living together again after living independently for quite awhile. ... For the record, I would like to say that Jenette's Mother has not once made any overt or covert move to dictate or in any other way control our joint family sessions.

She told me today that she had been wondering when the bubble would burst and we would suddenly begin operating "like an institution". She no longer entertains any such misgivings. It is small wonder that this mother had a few doubts at first. She did not come right out and say it, but the impression was strong that she feels that we know what we're doing. She has confidence in our team and is grateful that "someone" has Jenette's best interests at heart. Today's session has served to strengthen my conviction that we are on the right path with Jenette and her family.

Anyway, here I sit doing my time. I have not 'reformed'. That word is full of shit to me. But I am progressing pretty fast, that's something new for me. I expect to be out in time for school in September. I had my sixteenth birthday in March and I feel younger and more relaxed than I did when I was fifteen.

I look quite a bit better also. I have colour in my face now and I gained weight too. I weighed 105 when I was busted. That's bad since I'm five foot six.

I don't see or hear from anyone I was with before. I don't even know if they are dead or alive. I hate to admit it, but I really don't give a damn about any of them, except for my poor sisters.

9 July: Care Worker Notes

We have reached an impasse. Despite continued encouragement towards additional staff contact, Jenette no longer responds positively and is asking some unanswerable questions. She continues to retain her independent nature and repeated efforts to strengthen her motivation towards convincing staff of her sincerity. She now rebuts: "Everyone keeps preaching to me to be myself and not be phoney – be the real me! Well, I am being me and if I tried to act like most everyone wants and expect me to act, that would really be phony!" ... I still contend that the major problem area is still uncertainties around the mother/ daughter relationship, and the only sure way to find out about this is to have them spend some time together away from a youth justice institution. All of the high-sounding phrases such as "truth", "honesty", "personal integrity", etc are beginning to sound a bit hollow even to me. I do need to find out from Planning Board what the hell is further expected since the goals which were set early in our relationship have been realised. If anyone is under the illusion we are going to mould a positive super-citizen out of this girl, I got news for them!

I will be going home from here to finish high school and go to modeling school.

I hope no one ever asks me to be a prostitute again because I'll spit in their faces. I've got too much pride and self-respect for that kind of shit.

And I still sit and worry and cry about my sisters – both dead and alive – my sisters of pain. …

The End of Jenette's Short Story written while in the Secure Unit.

Addendum

Discharge Plan

Jenette left the secure unit on extended furlough to live in the home of her maternal grandparents in a rural part of the state. After 8 weeks she moved back into the city to live with her mother until such time as they could together move nearer to her Maternal Grandparents.

Addendum to Discharge report – Four Months Later

Jenette made contact with her juvenile parole officer reporting that she was engaged and planned to marry a Black man whom she had met in the city. They ran away and were apprehended in San Francisco at the end of October. On returning home under police escort and back to the institutional setting from which she went on furlough, Jenette was diagnosed with serum hepatitis contracted during her absence without leave, apparently from shooting up amphetamines intravenously.

A four-week rest program was initiated under the supervision of health professionals and counseling that reviewed what had happened with her short-term plans upon moving home the first time. After 5 years of institutional involvement with the youth justice system, we have reached the point with this 17 year-old young woman where little more can be done. Her only plan is still to return to her mother's home for a few weeks and then live independently when possible. While Jenette has made considerable progress towards preparing for independent living, it is our general impression that she still has little regard for the impact of her actions on herself and others, and that she will do as she pleases, regardless of the consequences.

If possible, Jenette should be discharged from the youth justice system with a strong recommendation that she be handled henceforth as an adult, accountable for her own actions. Her use of youth justice services overall has been poor, and while she remains a young woman with enormous potential, the prognosis for her future at this time must be considered marginal.

23 September: Care Worker Notes

I received a collect call from Jenette tonight about 8:00 pm. She said she was okay and was leaving the State within a few moments after this phone call, to get married. "He's Black, but has a square job, two cars and a nice apartment – and he's not a pimp!" I told Jenette that her Mother and a lot of other people were really worried about her – some were imagining all kinds of awful things which might have happened to her. She said she knew this but she was okay. She went on to say that this was something she could not discuss with her Mother, because Mother would only get upset and start making derogatory remarks about "niggers"

– they had been all through this many times before and always with the same results. Jenette then asked me if I would call her Mother and break the news of her impending marriage. I told her it was not my responsibility to do this for her – she should face up to this herself and not use me as a cop-out.

Jenette said she realized she was trying to get out of an unpleasant situation, and promised she would call her Mother before getting married. I asked Jenette point blank if she had thought the whole thing through because it was a very serious step she was contemplating.

She said that she had thought of little else recently. Jenette thanked me for listening to her and I reminded her of her obligation to her Mother and we said goodbye.

Apparently she does feel some obligation or responsibility towards her family because Jenette rang her Mother right after talking to me. Then Mother called me and we compared notes. We basically received a similar story. Mother was even invited to speak with the guy Jenette was with. She explained that the guy made pretty good sense and was quite cooperative, going so far as asking her if she would allow herself opportunity to get to know him, and let him call on Jenette at home since he did not want to get married without the Mother's blessing. She felt this was a fair approach and told him so, but also made it plain that she was not very happy over the methods he and Jenette had used so far. Jenette and her guy agreed that the two of them would be in contact with Mother within the next couple of days and see what could be worked out.

The authors heard nothing further from Jenette after she went on parole. Her mother received recognition for her work within her Native American tribe in the same rural area where Jenette spent time with her grandparents. We hope Jenette made it ok. She was a survivor, and she would need all the survival skills she could find.

Aliese's Reflections

Jenette and I were close friends and there was a bond between us because we were both of mixed blood – Indian and White. Both of us were very light skinned and "could pass" for being White. That always put us in unusual positions and gave us a lot of insight into the racism that was still very rampant in the 1970's in the United States. It is so strange looking back now, forty years later; on my Sisters of Pain because for the most part we did not really discuss our families. We did not share the stories perhaps out of embarrassment, but also because we were just talked out. Sometimes you lose your power when you share too much of your life, your feelings, your sorrow. It makes you vulnerable and we came from a world that would chew you up and spit you out. Besides, who wanted to talk about how messed up our families were, when we could talk about cool stuff like boys. After all, we were teenage girls! I never knew she was involved in prostitution and if she was, I think it was very briefly.

At the time of our incarceration, none of us had any idea that there was such a level of planning in the way we were managed. I mean we all knew the staff were working together, but not the level of purposeful engagement which is unfolded in the pages to come. I can smile now. But then again, I am reading and reflecting on this, forty years later.

This was a totally new approach to reforming juveniles and in retrospect, we were trying to keep up with all the changes in our lives in this locked-down and high security "home", and the world was rapidly changing around us. Also on our plate was trying to figure out how to cope with a whole new set of problems we were facing. Our problems. In the past, we never really had to do that. Otherwise, many of us would not be here at this facility. We had to learn a whole new set of rules, and for many of us, deal with an unknown future. None of this was easy work, neither for the young women who were locked up, nor for the staff.

The pressure was unbearable at times, for all of us. This was a time for forming alliances and later redefining what healthy relationships would be in our lives. We did not know this would be an ever-daunting, ever-changing task as we evolved from young delinquents into young women. As I look back now, I can see that we were the fortunate ones.

New interpretations of policies and social working were moving away from shock treatments or rituals designed to "break us" through demeaning and degrading practices such as placing us naked and handcuffed to our beds, and generally depriving us of any emotional connection.

In reading the notes from July 9th, where the staff felt they had reached an impasse, and that she was being accused of being phony, I wonder if Jenette was probably trying her best to just breathe and deal with the everyday stuff. Be yourself, means to let your hair down, relax as you would in a safe place where there is no condemnation, no judgment, and it is okay to NOT be perfect or well-mannered. I am sure there is some truth in that, as well as her simply not wanting to deal with some high pressured issues. To truly conform meant to lose your identity and that is the one thing we had left as our souls were lost at that time in our lives. Sometimes you just wanted a break from it all, like spring break at school.

Jenette had it pretty tough and she had to go back to her home where all awaited her and a home life and community that had not evolved with her. Lucky in some ways she had a home and a mother to go back to. That's what you would say when you had "no family", like me. Later, when you come to realize how dysfunctional home life was for many, you counted your blessings if – like me – you were a lone wolf. It was a wonder anyone of us kids survived and I am sad to learn that many of us did not. While I cannot say that I know what it felt like to be Jenette, what I can say is most of us had very similar problems. Finally she landed here at the secure unit where she was given the opportunity to make real life changes, to learn to form healthy relationships with adults and figures of authority, and given the time to muddle through the healing process, self-awareness process, and basically grounding her long enough to attempt to reach these goals.

Those of us who have become healthy adults no longer blame our parents, the staff, or the system. I feel very blessed and fortunate that I was placed there along with Jenette and the others, "to do the work". We are all just a work in progress, no matter how successful we are, or where we are in our walk in life. We were fortunate that we were being given the tools to engage life and learn how to make real changes in our lives. We had to get to the root of our problems, face them, and learn some coping skills while trying to grasp these new expectations that we placed on ourselves, as well as trying to please staff. What we learned in the secure unit was more than anyone else had ever taught us. We simply needed the tools to survive in our world, then we could get busy and conquer that world of yours.

We were always surprised with our Social Worker, because he had such a knack of really understanding what he was observing, not just with us personally, but also within the system itself. There was an example in the Social Worker notes dated May 19th where a small statement was made that would have gone unnoticed by many a carer – noting that Jenette had her shit together. Most people never really listened. Our strength, our wisdom, fortitude, willpower, "stick-to-it-ive-ness", our very core, comes through small steps of awareness and enlightenment. It is so refreshing to see the Social Worker recognizing the small things. In his own discovery and true compassion, he was able to project a new sense of awareness into Jenette, who still does not understand the power she possesses. She can make changes in her life, if she is willing to make the efforts.

Changes – we were in the middle of changes within a system, but still caught in the old ways of judgment, condemnation, and punishment. Some of that was coming from within our own souls, but not all of it. Many of us up to this point had heard nothing but condemnation from one source or another. To top all of that, we had to deal with guilt and shame: soul-killers – those two emotions will cripple you for life. There were plenty of feelings to go around, plenty for everyone to share, but most often, everything was left to the young person to deal with alone. At least here, and now, at this place, we were learning how to deal with the guilt and shame that had been our burden.

Our Social Worker was such a breath of fresh air to us. He understood because he cared and he listened, (not just from a doctor's point of view). What saved us and helped us, was that he truly had heart and was human in his approach. He could not help but reflect that. He was also young and seemed hip in his ole square way (compared to us incorrigibles) and that was a help to us too, he had a better grip and understanding of the world in which we lived and I don't think we felt as condemned by him as by some of the others. You must establish trust first and let me tell you, that is not an easy task and I still battle that today.

I know it was not an easy task running a secure unit. Staff had to watch our every move, careful of our safety, keep a structured program, and try not to bring their own prejudices with them, and oh yeah, count the silverware after every meal. We always vied for the attention of the Social Worker, as he seemed to spearhead more of the out-of the-box thinking and would go to bat for you, the extra mile like letting Jenette see her sister and brother. It was a simple act of kindness, a human thing to do – but yet in *that world, and at that time, he could have been reprimanded and possibly lost his job.* You have to be willing to take risks emotionally, at least, to reach out to a kid. Otherwise, you are just another authority figure flapping your jaw. And it was nice to read the Social Worker's notes about the mother and that he too, was questioning everything he had read in the case file.

You have to heal the family unit, if you expect the child to re-enter the same environment. Everyone had to re-learn how to do things together, how to break old bad habits, learn how to communicate together, and to co-exist through all those years of pain and heartache in the past. It is not an easy task – for anyone – and certainly not for a young woman who has been wounded so deeply, or for a family who thinks all the problems stem from the troubled youth. Parents were in as much denial as anyone.

What touched me so deeply with Jenette is living through her words, understanding her choices and seeing life through her eyes. My life was very different from hers in many ways. But I totally understand that her value system had not changed. She was still just trying to survive in her own way and what she understood, trying to fit into the material world and obtain the things that the world taught us meant success: marriage, nice cars, a decent house, and some extra cash. That was her view of the world and success, to whatever degree.

We were all in such a hurry to grow up and prove ourselves to everyone. I know "they" felt her chances of success were marginal according to the notes, but what I think they failed to see here was a young woman who had survived a pretty harsh world thus far, and that she had a grasp on what life could be. She just hadn't figured out all the mechanics of putting all of that into place. I would like to believe that with a few more years under her belt, she came through with flying colours. But then, I always like to hope for the best. I hope she was able to overcome the hepatitis.

I will always remember my sister, and the powwow we attended together, where we camped and shared our war wounds. I know that someday we will meet again in another world.

Making Connections

One cannot engage with someone in any meaningful way without connecting with her or him in some way or another. Without meaningful connections, a social worker's interventions – as with the interventions of child and youth care workers – will have limited effect. It's easy to blame 'a young person' when she or he is unresponsive. We claim that it's the Carer's or Social Worker's obligation to make connections with each young person for whom they are assigned professional responsibilities.

Jenette presented major challenges for her White, male social worker of provincial middle class background. As an experienced teenage prostitute at the age of 16, Jenette probably viewed me as she had other White male authority figures, whether youth justice caseworker, policeman or trick. Jenette was 'beyond my ken' as one might hear in Scotland. Her life experiences were so different from what most 16 year olds have experienced. Relationships for Jenette were instrumental, in other words, what can I get out of this person. My connection with Jenette finally came through her writing. Jenette wanted to write her story – the story around which this volume was fashioned – and I offered her the use of my portable typewriter. We ended up talking about what she was writing and where she thought the story was taking her. When she was finished, Jenette gave me a copy of her short story.

Sometimes a failure to connect or engage with a young person gets rendered as diagnostic justification for 'what's wrong with this young person'. Like Jenette, almost all of the girls in this secure unit had suffered from such labelling. All were recidivists in one form or another. We argue that relationship – not case management – is the foundation for all child and youth care work. Making connection is the foundation upon which any social work relationship builds (Brendtro & du Toit, 2005). A social worker or child and youth care worker connects with a young person, and then engages with him or her as he or she lives their lives. Helping a young woman nurse her child, assisting parents to prepare their garden, teaching a young man to shoot a basketball ... all such engagements are powerful when a young person is connected in relationship with another.

Social workers and child and youth care workers are required to give conscious thought to the ways in which they engage with a young person – indeed engage with anyone – giving respectful attention to protocols associated with engaging someone from cultural traditions different from one's own (Fulcher, 2003). Simply trying to understand, as well as contemplate, different relational starting points can present major challenges when seeking to make cross-cultural connections. One's own personal experiences of acculturation and socialisation impose taken-for-granted assumptions and create a cognitive mindset that is not easily altered.

Rituals of encounter between carer(s) or social worker(s) and children or young people have developed through cultural protocols. The meaning a child or young person gives to culture – including youth group or gang culture – is constantly evolving as young people seek to understand and adapt to their current predicament and daily experiences in any new living environment. Each encounter requires that a *cultural lens* be included in a social worker's or child and youth care worker's essential toolkit of competencies. Like transitional objects, rituals of encounter strengthen purposeful communication with young people.

Being in relationship is not the same as 'having a relationship'. Everyone has relationships but 'being in relationship' means actively engaging with another person in a deep and profound manner which impacts both the young person and their helper (Gannon, 2008). A child and youth care worker recognizes that they live in a relationship with a person where each has contributed to making that relationship what it is (Fewster, 1990; 2005). It also means engaging in social work or case management relationships and the personal/professional authority that shapes such relationships over the course of time.

Relationships build upon a history that shapes it and our ways of being in that relationship. Writing about social work practices in the United Kingdom with young people in care, Thomas highlighted the importance children give to relationships. These included "the continuity of this relationship, reliability and availability, confidentiality, advocacy and doing things together" (2005, p. 189). As Fewster said, "Being in relationship means that we have what it takes to remain open and responsive in conditions where most mortals – and professionals – quickly distance themselves, become 'objective' and look for the external *fix*" (2004, p.3).

Meeting people 'where they are at' involves being with people where they live their lives but is also more than that. It means accepting a young person or family member for how they are and who they are – as we encounter them. It means responding appropriately to Jenette's developmental capabilities, accepting her fears and hesitations, celebrating her joys and enabling her to be who she can be in our interactions together (Small & Fulcher, 2005). Krueger argued that interventions must be oriented to a young person's emotional, cognitive, social, and physical needs (2002). Just as a forest guide meets others at the start of their journey, so does the social worker or youth worker meet a young person like Jenette "where she was at" as they start working together.

Every young person and family is unique. This means that all of one's interventions must be tailored to fit that young person and/or family as we understand them. It means being flexible in our interactions with each young person or family member, recognizing that no one approach or intervention applies in all situations. Just because we responded in a particular manner when engaging with one young person from a different culture, it does not follow that all young people from that culture will respond in the same manner. Just because one young person liked a joke when they were experiencing pain, it does not mean that another young person will respond in a similar fashion (Digney, 2007).

Just as social workers or child and youth care workers are acknowledged as individuals, so it is with each young person or family member with whom we work. We must remain flexible, preparing to modify our approach and our way of being as appropriate with each unique young person or family member we encounter – '*one size does not fit all*'. 'Group interventions' where every child or young person receives the same consequence for specific behaviours make little sense. Without connections that underpin working relationships with young people, their family members and significant others, very little serious work will be carried out during their involvement with out-of-home care.

Questions for Small Group Discussion or Guided Reflection

1. How might the adolescent development of a young woman like Jenette be shaped through a history of sexual activity as a 15 year-old with multiple males, females, and three-some male-female partners at the same time?

2. What might be said of Jenette's cultural identity as a young woman whose grandparents were elders in their Native Indian tribe and whose mother later assumed respected elder standing?

3. How might you start making connections with a young woman like Jenette if she was assigned to your social work caseload or start engaging with her in a youth work mentoring role after school?

4. As a young woman of mixed Caucasian-Native American ancestry, how might one explain Jenette's identification with young Afro-American men and women and the ways in which her relationships with different pimps ended?

5. What did you note about the relationship between Jenette's mother and her daughter; and the relationship both mother and daughter sought with one particular male care worker at the secure unit?

Room 2
Suzie – *Relational Care*

4 August

Dearest Lonny Rae

Hey Beautiful Man! I know you have been worried about me not writing. Well Sugar, I couldn't write before I got permission because you are in jail. They got some kind of a rule that says we can't write to adult jails and institutions without special permission.

I can only write you four letters a week, but you can write as often as you want. So please write – the letters might be censored so don't be talking too slick because I don't want these people to misunderstand what you are saying.

Anyway, I am in a maximum security cottage. It's just like jail as far as I'm concerned. I have a Review Board in 6 months. If they feel that I'm ready to leave before then, they'll give me one sooner. So I got to work.

My counsellor is a pretty hip dude. He is for real and seems to really care about what's happening with the young ladies in here, which is really nice to know.

I'm okay, except my head is all messed up about being here. But I am really going to get myself together so that I can get out and be with you like I should be.

Baby, if the drug house thing goes through, lay and stay cuz it's a lot better than the joint. And Baby, I can't even imagine you going to the joint. I don't want to see you there. Just get it together because Baby, I love you – you're my whole world. And Baby, we got to work it out and live together – eventually get married.

Baby I got that on my mind – us being together! As far as I can see, that's the best thing I have got to look forward to. I know that we can be together eventually. Like you said, I'm not like any other woman you have ever known. I won't ever leave you again. Just like that song "If loving you is wrong, I don't want to be right". It's true. We just got to get it together, and keep it that way. Okay Sugar?

I know Baby that "we can make it if we try" cuz "you're the best thing that ever happened to me". Do those two sides sound familiar? I know you remember Sly Stones – "you can make it if you try". And that's what it is.

Another thing I've noticed about my caseworker is that he thinks I'm somebody. He didn't put me down at all. He thinks I'm somebody. And the thing that's so beautiful about it is he doesn't know hardly anything about me, but he gives me my 'propers', and acts like I'm somebody. I sure do appreciate that.

Baby, you know what I expect from people, but not a whole lot of people realise how important it is to respect and be respected. I know how well you know that – just as I do. But Baby, maybe it will be cool for us pretty soon. My caseworker feels that I don't really have a home (just as I do) anyway, I guess when I get paroled, I will get a self-parole. This means I won't be living with my parents or anything. I guess a self parole takes longer, but it will be better – we can most likely get married then.

I am so excited, Baby, cuz it seems like things are looking up! I know that as soon as I get myself together, I'll be able to leave. It might take awhile, but like I said, it will be for the best.

Evidently there is someone here who takes pictures that look like professional pictures, so I'm getting my picture taken so that you can have one. And tell "Mama" she better get on her job and send me a picture of you cuz I really got to have one.

I'm pretty tired of broads – I want to see my fine man! So Baby, please get a picture to me quick! Alright? I'm planning to get my hair cut – in a long shag. I hope you'll like it. Tell me right away because I'll probably get it cut this week! Alright?

It's hot here. Our cells are made of brick – and we only have one little window that opens, and that is the only source of air we have. It's way too hot at night. Last night I got up and put cold water in a towel and slept with the towel on me. I was still awake around midnight – and lights out is at 10 – so I couldn't sleep for the longest! But later on, I finally cooled off cuz the towel was so cold, I almost froze.

I wish my Dad would hurry up and bring me some cigarettes. I don't know when he's coming, but he better try to hurry up and bring some cuz I'm dying without some. Right now, I even wish I had non-filters. Anything. So my Dad better get on his job. He be telling me that things is cool. I wish he'd just come on! Well, well.

Baby, I know that you know that I miss you. You better know that anyway. Cuz I been missing you Sugar! Yes I have. Baby you don't even know how hard I cried when I heard that I couldn't write you without special permission. I guess I just figured that I wouldn't get it.

This guy is so nice – it takes a caseworker with for real emotions and capacity to care about "his kids" to realize what a young lady goes through when she doesn't have her man by her side. I just got to be with you. Got to be with you soon. I know it will happen.

Sometimes it's hard to look really good in an institution. I know you can understand that. It seems like I can't look the way I want in here because there are so many restrictions. I can't wear eyelashes so that messes things up a little.

I gave the Bitch who snitched on Willie the mental charge of her life before I left juvie. I got Anne, who had moved out to come back for a visit. She came in, and Sharell (the Snitch) was sitting down at the table. Anne came up to me and said "Hi Lady – Is this the Snitch?"

I said "Yeah"

She said, "Well hey Bitch, you snitched on my Man!"

Sharell looked really surprised.

She said, "Yeah, well he was gonna kill me".

And Anne said "Well he wasn't going to, but he is now," and took Sharell to the window.

Sherell looked out, and all she could see was a Black man sitting with a lady with long black hair and another dude.

Sharell said, "Is that Willie? I thought he was in jail".

Anne said, "Well I'm a good woman – and I love my man. Now he is going to be sitting outside the day you leave, Bitch. And we're gonna be waiting for you. Don't go saying anything about anyone telling you this either. Our alibi is too strong and they'll just feel that you are lying."

Sharell was so scared that she just went to her room and said something to staff. I don't know what it was she told them but when she came out, I hit her right in her stomach. I know I warned the Bitch! Anyway, she tried to cut her wrists the other night, but I told staff and she had to go to Security. Staff asked me was it all in Sharell's imagination, and we said yeah. And Staff said, "Well Anne's with Al anyway, she's not with Willie".

And then I had this dude who is a friend of Anne's sneak up outside of Sharell's window and say, "I'm gonna kill you, Bitch".

Evidently they are thinking of sending the Bitch to the psychiatric hospital. I know I be slick sometimes. I hope she goes too!

Well Sugar, I'm getting so tired of this ugly ass place and I ain't been here but for 4 days. That ain't just but for just a minute – So I know things will have to start going a little bit faster!

This place isn't really all that bad, except it's boring, and I hate being locked up. I know that you know that! Well, I guess I can't really say anything cuz I'm here and I better just try to make the best of it.

But anyway Baby, this letter writing to you is a privilege – evidently not too many young ladies get this. So Baby, don't write anything about running, pimps and hoes, or anything because this cottage goes by something that is called positive/negative.

Running, talking about the fast life, or drugs or something like that is negative. I don't need to dwell on negative things. I got to put them out of my mind to get out of here.

So please don't write those kinds of things because 1) it might get my writing to you taken away and 2) it might get my head in the wrong place and I got to deal with the positive future, rather than the negative past. I hope that you understand this.

So Baby, let's get it together and show these people just how much we care for each other. Also Baby, have you considered going to school up there at the jail house? You're a Trustee aren't you?

Do you get to go up to the recreation center? You can shoot pool and stuff up there. We don't have a pool table but our rec center has one. I don't have my privileges to go there yet, so I can't go like most of the girls can.

My detail here is bathroom. At least the broads are clean. The broads at Juvie were disgusting. They didn't even bother to take care of themselves. So here my job is easier.

I just have to mop and generally clean up. Bathrooms are an easy detail here. I'm going on a diet – also exercising. Trying to get myself looking good. For you!!

I start school tomorrow. We go to the school here in the cottage.

Here's my schedule of what I do all day:

7:00	Get up, dress, make bed, empty waste basket, sweep and buff floor. Open my curtains and straighten up the shelves.
8:00	Eat Breakfast – Do Detail
9:00	Go to School
12:00	Eat Lunch
12:30	PE and exercise
2:30	Rest and Free Time
4:00	Rec Time for girls who have privileges go swimming or to the rec center
5:00	Eat Dinner – rest and free time
9:00	Detail
9:25	Go to Room
10:00	Lights Out

Pretty crazy, huh?

Staff here is pretty cool. Talking to staff discussing problems is a major part of getting out. They are pretty easy to talk to. Seems like they always have the time – they're never too busy!

Well Sugar, I got to go cuz its bed time. I'll write again Tuesday. Love As

Always, Your Lady Love.

Goodnight Sexy Baby. Love!! This letter doesn't smell good cuz I don't have my perfume cuz it's glass.

Each young woman spent her first 60-90 minutes upon entering the secure unit for the first time, locked in a room talking with their new caseworker and compiling a list of "I Statements" about their life journey which brought them there that day.

1 August: 28 Points about My Life Journey as of Today

1.	*I started to know that I had problems when I was about 5.*
2.	*I didn't have a home, nobody loved me and everything I did was wrong.*
3.	*I got beat up by my stepmother when I was about four until I was about eight.*
4.	*Then I went to my Grandmother's house to live.*
5.	*Things never did get better with my family.*
6.	*When I was about 12 I ran away for the first time.*
7.	*I ran away to be with some dudes.*
8.	*From then on I started getting into more trouble and running with the wrong crowd.*
9.	*I was the terror of my family. Nobody else in the family got into trouble.*
10.	*They (my family) started saying I was like my Mother who they called a junkie, a prostitute, a no good.*
11.	*I decided, "What's the use?" If that's what they thought of me, that's what I would be.*
12.	*My caseworker at the Youth Center made me meet my Mother when I was 12. I didn't want to meet her at first, but when I did, I liked her.*
13.	*Then I couldn't see her after I got out of the Youth Center.*

14. So I ran way to be with her and the court said I couldn't see her again.

15. My Grandmother made me have an abortion when I was about 14.

16. I kept running away and they sent me to live with my Dad.

17. I still kept running away. They put me in a foster home and a drug treatment place. Started using heroin when I was 15.

18. I finally went to live with my Mother. She is always drunk or on the verge of being drunk.

19. I started prostituting. All my money was going to support my heroin habit.

20. I was going in circles and didn't care.

21. I got nothing going for me so what's the use.

22. When I get down or feeling depressed, I put an act on so nobody will know.

23. I sing, dance, make jokes until I can be by myself, then I just cry.

24. Sometimes I can't even cry and that's when I feel the worst.

25. The only person I got going for me is Lonnie who's in jail right now.

26. Everybody tells me not to manipulate. But when I don't, I don't get anywhere and things work out for the worst.

27. I am going to have to make it on my own. I don't think I can ever have a family that care about me.

28. I just want to be secure.

Suzie

8 August: Care Worker Notes

I asked Suzie's Grandmother not to give her any rescue messages. Grandmother and Aunt both agreed. I also told them even though I granted them an hour's visit, it didn't mean this would be continued as all visits were evaluated for what benefits they offer each student. We haven't had Suzie's initial Board to make any of these decisions. Grandmother said she could come every week and probably would if allowed. I question the helpfulness of the frequency of that many visits.

Grandmother and Aunt were well dressed and wanting to be helpful. She brought a whole bunch of stamps which I put in the book for letter recording. Told me Suzie could call collect if and when she was allowed. She talked about Suzie being a good girl and attending church until after she left their home.

Asked if any of her clothes needed dry cleaning and offered to have it done. Told her no as our clothing lady said they were all fairly clean. I get the initial impression that she will be overly helpful, and thus interfere if visits aren't controlled and or limited.

13 August

Dearest Lonny Rae

Hey Sugar. I was reading some of my old letters from you and crying because I miss you so much. It's like I just got something inside me that keeps calling your name, reaching out for our love. Cuz Baby, I know it's for real.

Baby, we got to cut this game loose. It never has gotten us anywhere but in jail and in trouble. We haven't gained anything but trouble through all this? I know it's hard to feel that the game ain't no good because we can look at the successful players and their ladies and look at what they've got – but even the best of them have a downfall.

And we are having our downfall early in life – we'll be fools if we go back to the game. And changing our location won't do anything. We can get busted anywhere else just as good as we can here. We've both got records. And if we just got a speeding ticket they could look back on our records and know what we have been busted for. They would be just waiting for us to do the same thing there.

Why can't we just be happy? Is your idea of happiness a Cadillac, diamonds and furs? Well Baby, money and possessions aren't any good unless we're happy. And this has been the saddest time in my life and I know you aren't enjoying yourself up in that funky jailhouse either.

Baby, we'll never get anywhere in the game. It just isn't real. As far as I can tell, none of it is any good.

And do you want to spend your life in jail or the joint? Or do you want kids, me, a nice crib and happiness?

Baby, we got to make our decision – and quick!

I just hope that your's is the same as mine's. Do you want to cut the game loose and not have the fast life, or do you want to stick with it and not have me? Decide Baby, cuz I'm being honest. That's how it's got to be.

I got to look out for myself too. I can't be used – it just doesn't lead me anywhere. If we're together, out of these jails and I keep on whoring, our love will not keep me from getting busted. The only thing that will keep us from getting busted, is cutting the game completely loose.

Lonny, look back. It hasn't gotten either of us anywhere in the right direction. Sure, we can always think up an excuse to justify why we don't have things, but it still all boils down to the same thing. We're not together. And what good is a Cadillac if we're not out in the streets to ride in it.

15 August: Social Worker Notes

Mrs M and I talked with Suzie this morning and explained about her 10 year-old half-brother's death. Her first reaction was sobbing and repeating that she couldn't believe it. Then she pulled herself together and rambled on a about a lot of unrelated stuff.

We later talked about having to manage our own feelings of anger towards Suzie for the way she was handling the news of her half-brother's death, found at 6:15 a.m. hanging from a rope attached to an old swing set in the back yard of the family home. Her Grandmother will be down this evening to share more fully with Suzie what happened.

Second half of the afternoon, Suzie was much the same – listened to music, danced and chatted with various girls from time to time. She went out on the patio with Ali and they talked for more than a half hour. Suzie was by now becoming increasingly pale and was beginning to show a little agitation. She talked quite a while with Mrs Y before dinner. Through dinner Suzie chattered away with Mrs F and girls at her table – trying hard to think of anything but her little brother. A lot of disruption around the cottage and the resident group was fairly itchy.

As far as I can see, we better just give it up now and try to have a future – despite our records. If you can't accept it, well Baby, say Good Bye to me cuz I ain't gonna destroy us. I'd rather just end our relationship now than to keep on trying to build it up and have it all fall down.

I hope you really understand what I'm saying. I am going to square up and be real and enjoy my life.

Like William DeVonne says "I'm thankful for what I got, although I may not drive a great big Cadillac ... Gangster whitewalls, TV antenna in the back ..." See Baby, I feel like I have uplifted my mind to its highest place in the game, and that's deciding to cut it loose. I know you can understand where I'm coming from.

Baby, can't you see that all I want is you? Let me be your motivation – if nothing else quit because you want to keep me.

I'd rather you quit because you care about yourself. Cuz Sugar, you deserve all the good things in life – a good wife, sweet children, all of those things. It's just a matter of you wanting them.

I wish I was writing you and saying that I was leaving out of this place and I will be seeing you, but I cannot say that. I am not leaving yet, and probably won't be leaving for a long time.

I want to do my best and show these people that I really do not need this place. I don't think that the Family House thing even has a chance. I've written two letters about it and still haven't gotten an answer. So I really am thinking that the whole thing must be just completely dead.

Well Sweetheart, I know this letter isn't going to get to you probably ever. Maybe someday. Baby, I do love you.

I guess I wrote this letter just to get my feelings out. I did mean every word I said though. Even if this letter never gets to you, at least I'll know where I'm at.

Love As Always,
Your Lady Love

15 August: Care Worker Notes (cont)

Suzie became more anxious as time wore on after dinner — asking one staff or the other when her grandmother would arrive. Intermittently she would return to the music, dance awhile, talk a bit and a couple of times, stood staring out the front window. Mrs Y finally called at 8:10 p.m. and found out that Grandmother felt it was too late to come down; she had been very "busy".

Mrs Y requested that Grandmother come as soon as possible since Suzie needed a family member right now! Grandmother and Aunt arrived shortly before 9:00 p.m. We cancelled the 9-10 swim session, and placed the rest of the girls in their rooms at 9:00 p.m. because I had to leave for a campus Security tour and didn't want to leave Mrs F with such a high group all by herself.

Another Carer continues ...

Suzie's youngest brother found their half-brother and tried
to get him down from the swings, but failed. Nothing was
said about where the parent(s) were at that time — 6:15
a.m. Then the police were called and so on. Suzie cried really
hard for a few minutes. Grandmother gave Suzie very little
comfort at first. She told us the funeral would be Monday at
3:00 pm. Suzie asked about her family but little was said.
She broke down several times but was given little comfort
by her family. I thought they were sort of cold. Suzie started
talking about the death and cried. Then Grandmother
started to cry a little and gave Suzie a hug. Suzie said she
wanted to go to the funeral. They talked of proper dress.
Suzie told of her future plans. I ended the visit at 10:00
p.m. Grandmother asked us to let her know if Suzie can go
to the funeral.

When we got back in the cottage, Suzie asked to call her
Father. We let her. While in her room, Suzie told of how her
Father seemed unaffected by the death. We talked about
death and she recalled a lot of incidents with her little
brother. Just before I left, Suzie told me she was really
surprised by how much staff really care here. She said it
really shocked her when she saw Mrs F cry.

Stated it was really strange because she feels closer to me
than she feels towards her Mother or Stepmother because
she knows I care. Suzie used to be beaten for crying when
she was little, and on the streets she had to learn not to
show emotions. She finds it hard to accept the fact that
tears are okay here. There's so much more to say but I'm so
tired, it is 2:00 a.m. More later.

16 August: Care Worker Notes

Back again – refreshed I think (?) Tonight I talked with
Suzie and she felt very relieved because she's allowed to go
to the funeral. Suzie's having a very hard time sleeping
tonight so Annie left the light on for her. I sure hope that
I'm doing things right. It's such a draining experience for me
because I never thought I could really help as much as I have
with Suzie. Oh, and I forgot! Suzie's Grandmother told me
that her half-brother could have stood up when he was
found hanging from the swings. His feet could touch the
ground.

Another Care Worker continues –

Thanks for the information about the stages of grieving we
might anticipate as Suzie's lives through her grief process
over the hours since learning of her brother's death. The
strangest part of the entire episode was the fact that Suzie
did not really break down and off-load any appreciable
amount of feelings or emotion until her Grandmother and
Aunt had gone. I guess that is about denial.

 The first real break occurred while Mrs Y and Suzie were
still out front after the relatives left. Mrs Y held her and
comforted her so that Suzie was able to cry openly.

After Suzie talked to her Dad, she was back in control of
herself pretty well, but her expression was DEAD! She came
and sat in the office doorway and talked almost
compulsively. I knelt beside her chair, held her hands and
talked to her quietly and this was all that was needed. I've
never seen anyone fight so hard against crying!

But she did cry, a great deal! She never really stopped talking throughout although it was not entirely coherent. There was anger, self-recrimination, frustration, puzzlement and downright anguish. She admitted that it was hard for her to cry — trained from early childhood not to cry and this was strengthened by her street experiences.

Finally, Suzie pretty much ran out of steam about 10:45 p.m. Mrs Y stayed with Suzie for another half hour or so, and we left her door ajar. By then the prescribed Valium had hit with full force and Suzie was really drowsy. When checked at 1:00 a.m., she was sound asleep and her door was locked.

This has been a heavy day folks. But it has only strengthened a conviction that I am pursuing the right profession! I will admit, however, that I'm willing to step aside and let some other team members help Suzie through the next few days which are bound to be rough for her. I think this entire experience here with us tonight will have a profound effect on Suzie. It's probably the first real lick we've gotten in for the "Good Guys"! One additional item: Suzie has requested that Mrs Y be allowed to accompany her to the funeral if Suzie gets permission to attend.

Night Staff Note —

I also dealt with Suzie tonight and answered some of her questions about death. She really appreciated the fact that staff here care about her. I would certainly agree for her going to the funeral if a caring staff member could go as a buffer between Suzie and the family. I think she needs this funeral to really face the reality of her brother's death.

28 August

Dear Sir

We would like to express our appreciation and gratitude to you for bringing Suzie home for her little brother's funeral services.

We wish she could have been here longer, but we understand.

We have been hoping that somehow this whole tragic situation might have a beneficial effect on Suzie's attitudes.

Thanks again.

Father and Stepmother

5 September: Care Worker Notes

I talked with Suzie last night. She's a very confused girl, quite afraid of the future and the unknown. I asked her about the letter writing the night of the funeral and she said she wrote to a "wanna-be" pimp to tell him off and get rid of hostile feelings she had felt all day.

The other was to a guy she met at juve. They've exchanged letters a couple of times and he's not a pimp.

Suzie feels that she has to compete with her stepmother for her father's affection. It always was that way and it always will be that way.

Suzie said that she keeps reverting back to her old ways because she feels comfortable there. She doesn't feel comfortable with the changes she's trying to make. She is very disappointed in herself because of her past and for not feeling she can make the necessary changes. I encouraged her to keep working on it.

Apparently she has an older sister (don't know if this is her real sister or a sister from the streets). This sister who's 24 now was here in this same institution some time ago! She was involved in prostitution from the age of 13 — is still involved and also a junkie. With something like this hanging over her head I can see why it might affect Suzie's outlook!

I feel that Suzie and I can talk openly but she is cautious about what she says at times. I asked why she feels that Daddy denies the beatings she got? She said because Father really loves his second wife, Suzie's stepmother and just puts the beatings out of his mind. She didn't think her Father knew about all the beatings. Stepmother told him she spanked the kids which Suzie claimed were actually beatings. Suzie said it is possible the things she remembers get distorted a little because she was very young at the time.

We draw our own conclusions!

September 11: Care Worker Notes

I talked with Suzie tonight about her Grandmother. She told me that she and the Grandmother never have been able to talk about anything serious. Grandmother always avoids problems as if they didn't exist or just accepts them without questioning.

Suzie told me that from what she could gather the Grandmother was very jealous of the women in her son's life. She told me that when the Grandmother found out that Suzie's mother was pregnant with her older brother, and then Suzie, her Grandmother offered to pay for abortions but the Father wouldn't hear of it.

Grandmother has always given Suzie anything that she wanted and that when Suzie lived in her home, the Grandparents were really strict with her.

They didn't allow her to date or go any place without them taking her. If Suzie wanted to spend the night at someone's home, Suzie's friends had to come spend the night at their place. They were very protective.

Suzie shared that the relationship with her Grandmother has been only a give and take thing around material possessions but they didn't talk about Suzie's problems. Instead, there was just idle chit chat.

September 11: Care Worker Notes (cont)

Suzie's Grandparents came to visit tonight and I had a chance to talk with them. I asked whether they knew about the beatings Suzie got when she was little.

Grandmother told me that Suzie was definitely beaten by her Stepmother and that her Son and Suzie's Father knew about some of these beatings but that he was usually working swing shift and this is when the Stepmother beat the kids. Grandmother told me that she got Suzie and her older brother one time and there were marks of the beatings on their bodies. Suzie's Brother had big open wounds on his body where his Stepmother had beaten him with an electrical cord and Suzie had old marks where she too had been beaten. She told me that at one stage, the Court was involved with Father and Stepmother about the beatings and the Grandparents were given custody of the two oldest children for a short time.

The Grandparents described Suzie's Father and Stepmother as very unstable people with a lot of problems which they take out on the kids. The Grandparents think their Grandchildren have been abused by both parents and they have not received as good care as they should have received.

9 October: Summary of the Planning Board Meeting

The tragic death of Suzie's half-brother had a profound impact. Her entire manner of functioning in the living unit has changed. Staff who accompanied her to the funeral have developed a close working relationship with Suzie. She has functioned very positively in the program and become something of a positive influence. Considerable work has been done with the family around sorting out various intrigues that prevent everyone helping Suzie formulate a placement plan which can be most helpful to her.

School Functioning: Works quite well in all areas of school. She needs tutoring and reassurance during times of stress. Suzie tends to fall apart under pressure.

10 October

Dear [Social Worker]

I'm writing to you regarding Suzie. I understand that you are her caseworker. I was wondering when we will be able to communicate with her. I didn't want to write her until I knew it would be alright.

I have a lot of her personal belongings I know she'd like to have if they are allowed. She has quite a few records, books, and good clothes which I would be glad to bring.

Could you please let me know how she is progressing? I know she has a bit of adjusting to do, but she is a brilliant and beautiful child. With the right guidance I know she can become a very lovely and intelligent young woman. She had a very disturbing childhood and when she came to us, I know it must have been a tremendous change for her.

Learning about us and our mode of living must have been a challenge, making it hard to understand and respect our values. I'm sure if I would have had more patience and knowledge I could have perhaps prevented what has happened to her.

I hope you haven't got the impression from Suzie that she was unwanted or unloved by us. We miss her very much.

Thank you for helping her, and please contact me as soon as possible about writing and visiting privileges.

Mother

Addendum

After the funeral, Suzie turned around in the attitudes and behaviour she demonstrated in the secure unit. She invested energies into catching up on her formal education, and continued to see Grandmother and Aunt who lived near the institution.

After five months, Suzie was transferred to an open unit on campus where she continued to do well at school and received formal recognition for her positive efforts. She began home visits with her Grandmother and successfully transitioned into parole with a condition of residence living with Grandmother.

Three to four months after parole from the institution, it was learned that Suzie had gone back to the city and The Game. She worked for a new Pimp after a fight with her old one. Not long after the fight with her old Pimp, Suzie died tragically in a hit-and-run accident – a Sister of Pain dead at the age of 17.

Aliese's Reflections

One thing that stares at me starkly was the death of Suzie's brother. It is likely that she never recovered from his death. Death is a hard hit for anyone – at any age. Staff's comments on the manner of Suzie's grieving process surprised me and the hint of disapproval was disappointing to read. I am sure they were well-intentioned and after all, they were just adults, as we were children. I think we have learned much about grieving in particular, in the past 40 years. To carry the pain of a lost sibling when you are in this type of place must have been very dark for her indeed.

When you have gone through the gamut, you learn very quickly how to engage with adults or those who are in authority over us. We had to maintain some kind of balance on this constant tight-rope. Even in the so-called "good homes", children were to be seen and not heard. It was always some kind of double standard with adults and you never really knew where you stood with them. I hadn't expected to read that the caregivers were surprised at Suzie's lack of response while her family was present. This is something I would have totally understood and expected. We were first and foremost children, even if we were delinquents or incorrigible; there is safety in shutting down, and to become small.

Suzie's inability to cry and really connect with her own self and her own feelings were in part due to her upbringing. I think staff should have been more conscious of this at the time. I know they were all doing the best they could though and trying their best to just reach this girl before she slid off the slippery slope.

It was nice to read that Suzie recognized and appreciated the extra attention, the extra mile staff went on her behalf, and the genuine caring of staff members. This was probably the first time she had witnessed any adult showing any real compassion. I am sure it had a profound effect upon her. You should note that it took this young woman a lot of courage to admit to staff that she cared more about them than her own family. Suzie was going out on a limb and that made her very vulnerable. She was brave.

I will never fully understand the whole pimping and whoring thing. The need to be needed is one thing, but the "need to be abused" means that was probably the only type of love she had experienced up to this point in her life. Normal was the constant chaos, feelings of terror, the rage, the beatings, the abandonment and the daily search of escape – that of course is where the drugs and/or alcohol came in. I mean look at this kid – in the system at the age of five or earlier. Prostitution was quick money and it was also one of the only ways to earn money, or you could get into stealing. Living on the streets, keeping it together on your own was tough and there was safety in having a pimp and easy money for the boys or men who claimed such a title.

I know in my heart this child was probably pushed to her death in one fashion or another. Whether the pimp pushed her after an argument, or maybe she just stepped out in front of a vehicle to end it all. I guess we will never know. It only takes a second to revert to old habits, to have knee-jerk reactions, and old ways of thinking – and then it all takes over and has the best of you. So very sad that she never gave herself a chance, that she didn't believe in herself or find her spirit. But then the system did a pretty good job at destroying this young and beautiful woman, and my sister of pain.

How do you know when you have got through to a child? And even when you have, there they go, right back from where they came? Their proving grounds, their real world where life is not controlled and life's events are not always planned or pretty. It is a not much of an option and most of us young ladies did not have many healthy options. We all did the best we could. I would like to think that the family did the best they could too, but scars run very deep in this family – tragic.

Relational Care

Relational Care requires that one directs attention towards what is happening between a child or young person and his or her carer(s) or social worker. Garfat (2008) called this the '*co-created space between us*' or, as Bellefeuille and Jamieson noted, "*relational practice is a dynamic, rich, flexible, and continually evolving process of co-constructed inquiry … [where] meaning emerges within the 'space between' the individual, family, or community*" (2008, p. 38). Relational care is a central feature of effective practice, whether in child and youth care or social work. This *co-created space* between a young person and their carer(s) or social worker represents the 'hub of the wheel' around which all other practice efforts revolve. Elsewhere we called this *co-created space* between us *the relationship* (Fulcher & Garfat, 2008).

Relational care involves more than just 'having a relationship' (even a good one) with a young person like Suzie. As we see here, a working relationship had to be established with Suzie and 15 other young women – each with significant personal needs and challenges. Relational care involves working to establish and maintain a co-created relationship. It thus involves more than simply focusing on the individuals in the relationship. By focusing on the '*co-created space between us*', a social worker or child and youth care worker acknowledges how both parties to the relationship create, and are influenced by, that relationship (Fewster, 1990). This feature of relational care, sometimes called 'mutuality of relationship', actually builds from rhythmic interactions that evolve between the parties over the course of time. Stuart argued that "the relationship is the intervention" (2009, p. 222). Relational care requires that a social worker or carer focuses on relationships, or as Smith argued, "*building appropriate relationships and using these to help children as they grow up is our primary endeavour*" (2009, p. 120). Because of these distinctive features about practice in out-of-home care, Milligan gave a timely reminder that residential child care is not social work case management (1998).

Care does not follow simple formulaic patterns of cause and effect as championed by managerial ways of thinking. Relational care outcomes are achieved through messy and non-linear processes in which relationship-building and purposeful activity come together to infuse children and young people with optimism about their future life prospects. This requires a shift beyond a simple, instrumental focus to consider what are essentially three moral questions posed by Moss and Petrie (2002): (1) Who are children? (2) What is a good childhood? (3) What kind of relationships do we want to have with children? Such a view was reinforced in the UK House of Commons Report on Looked After Children (2009).

Few in social work or child and youth care would deny the importance of caring relationships. However, there is a danger that asserting the importance of relationships in relational care becomes a warmly persuasive but largely empty phrase. Putting relationships at the heart of practice challenges contemporary ideas about risk and what behaviours might be considered 'professional', often associated with qualities of objectivity and detachment (Meagher & Parton, 2004). According to Fewster, there is a need to ensure the experience of intimacy and connectedness in caring relationships while maintaining appropriate boundaries. The trouble in current climates is that we confuse boundaries with barriers – boundaries are individual and personal whilst barriers are reactive and impermeable. Fewster (1991) concluded that practitioners should heed professional exhortations to put objectivity before experience. It is important to recognize that what we bring to the caring role as persons in relationships is of greater significance in providing relational care than professional role behaviour.

Relational care invites one to attend closely to the dynamic of *rhythmicity* in relationships, or shared experiences of engaging in a synchronized, dynamic connection with another or others (Maier, 1992). As a mentor and friend, Henry Maier's ideas were particularly important at that time, and are as valuable today as they were then. Rhythms of coming and going, rhythmic rituals of acknowledgement, patterns of play or 'hanging out' amongst children or young people, simple repeated gestures of greeting at the door of the family home, special handshakes on the street – all are examples of the rhythms in which one might engage and experience with others. Connecting in rhythm with young people helps to nurture and strengthen connections and a sense of 'being with' that person. While working, regardless of location, a relational care approach invites one to pay particular attention to the rhythms of that person's, or that family's life, thereby strengthening opportunities to enter into rhythms of connectedness and caring with them.

Relational care *also* means that a social worker or youth worker attends to important developmental characteristics of individual children or young people (Maier, 1987). Rather than simply reacting to a young person's behaviour, relational care responds to that young person in a manner which is proactively consistent with their overall stage of developmental and personal needs at the time (Small & Fulcher, 2005). Here one considers development not from a chronological perspective but rather from a capacity perspective. This enables us to consider each young person as an individual with strengths and challenges in different areas. When thinking of families, it is also important to consider their developmental characteristics and potential. Most families do not develop according to some predetermined plan.

Two weeks after Suzie arrived in the secure unit, her little brother was killed whilst playing in the back yard of his home. Two weeks did not give much time for relationship building to progress with Suzie. Life events such as the death of a close family member or group home resident have a dramatic impact on relational caring. Being a Mormon family, there was special meaning given to whether Suzie's little brother had died an accidental death while playing on the swings, or whether his death was a potential suicide. Such distinctions are very important in determining whether a Mormon family might be united together for eternity. For Suzie, relational care had to take all these factors into account.

Before leaving to attend the funeral, a special point was made with Suzie about the accompanying care worker and me ensuring her personal safety and her personal return to the secure unit after the funeral. Suzie was told that we were carrying handcuffs in case these were required to guarantee her safe return as a ward of the court placed in out-of-home care and supervision. We told her that we hoped not to have to use them, but would do, if that was required. As seen in Suzie's case, relational care is provided within a mandated authority or legal context that cannot be ignored.

Everything occurs in a context that is unique to the individual, the helper, specific moments of interaction and the history of such interactions. While some elements of context may be the same (e.g., national and regional policies, agency philosophy, regulations, physical environment, etc.) other elements of context (e.g., cultural traditions, personal histories of being cared for, previous relationships with adults, developmental stage, etc) vary with the individual interactions between carer or social worker and the young person (Fulcher, 2006). No two contexts can ever be the same. Relational care involves constantly reviewing all these elements so as to 'understand the moment' more fully.

Questions for Small Group Discussion or Guided Reflection

1. What are the core elements of relational care?
2. How is relational care different from say, forensic care?
3. Explain what is meant by rhythmicity in relational care and demonstrate (perhaps through role play) how one might identify rhythmicity in interactions with a young person?
4. What rhythms or elements of rhythmicity were noted in the accounts of Suzie's relationships with her boyfriend, her father and stepmother, her siblings, her grandmother and with selected carers?
5. In what ways might relational care nurture youth and family participation in decision-making around daily activities in life-spaces at home, at school or elsewhere in the community?

Room 3
Nita – *What does Cultural Safety Mean to You?*

12 September

Say Lady

How is everything for you? Eye just thought eye would write you to see if every thang is cool. Of corse you understand what eye am saying.

Hay, why haven't you written me back? Eye thought we had a little understanding that was very cool for the both of us. Say Mama, eye keep getting this strange feeling that won't seem to get right. Eye don't know why eye think of you every day. Eye gess it is because you are obligated and deadicated to me and you don't realise it.

Say Baby, eye remember all the sweet things you used to say to me and how good eye would fill after reading all that sweet stuff. Look Nita, eye shore miss seeing you cute and foxie and so sweet face. And Mama, every time eye thank of you, eye thank of all the beautiful things life has tot eye am say offer. Can you dig what eye am saying?

Say Baby, we can socialize with society and acknowledge our game and get on down 'cause Mama, eye can school you for the sporty season and we can be happy for a long time. And dig this, eye got a ride, so Baby you aint got to walk. Just as long as you play your role, every thang is cool. And "me"? Baby, eye all was play my role.

Hay Baby, eye got a love deep down inside, do you? Eye can amagen you but eye want to hear it from you. Cause it will make me feel much better in side, dig?

Say, eye got to go to basketball practice, so eye wait to hear from you before eye go on.

P.S: You got me talking in my sleep. Write back if cool.

Your Man

12 September: Social Worker Notes

Nita presents as a 17 year-old young woman who is socially resourceful and capable of functioning reasonably well in the community. She has turned to a fairly delinquent peer group and through such involvement got into trouble. Two questions that are likely to become the focus for our work with Nita are (1) what is causing the depression which she acknowledges at times can be quite intense; and (2) what is the source of physical tension in her relationships with others. Nita will likely be a fun kid to work with but we must move early to reach out with the message that we are interested in her.

Everyone should be aware that Nita will probably gravitate to the negative peer group and this will be mediated somewhat if staff make a point of seeking her out early. Nita should be considered a high security risk at this time and probably will remain so until relationships with staff begin to evolve.

I've told Nita that she can plan to be here for at least 6 months and that the average stay is from 6-9 months. Some girls stay longer depending on how they are dealing with the problems that brought them here.

We've seen many girls in much worse shape. Keep on your toes as I know you will. Here we go again!

14 September

Say Mama

How you been coming? Eye hope its cool Baby. Cause it aint for me. You know eye can't really juge you and eye can't tell if you are for real but eye hope so cause "im real, ya dig? You don't know how eye fill about thangs do you?

Eye hope we never part cause eye got a love for you and eye want you to understand this cause my one decier is to love you. Belive me Baby.

Come time to time eye think of you and wonder if you really miss me and love me like you say you do. Is you for real Baby? Let me know cause it will be very soon for us to get our self right and find out first were each other is coming from.

Say Baby, eye don't know if eye should consider you my main Lady or what? Cause you never tell me nothing. All you tell me is you miss me and you love me witch is cool but can you tell me how much you love me cause eye don't know. And eye hate to thing the wrong thangs ya know.

Well Baby, eye can't seem to remember your face and eye want to so why don't you send me a picture of your self. Baby, let me talk about the good thang like the love eye got in store for you cause eye know you need it. And it is going to be good to you and good for me.

Cause eye need it just as much as you do. So we gon make it good for the both of us aren't we (you know were I'm coming from). Say Nita, when eye get a chance to see you then the conversation will get better. So then eye see the expection on your face.

Baby eye got to go but you will hear from me again. Like eye sead, tell me how much you love me, cool?

Your Man loves you!

1 October: Summary of the Initial Planning Board Meeting

Nita is a 17 year-old Afro-American girl committed by Juvenile Court for a series of charges dating back 3 years, including shoplifting, assault, robbery and running away. She has had difficulties in school and at one time was suspended by the school system after an assault on another girl. About two hours after the court hearing which committed Nita to this institution, Nita attacked a Youth Center staff member with some other girls, stole their keys and escaped from the facility. Nita's whereabouts were unknown for several weeks. She was apprehended after another assault and attempted robbery, then returned to the Youth Center. While awaiting transport to the institution, a note was intercepted which Nita had written to another girl requesting that she call Nita's sister and sneak a gun into the Youth Center. Nita's activities while on leave from the Court indicate that she is a high security risk, potentially dangerous.

Personal Care Plan

Nita is able to talk indirectly about her assaultive behavior, describing this as coming from the fact that she has a violent temper. With encouragement, Nita shared how she used to express strong racial feelings. She feels that she has been discriminated against by the "system" because she is Black and has added that it seems that most of the kids who get sent up are Black kids. These racial feelings may make it hard for Nita to trust or relate to White authority figures. Establishing a trust relationship with Nita will take a long period of time as trusting is something she has not often experienced before. She will need extensive support in order to begin talking about what is inside of herself. Working with a Black counsellor would probably help Nita feel more comfortable in relating to someone from her own race.

Nita will need to learn to deal with her feelings about herself and her family since she is the only one of 7 children to have got into any serious trouble. Re-gaining control of her assaultive behavior is a priority for all concerned. It should be noted that in past group living situations, Nita has proved to be a very negative influence. Her few friends have been the most hostile and delinquent characters in the group. At first it was felt that she was a follower but it soon became evident that she had real leadership capabilities. Nita was very good at getting the weaker and more immature girls to do her bidding and then sit back from the action to enjoy the results. She introduces a subtle quality of instigation in her interactions with a living unit peer group.

Since entering the living unit, Nita has made a great many attempts to avoid attention. There is evidence that she has been putting pressure on peers to get what she wants. She has made every effort to avoid talking to staff. Respond to her physical symptoms with sensitivity, being aware that Nita has terrific tension-based headaches. Attend to her pain as directed by the medical doctor and help her reflect on why she has the pain and what may have led to it. Let her know we are interested in her and her future. Nita has promised to seek staff out for medication for her headaches so use such opportunities to connect and nurture a relationship. Nurture the little girl part of Nita's make up while at the same time remaining wary of her security risk as a 17 year-old.

15 October

Say Lady

Well how's every thang for you. Fine eye hope cause its the same oh same oh for me.

I got back from pass a few days ago and its been a little change as for the people thay are trying to make it.

Say eye haven't haeard from you in a long time and eye still miss your sweet face and every than gels.

Do you know eye got a new ride? It is very sporty and eye can't wait tell you get a chance to ride in it. And eye bet it well look more prettier with you in it.

Baby I hope everything is still cool for us. Eye mean as for our little understanding cause eye shor want to be your man and make thangs cool for us in that big world out there. Can you dig it? Cause I can.

Mama eye need your love cause eye don't thing eye can make it without you cause you are my life. Baby I want to tell you this. Eye used to think about living and how your fill loving like a long, low gentle soft lazy river kind of thing. And sometimes it is, but along with it something els has happened to me.

My feelings are strong – all of them. They're in tense as hell. Eye see better, feel better, hear better, touch better, but better isn't what eye mean, eye mean they've all become crystal clear and strong – so wonderfully strong...

Baby eye got to go so you be cool. We will be together soon. Write back.

Your Man

16 December: Social Worker Notes

I met with Nita's Father today. He seemed a very level-headed guy who is honestly concerned about the wellbeing of his next oldest child. He works at the County Jail so can relate to what this secure unit is about. He said he talked with Nita about not getting into mischief with Edna who has just arrived at the unit. They are long-time friends and got into trouble together. I said we would support his message. He said that it probably didn't make sense to try and separate them as it will probably be good to make them behave together. After all, Nita lives just up the hill from Edna. Father said he had some trouble with visiting on the weekend, so I asked him to contact me before coming and we'd try to arrange a special visiting time.

3 April: Summary of the Planning Board Meeting

Nita has shown improvement in all areas since her last Board. She is able to seek staff out and counsel with them about herself and her plans, although "plans for the future" are still vague and non-specific. There is still reluctance to closely examine fears and apprehensions about her mother's mental health problems with Nita wanting to take care of her mother. Nita accepts support from female staff. She is hesitant in group meetings, usually saying very little while taking everything in. She now admits to having spent more time worrying about her friend's problems than her own. This is a situation that has now definitely changed. Nita is to be enrolled half day in the open campus school during the afternoons.

Current school performance: Health – recently lacked self-confidence and seemed to view criticism as rejection. Does follow through on work; English – puts in a lot of effort and takes pride in her work; Math – not very realistic about her abilities but has made a lot of gains within herself; History – tries hard, more willing to accept help from teachers now; Remedial Tutoring – always gripes about work, still reads too fast but is improving and knows this; Typing – moody, sometimes not serious about the class – just putting in time. Detailed instructions completely throw her.

7 May: Social Worker Notes

Nita is really in good shape in spite of the reception she was given by one Cottage on campus. She wants us to pick whichever Cottage we think will be best for her. She offered a couple of suggestions and I agreed that she was being fairly realistic. She continues to amaze me with her new-found confidence. She is joking more and seems genuinely secure in her relations with care staff. Thank God for good staff who were able to 'move in' on this kid the way you did over the past week. It allowed her to use the initial rejection of a place on campus as a real personal growth experience. Thank you.

16 May: Care Worker Notes

Nita told me all about her furlough today. She started right at the time she got home — calls from everyone — it seems the family called everyone before she arrived home. She answered phones and said Hello to everyone and their dog. Relatives in droves. They had BBQ and "Mom makes the best homemade ice cream"! The family had a surprise Welcome Home Party for her. She went for a ride with some friends of her younger sister and her cousin. They had a flat tire and it was late, late when they returned home. Papa took her to the bus and they waited but they didn't know which was the correct bus. In the end, she got the morning bus. Nita was upset this morning because staff kept asking her if she had any dope last night. "Aw's tired and sleepy — aw did not go to bed at 9:30 p.m. all the time." I buy her story — it sounds too much like Nita to be anything else. I also think we should call Exit and get them going on her application.

20 June: Social Worker Notes

Nita did a super good job in her Exit Cottage interview. They were impressed by how she thought before she answered questions. If she didn't understand, she asked for an explanation. She asked questions about how the place runs, etc. She moves in tonight and we write up the contract after school tomorrow. They felt she was the kind of kid who fits with what they are about!!

21 June
Handwritten Application to the Exit Cottage Placement Committee

My name is Nita, age 17 and a half and I was sent to this institution by the Juvenile Court for Robbery, Assault, Shoplifting and Truancy. I've been in the secure unit for 8 months and have completed Grade 9 in school.

My accomplishments since being here:

1. Learn to communicate with adults.

2. Learn to identify feelings and deal with them.

3. Deal with my prejudice for White people.

4. Learning to make decisions and decide what is important to me and my future.

5. Attempt to catch up on my education.

6. Realize that money and clothes are not important (At least they are not the most important things in my life.)

7. I have learned that life is not all fun and games.

My Parole Plans:

1. Go home and live with my family.

2. Vocational School (job training).

3. Part-time employment – Hospital or Public Library

Exit Cottage Plans:

1. Having the opportunity to be responsible for myself without supervision.

2. Be responsible for my own leisure time.

3. To have opportunities to investigate job training.

4. A chance to demonstrate my skills of communication and relating to adults before leaving the structure of the institution.

5. The secure unit is not designed to fill this need.

I will know that I no longer need Exit Cottage when I have achieved the above goals. It will take me approximately 3 months to accomplish these goals.

JUVENILE PAROLE CONTRACT (Pre-Release)

Certain conditions of my release have been discussed with me, and I am aware of the specific regulations restricting some of my activities during this period. In accordance with this Agreement I will:

1. Obey all federal and state laws and all county or city ordinances defining crime.

2. Obtain prior approval of my Juvenile Parole Counselor before changing my residence.

3. Obtain prior approval of my Juvenile Parole Counselor before leaving the State.

TRANSFER TO EXIT COTTAGE TO
COMPLETE THE FOLLOWING

1. Finish Summer School.

2. Get to know my way around the local towns in order to learn how to find my way around in new places.

3. Go home every other weekend to visit with my family.

4. Learn how to arrange transportation on my own by either buses or trains.

5. Assume personal responsibility for all my actions, respecting the rights, privileges and property of others.

PROJECTED PAROLE DATE: 9 August

Nita, 21 June

Addendum

As planned, Nita returned to her family home on parole. Nothing further was heard from her, nor did we receive any further news about her. We hope that was good news. Nita was a capable young woman with strong family support but inner city life as a Black family is filled with many challenges. Nita deserved some breaks in life!

Aliese's Reflections

Although there was no news on what happened to Nita, I would like to believe that she made it through to the "other side". She had a solid family who supported her and loved her. She also had a father who seemed to have wisdom about her neighbourhood friend, and his keen perspective on prison life, due to his job, was certainly stacking the odds in her favour. It was fantastic to read about her huge family gathering on her furlough as her "welcome home" visit. I mean, while she had a lot of work to do on herself in the months to come, I can't help but think how very fortunate this young woman was.

The sad note here is the boyfriend who wants to school her and get her ready for the sporting game. There is not much mentioned in the notes but I can imagine Nita's feelings on this. Here you are, ripped away from your family and your life, nothing is really familiar to you in the sense of belonging. She knows she is at the end of the road and this is a make it or break it, sort of last chance go 'round. As a young person, it is so hard to pull yourself away from your "loved ones". These loved ones were your good friends, allies, your comrades, and in this case your pimp. That is something we had with our friends, a sense of belonging. While it may not seem like much to some, it was something big for all of us. Our bond. Us versus Them.

Now here alone, locked up, away from all you know, and being forced to contend with your whole life at one time, it was natural for us to continue correspondence with people from the past, even if they were not considered the most desirable. It was in your comfort zone. You would do anything to keep contact, to have something from the outside world. You day dream your time away, with the desire to get right back to it. It was a game we played with ourselves. Keep the fantasy going. Some connection with the past made us feel safe in who we were. We belonged. Yet the struggle to REALLY fix our lives was nipping at our thoughts too.

They (the workers within the system) never really understood the family condition and the generations of abuse and the after effects. They had not been taught about family dysfunction and they were not really dealing with the broken family – not yet, and not until this secure unit program. At least our social worker was conscious of that and he did make the effort to reach out, involve, and evaluate the real home life situation. He helped to guide the staff in the right direction and they listened. "They" also made the effort to get the family involved in family sessions during the visits. Social working was working better than it ever had. Great strides were being made, history, really when you think about it.

I believe that up to this point in Nita's life, it is highly unlikely that anyone had ever acknowledged her, had ever connected with her, and finally, had ever been a role model to her. I am certain she had never experienced any of these situations because it was not something that typically happened in institutions and all those relationships associated within that working environment. Forming any healthy relationships was denied and generally frowned upon. I would also note that there were probably very few who worked within the system who were African American, Indian (Native American), Asian, Hispanic or other minority races. At this point in time, I really don't recall any, though I am sure that was not the case.

Nita's aggression towards the other girls and her instigating situations for her own delight and entertainment was a defence mechanism. I am sure that in part this was to get some of the heat off of her as a "Black girl". She grew up with harassment being Black, African American, or of mixed blood. Those were the times. This world did a lot to instil racism – and it came from the authority figures as much as from ordinary citizens.

In the end, I am certain Nita was successful in her life, regardless of how long it may have taken her to find that success. She was very intelligent, had a great exit plan, and she truly understood that it would be her efforts that would change the world around her and her life.

What does Cultural Safety Mean to You?

Important legal and child welfare questions have been carefully reviewed before any child or young person is admitted to out-of-home care. Contemporary practices assume that all other options will have been considered before a care order is issued, or a mandatory sentence is handed down (Fulcher 2002a). In practical terms, it is still difficult to offer children, young people or family members a service guarantee that – at the very least – their lives and life chances will not be left worse off as the result of State administered care. The facts show, sadly, that children and young people, not part of the dominant White Eurocentric culture, are still over-represented in the caring systems of most Western countries (Fulcher 1998).

Cultural safety involves the state of being in which a child or young person experiences that her/his personal wellbeing, as well as her/his social and cultural frames of reference, are acknowledged, even when not fully understood. Cultural safety – in Australia they say cultural security – needs to become a minimum service guarantee offered to all children, young people and family members in receipt of health and welfare services. In early engagements between workers and young people or family members, selected rituals of encounter are commonly disregarded. Cultural safety involves much more than good intentions.

Cultural safety requires that each child or young person has reasons for feeling hopeful that her/his personal needs will be attended to, in terms that she/he can understand. Cultural safety also means that family members and kin are accorded dignity and respect (Ramsden 1997), and are actively encouraged to participate in decision-making with service providers about the futures of their child(ren). Ainsworth (1997; 2006), Gharabaghi (2013) as well as Burford and Hudson (2000) have shown how family participation in decision-making results in better long-term outcomes for children placed in State–mandated care. However, as Rangihau concluded in his New Zealand review of child and family welfare services for Maori peoples, "*at the heart of the matter was a profound misunderstanding or ignorance about the place of a child in Maori society and its relationship with whanau* (family), *hapu* (sub-tribe), *and iwi* (tribal) *structures*" (1986, p. 7).

Social workers and child and youth care workers educated in Western traditions of bio-psycho-social theories of child and adolescent development have been guided traditionally by values and customs founded in Judeo-Christian traditions (Payne 1997, Fulcher 2003). However, when working with children or young people from different cultural traditions, it is easy to make false interpretations of child or adolescent behaviour, personality development and family practices with deleterious effects on the lives of vulnerable children (Fulcher 2002b). As with First Nations, Hispanic and Afro-American children, New Zealand Maori children have also experienced racial disproportionality – overrepresentation in the child welfare system compared to their numbers in the population. Indigenous children have experienced extreme disadvantage from the application of Western psychological theories and methods used by social scientists to investigate Maori character structure. Post-war research identified alleged character deficits that informed New Zealand government policies with negative impact on at least three generations of Maori (Stewart, 1997).

When culture is viewed as reflecting intricate, highly patterned systems of social inheritance through which each group of people attains and maintains the separate version of the humanity of its members (Mead & Calas 1953), it is easy to see why cultural safety requires careful scrutiny. Child and youth care workers and social workers need to acquire and maintain minimum competencies – building on personal sensitivity – actively learning about cultural practices and rituals of encounter that ensure cultural safety with local ethnic communities (Leigh 1998). Simply trying to understand, as well as contemplate, different relational starting points can be a challenge. Each worker's acculturation and socialization experiences leave her or him with taken-for-granted assumptions and a cognitive mindset about culture that is not easily altered. The practical result is that some children are treated as "having culture" whilst others are more socialised and adapted to the ways of the dominant culture.

Rituals of encounter between worker(s) and children or young people have developed through cultural protocols. The place that a child learns to call *home* and *my people* has a particular history, with a political, economic and social legacy. The meaning she or he gives to culture is constantly evolving while seeking to understand their current predicament and adapting to any new *home environment* or experiences. Each encounter with a child and her/his family requires that a *cultural lens* be included in one's essential toolkit of professional praxis competencies.

When workers of urban and European ancestry are not first aware of their own culture and attitudes, then understandings of cross-cultural and rural-urban differences are likely to result in negative assessments of families and their children. Bi-cultural rituals of encounter that frame I-Thou relations form the basis for rhythmic interactions at the core of care (Maier 1979). Rural and cultural differences – and the impact these have on each young person's life journey – are closely enmeshed within the meanings that children and young people give to their experiences with carers. Only when cultural predictability is combined with feelings of personal dependability in caring relationships is a child's whole being cared for pro-actively.

Rituals of encounter that ensure cultural safety whilst engaging pro-active expressions of caring are important if social workers and others are to break cycles of cultural racism that disadvantage some young people in care more than others. Each worker must learn basic cultural practices of those living in their home region, or cultural traditions which children or young people bring with them into care as asylum-seekers or economic migrants from war zones or escaping natural disasters. It is insufficient to expect children and young people in care – or their family members – to perform as the teachers of those employed to work with them.

A key objective of cultural safety in professional education is to ensure that each worker "*examines their own cultural realities and attitudes they bring to each new encounter in practice*" (Ramsden & Spoonley 1993, p. 163). Such examinations are frequently characterised by uncertainty and emotional tension as workers move beyond their own ethnocentric worlds to explore cultural knowledge and assumptions quite different from those to which they are accustomed. Praxis knowledge and skills must extend beyond the limits of personal life experiences to embrace practice competencies beyond our own ethnocentric understanding. It is one thing to acquire knowledge about culture and cultural differences. Cultural safety involves learning hard lessons associated with cross-cultural living beyond one's personal comfort zones.

Questions for Small Group Discussion or Guided Reflection

1. What does cultural safety mean to you?
2. In what ways might explorations of culture – more than race – offer useful information and helpful guidance for working with young people and family members from cultures other than the dominant culture?
3. What racial and cultural influences helped to shape Nita's life journey that led to her admission to a secure unit for juvenile offenders, and what cultural influences might be re-activated to help Nita stay out of the system?
4. How might cultural safety enhance the quality of relational care offered to a young woman like Nita?
5. What legal requirements and State-administered procedures are required in order to obtain authorization for a young person such as Nita to leave an institutional placement and return to her family home still under supervision by a court appointed social worker?

Room 4
Linda – *Pain-Based Behaviour*

27 March

I'm sitting here in the room of loneliness after movin here. Thinking about the times to come and watching outside my window covered with bars, seein how the wind blows the top of the trees softly. The sky looks grey and I can almost hear the sky calling out to the loneliness of a little girl.

Here I sit on the window sill of this lonely room. I hear cars and trucks driving by fast to get where they are going. Airplanes are flying high up in the sky. I hear the train that comes by every 4 hours, sometimes every two hours. I hear people laughing. And I hear others crying in their own rooms of loneliness. Someone is yelling "Let me out, I want to be free! Don't treat me like an animal".

But here I sit feeling that I am no longer a part of this place. I shouldn't be a part of this "massterwad" inside world. I should be a part of the "massterwad" world of the outs where there are millions of people, stores and places to go. But, no, I sit here in my lonely room waiting patiently for them to unlock the door and say "Good, you're free once again".

Some people are laughing to cover up their loneliness. Then they cry because they have crawled inside and looked at what the real thing is. I cry because I found out that you're only out to do one thing and that exists in both the massterwad world inside and out. And when you're in the massterward world inside, they help you so much and get as close and have an understanding and loving thing that they can get with you. Then they push you away and are there no more.

But I alone would like to know why do they keep me here and let me see what they are doing to me. If I knew it would be less strain on me and maybe I would understand. But no, I have to sit here, pushed away from the staff that I thought cared and was beautiful. I felt close and loved, and who gave me a home. But now my eyes see a different thing.

My eyes tell me I'm being pushed away cause it's hard to let me go. They're trying to get used to me not being here. But my mind won't take no reasons because my mind keeps saying if people care as much as they say they do there will never be an end of that understanding and care. And then they ask me why I don't let people get close to me. My mind only knows that you'll wash away like a ruining stain in the end.

I will live on cause I know I have my own life I want to live and there won't be people around to make me think or make be do what I don't want to do. Only I can make my own decisions and follow my own path.

From now on, I will only keep in my mind that the people who work in this world inside have a job to do. They don't get paid to love me. They get paid to help us get it together and I have a job to do. That is to go and follow my path of life and not get wrapped up in or too close to these people in the inside world.

I will always be following the path of my life and I have no time to stop and get so involved with the people inside. I may forget where I left off on my life path because I only got a life time. If I was to do what I did in the inside world everywhere, I would have nothing to show at the end of my life, nothing I always wanted.

I will live on and will get back on my life path and walk and work and get what I want. When I leave this place, we say our goodbyes and leave our tears. We will both remember that you got your job and I've got mine. And mine is to follow my own life path.

Linda

Linda is a 16 year-old Caucasian female committed on a technical charge of incorrigibility. She has been known to the Juvenile Court for 3 years for curfew violations, running away, drinking and drug use, truancy and incorrigibility – at home and at school. During her 6-week assessment, she was seen as a loud, argumentative and disruptive girl who instigated because of the resultant excitement. She was placed for 13 months at an institution for younger teenagers in a program that used a *guided group interaction* approach. Linda absconded 12 times while "in that program" and altogether was in residence for about two-thirds of the time. Her longest continuous stay was for 2 months. While on run from that institution, Linda was involved in a variety of serious behaviours in the community, including prostitution, problems with and threats from pimps, theft of stereo equipment, and heavy involvement in drinking and drugs which recently included heroin. Linda attended thirteen different schools from kindergarten to the 8th Grade. She was retained in the 1st Grade but managed to earn average grades in spite of her many school transfers. By the 6th Grade she had few goals and made little effort to succeed academically, but she had a good sense of humour and was a good athlete. She says that she hates school and manipulates her way out of class. Linda says that she plans to quit school as soon as possible and get married. She was very quick to inform her teacher during a timetabling session that she was "dumb" and if placed in regular classes, she would only flunk them. She is in regular classes with the exception of developmental math and achieves at approximately 5th Grade level.

28 March: On admission to the secure unit, Linda offered 7 statements about her life and her plans while staying there.

1. *At the other institution, I learned how to depend on other people but didn't learn how to handle myself on my own.*
2. *At times I can handle myself but when I get in a down mood, I quit caring.*
3. *When I quit caring, I take it out on other people by getting them down too.*
4. *At the other institution, I would get other people down by AWOL talk and usually take them AWOL with me.*
5. *When I'm down I don't feel like talking, but keep pushing me to talk.*
6. *I like to figure out people and if I find staff who are only trying to help me because they are getting paid, then I usually avoid those people and try to find a way to put them down.*
7. *I need to feel that people care about me or I just don't care at all.*

28 March: Cottage Report

Linda is very resentful of her placement at this institution. She goes out of her way to avoid staff. Her reaction to counselling or corrective criticism is one of denial and anger. She is an experienced talker and has a full bag of tricks. She has gathered a following of weaker peers to listen to her bad-mouthing the institution. She put across a very tough image with her talk and mannerisms for a girl who expresses much desire to be a woman. She is considered a high security risk. Linda is not a willing worker and requires constant supervision from staff and reminders and prodding from peers. She is a lazy girl with no apparent home making skills which show up in her room care and detail. Personal grooming shows no pride or interest. Linda prefers Black male relationships and has been confronted by her peers about this which she accepted with complete indifference. Her overall attitude is one of open defiance and hostility. Linda leaves the impression that she is capable of being physical.

24 April: What People Want But Don't Know How To Go About It

I have been around a lot of people. And a lot of them will say to me when they have only known me a week, two weeks, maybe a month. They will say "You play games".

Well they will think they know me. But it's like saying I have seen God. Nobody has ever knowd me, not my Mom or my Dad. They would be the people who should of knowd me but they never. I'm the only one who knows my self.

And then they say, "You have to trust people". People say, "I can understand you. I can help you. You can trust me".

Them are people's words they know but they don't know to work them words. The people who help me are people who can take me for what I am, what I do and how I do it.

I been as for real as real can get. But what those people say "You play games". I have played games before and the game playing was for real.

I would tell them I play games and then I tell them the real thing how I feel and everything. Just because I had said, "Hey, look I play games. I can't be for real.

I be for real and don't be playing no game. And then just because I said that to see what that person would do, and they said I play games. I play games to see if people know a game player from a real person.

And if they told me, "Hey, you don't play no games. You're for real. You just say you do".

That is a together person but never in years have I heard anyone tell me that. And that is because I never find no one who could understand me, why I do it, and what the reason is for hiding it.

I'm the only one who can understand myself and know why I do the things I do. Now I let it out. No one ever knew my game. And then they ask me why I don't trust people.

How can you trust anyone who can't really trust themself who don't know the person is game playing or for real? The day people can really understand them self and know a famous player who does play the life as a game and nothing but a game, that will be the day I would have trust in someone.

I'm glad that I know me and I'm a different person than any one else. I can see what is what. That is why I don't trust people they all think they know what a game is and what is a for real person.

It's only words. That is all it is. Trust is about big words that people use. They have to learn to know what they have to do for it. Unless they do, I would never trust people who don't know.

And people who can say, "Hey, I made a mistake about you". I'm looking at a person who knows them self. They also know a game player from a real person. I wish people could understand what is what.

Linda

26 April: Social Worker Notes

This kid is scared to death with what Board said about having our goal as "getting close to Linda". She is flabbergasted and is not at all sure she wants to let down the defences. But she is also pleasantly surprised at how good it feels. Move slowly folks and this is one kid (amongst many) who we better be damned sure of our motives in whatever we do with her or she could get hurt badly. Linda has never allowed people to get close before and to think of it in her shoes, it must be a very fearful prospect. She's afraid that if she learns to care, she will lose some of her strength and also have to leave here sooner or later. I explained that we weren't going to take anything away from her, only show her how to use caring as a way of becoming stronger. She isn't entirely sure about that but definitely not holding back as much. I explained that she could very easily control how close people get, and if she feels people are moving too fast, she can tell them to slow down until she can handle it. I feel as though this week has seen something of a breakthrough for Linda. Continue in a low-keyed fashion but live the message "I care about you!"

29 April: Social Worker Notes

Everyone please read Linda's 10 goals. I think she is trying and I've said, "OK, let's get on with making these goals a reality.

29 April: Care Worker Notes

Hey, this is a start and I'm not sure I believe it yet!

Read – Linda said that she can be herself when alone in her room and this is what she "really wants to happen".

29 April : My Golds

My first Gold is to let people help me and not think I know it all.

My 2 Gold is to try to do my school work and not to keep on saying I can't do it.

My 3 Gold is to be able to espet no for an answer and not keep on presserin and try to talk them into it.

My 4 Gold is to stop being so damn stubborn and esept it and deal with it for what it is.

My 5 Gold is to trust and let people get close to me and to open up so they can get to know me.

My 6 Gold is to try to get along with some of the staff and teachers I don't like instead of taking things out against them and back stabbing them.

My 7 Gold is to stop day dreaming about things in school and say, well I can't do it after the Teacher told me how to do it, and I did not listen to a word they said.

My 8 Gold is to accept the fact that I will not be able to go on parole from this place because I will still need help and not to be in such a hurry to get on the outs.

My 9 Gold is to stop saying I'm so together I don't need no one's help.
My 10 Gold is to stop covering up my sadness with my smiles.

Linda

---

31 July: Summary of the Planning Board Meeting

This Board comes one day after Linda was caught instigating – through the mail – a prostitution role with a boy at a neighbouring institution. When confronted about her behaviour, Linda projects most of the responsibility on the bad laws and the bad rules which limit her. She assumed very little responsibility for her own action in setting the boy up. She was most angry at being caught in this situation and expressed anger that the boy involved would also be reprimanded. This incident has brought to the surface what has been considered an underlying pattern of dysfunctional attitudes that has been prevalent throughout Linda's life. She tries to rationalize her actions by appearing positive in contacts with staff. Recently she seems to have gone underground in some of her actions, is still closely engaged with the more delinquent residents in the group. She has been spending more time with peers than she has spent talking with staff like she did earlier. At school she is working somewhat better in Social Studies, and also in English and Reading. Her best area appears to be P.E. as she is quite athletic. Still attempts to manipulate teachers to get things easier for herself but is getting along with peers during class.

3 September: Care Worker Notes

I took Linda out for a walk this evening and we had a pretty good talk. Maybe I should say she got out a lot of anger. She started out by telling me how angry she was at me. She said she was so mad at me that she could have stomped my head in the ground. I asked her why (I knew why) and she said because I was talking with another girl about her, and the threat Linda had made towards the other girl. I said Linda must have a guilty conscience. The other girl only told me about the threat Linda had made. Of course Linda denied making any threat that she would beat the other girl up on the outs if she ever ran across her. Linda became angry when I didn't agree with her. She stopped dead in her tracks and screamed. I asked if she was trying to scare me? If so, she could forget it because I don't scare easily. Linda then simmered down some. During the course of our conversation, the vulgarity got quite heavy. I said that I expected her to clean up her language, that she is a young lady and I expected her to act and talk the part. By the time we got back to the cottage she was in a better mood but I don't know if I even made a dent.

9 October: Summary of the Six Month Review Board Meeting

Linda is nearly 17 and was sent by the Juvenile Court to institutional care because of incorrigibility, curfew violations, running away, drinking and drug use, truancy. While on the 7 run away episodes from her first institutional program, Linda became more and more delinquently involved and worked as a prostitute.

From the start, Linda fit right into the secure unit peer group and talked with staff from the beginning. Her sharp tongue towards peers and superficial talk in testing staff undermined relations with both groups, at first. Her next actions noted a lot of ambivalence in the mechanics of daily living, a pulling together of reasoning ability, less anger evidenced in staff relations and a definite trend towards peer leadership as evidenced by her peer counselling and control of peer relations.

In anticipation of her 6 Month Review Board, Linda still says being a lady is the most important thing to her. Her interpretation of being a lady is unclear and confused and intermingled with wishes to be with her man, and in control of her own living situation. She likes Black-oriented things, especially Soul music. She states that she wants to make an honest living working in a real job. But so far, her main qualification would seem to be a dancer since she is well coordinated and strives to win in everything recreational.

Linda has tried to relinquish some peer control but is still a leader. At times, she accepts favours. She relates to staff with a winning smile but still gets quite flustered when she is put in a position where she is expected to talk meaningfully with staff. She acts like she is angry when talking at these times, and will often use an excuse to leave. Linda says she would like campus school at this time.

It was the decision of the Six Months Review Board that Linda was ready to leave the secure unit and move to another living unit on campus. She will start in half-day school while still living in the secure unit. As she gains consistency in handling her half day school, this will be increased to attendance full days prior to moving to the open campus program. School planning will focus on remedial reading and vocational training.

14 November: Care Worker Notes

I had quite a talk with Linda tonight. She was able to let her hair down tonight. I asked her about relationships with males, going progressively further back in time. I was careful to observe closely to determine if my questions might become too threatening or painful, but Linda really showed no hesitation or reluctance about any of it.

Some of the following information may already be known to some members of the team, but since it was all new to me, I'll pass it on. The earliest recollection Linda has of male/female relationships was at the age of seven. Her older sister's boyfriend who was a regular visitor in the home, one day told Linda he had something for her and if she wanted it she would have to sit on his lap. This she did reluctantly and he gave her a tape of a song she really liked, and as soon as she had it, she took off.

He called her back and asked her if he didn't rate more than a thank you. So she asked him what he meant. He said he wanted a kiss and Linda said, "I gave him the goddamn tape back because I didn't want him sticking his dirty old tongue in my mouth like he did to my sister". The guy finally settled for a kiss on his cheek and "I grabbed the tape and ran the hell out of there!

I wondered whether she had any other memories and just before moving on to something else, Linda remembered when she was really little that her first stepfather had tried to rape her older sister and she could recall the big family battle that ensued, culminating in stepfather being belted over the head with a baseball bat by one family member or another.

Linda also told of the time when she was 13 or 14 and on the run and had gone to the enlisted men's club at an Army base. She had gotten drunk and two Black soldiers had offered her a ride home. They drove instead to a secluded spot near some river and made her submit to each of them a couple of times before dumping her off in the city.

The story of her first attempt at prostitution would have been hilarious had it not been so tragic and degrading. It turned out that she serviced nine soldiers and only ended up with ten dollars.

I probed a little into her feelings and some specifics in the relationships she had been involved with in which she felt herself to be truly "in love". It came out that Linda never was able to really feel close to any of these men the way I interpret it. She said she just could not bring herself to hug and kiss them, or to even touch them, or sit close to them for more than a couple of minutes.

Any time one of them would approach her, she would feel cornered. If she was touched unexpectedly, such as being hugged from behind, she would jump a foot. I shared that I had noticed this reaction inherent to her make-up when some months earlier I had reached out and casually placed my hand on her shoulder. She had jumped like she had been burned. After that one time, I had avoided physical contact. Linda said, "Yeah, I noticed that".

I asked Linda, if she could, to describe her feelings about being "close" to someone. Here, she did have a little difficulty. She was finally able to get it out that she was "afraid", and after some coaxing, "being pushed away" that she was afraid of. This was not an easy admission for Linda and she immediately began getting defensive and started bragging about all her conquests — and how slick she was in manoeuvring them around so she could get anything she wanted.

I stopped this by asking how she regarded any of these people who allowed her to manipulate them, and let her get away with murder? She thought a minute and then seemed surprised when telling me she didn't have any respect for them. She thought they were "kinda dumb" for allowing her to move them around any way she felt like.

Linda explained how she hadn't really thought about it, but she had remembered that when sleeping with a man – even after they had been intimate – she always moved clear over on to her side of the bed and curled up into a ball before going to sleep. She could never recall "snuggling" up to anyone, either in or out of bed.

We then talked for awhile about the relationship which she and I had developed over the months we had known each other. Linda was pretty straightforward and pulled no punches. She told me that she held three different views of me – as a father that she always wanted but never had; as a man to whom she was attracted; and as a friend she felt understood her and in whom she could confide.

It was my turn to suffer from a few seconds of speechlessness. Recovery was rapid and complete as I realized that what Linda had just told me was very significant in the very noticeable changes she has recently undergone.

She went on to say that the note I had written to her a couple of weeks back had really made a strong impression, and she had dug it out every day since to read all over again. "You really convinced me", Linda said, "that I can be a lady. It's that important to convince everyone else that I can be a lady too!"

Linda confided that she had many times observed me giving girls goodnight hugs and putting my arm around others. She said that she envied that. Linda said she wanted that for herself but that I would never make the offer. And she simply could not bring herself to ask.

She asked if I remembered the first time Linda did ask for a hug good night? I replied that the memory was still vivid in my mind and described it for her. We were both able to laugh about it tonight, but it was not funny at the time. Maybe none of us will ever know how tough it was for Linda to make that first move.

At bedtime I walked down the hall with Linda and laid my arm across her shoulders. She got a little flustered when I pointed out that she hadn't jumped when I touched her this time. She didn't comment, just gave me a hug and hollered "good night".

8 December: Care Worker Notes

In our session tonight, it became clear that Linda has been blaming us for having to leave here and move to open campus. She is projecting her own very strong feelings about leaving onto us! If anyone has been guilty of doing any "pushing away", it has been Linda herself.

She knows what M laid on her last night is true – she must learn to function on her own. But she has become so deeply attached emotionally to a couple of us, and myself in particular, that the only way she has thus far learned to handle it is to begin shutting herself back up inside again.

Linda is back on track but the situation calls for some very careful handling from this point forward. Her concept of me as a caring person in relation to herself is really mixed up. Not all that surprising under the circumstances. There is a full-blown "crush" going on here and I'm gonna need some help processing it.

113

We spoke quite frankly about the situation tonight and Linda laid some "biggies" on me in an open and completely natural manner. There was nothing coy or suggestive at all – the kid has some pretty heavy feelings which need to be respected but must be worked out nevertheless. Let's not make a big deal out of it because ridicule, teasing or even kidding will end up shattering her.

It's more serious than I ever suspected – to the point where Linda is jealous of every attention I pay to any of the other girls. She recognizes that it is an unreal situation as evidenced by her attempts to handle it in her own inappropriate manner. We spent considerable time discussing warm, caring relationships and the normal feelings we all hold towards people we like.

The fact that Linda was able to discuss this at all was most impressive to me and is still another measure of how far this girl has travelled since she first came here. We talked at some length about "people" relationships and how there is nothing at all abnormal about feeling genuine affection towards another person.

I feel pretty certain that I was able to show Linda that our relationship was probably the first in her experience where there were no demands laid upon her – where she was not required to "pay" and that the caring and warm feelings bestowed upon her had no price tag attached.

I told her that we would help her deal with her own feelings, but that she was gonna be required to handle most of it on her own. She was reassured that I did not intend to alter my approach in any manner and that I would be available to her for counseling the same as for the other girls here.

Linda is clearly relieved after purging her mind of all this built-up material. She seems happy to have it out in the open between us, although it would not be surprising if she had second thoughts about "letting it all hang out" after thinking it over for awhile. This can be worked out with no ill effects if a little care and tact is utilized along the way.

11 December: Care Worker Notes

Linda is still showing a lot of ambivalence about leaving the secure unit and moving on to campus, and about it being "so soon". I reminded her that this was what she and all of us had been working towards ever since she arrived. I'm sure she'll begin to accept it after the initial shock wears off.

I gotta say, that spur of the moment idea about giving her a Memory Stone may have made an impression on Linda that nothing else we have done here even closely approaches! I admired her stone and commented on what a neat idea I thought it was, and she beamed all over the place. Such a simple gesture yet one which contains profound meaning to Linda!

Linda said, "they hadn't better send me to my new cottage straight from school like they did the last girl. I want you to take me over there when I have to leave here!" I explained — or tried to — that usually a girl made her move when it was most convenient for all concerned. Linda looked at me and said, "Convenient shit! What do I care for convenient? I care about feelings!"

We also talked some about saying "Goodbye". She said she will cry for sure when the time comes. I told her not to worry about it. We would all have to cope with our feelings and memories the best we could when the time comes.

That Linda is making a real effort to deal with her own feelings was evidenced by her timely, albeit reluctant, departure after we had spent a half hour or so together. She left saying, "I know you gotta talk to others and I don't want to hog all your time". I complimented her for her consideration and she took her leave.

Addendum

Little is known about what happened to Linda other than that she moved into an open cottage, attended school and moved forward with her life successfully. There was no other reason to think otherwise. Linda started living her life with new found confidence and learning more about relationships with caring adults. At school, she managed to cover the basics and completed the school year. Linda is remembered with fondness and a smile.

Aliese's Reflections

Well I had to laugh to myself, although none of this is any laughing matter. At first, I thought this was me. Especially since it started off with this whimsical reflections that sounded just like something I would write. And then reading along the description of all "my" charms and crimes, incorrigible, runaway, truancy, but then ... as the list continues, I realize this is not me.

As I read through this chapter, I recognise so many underlying common factors. In the comparing notes, I concluded that "all of us" had so many of the same thoughts, feelings, histories, and problems. You would have thought we all could have been "cured", so much more quickly, with all these transferable characteristics. Like a little cookie factory, with all of our problems being diagnosed, labels assigned to us –

sometimes frivolously – and without concern to the cause and effects of our cosmos. All of us neatly tucked away in little boxes to be pulled out and shown as examples, but I digress.

I don't think the system ever really understood children at that time. They would call you a runaway, but never look at the real reasons behind your wanting to leave. If you talked to someone about any of the hard and cold facts, you knew they would never let you go back home. So, you can see the quandary here. You would want to talk about the real stuff, but when you did, it was like it was held against you and you felt like you were being punished. While living at home, or a home where there was abuse going on was much better than being locked up, where you were under constant scrutiny, judgment, and control – and certainly no sense of freedom.

That is what was going on here with Linda. Her main goal was to get out of the institution and to get married. That meant safety to her, a new life for her, and control of her own environment. Note how somebody said in the care staff report where they called her lazy and lacking homemaking skills. I mean, really? Was THAT so important? When a kid is getting beat at home, physically abused (raped) by male figures, I am sure Linda wanted to improve on her talents of bed making and dusting. Please note: you were not allowed to have one hair in your comb or brush. It is so odd to me as an adult looking back on some of the rules and regulations.

What was so irritating, is we were constantly judged recklessly. Notes were written, notes were read, and by the time you got to the end of the line, you would have thought we were the worst type of person imaginable. Note again: being confronted by her peers about her associations with Black men – the prejudices were prevalent – but that is the world in which we lived. We KNEW this and we lived in the real world "on the Outs". We were judged constantly by our peers, the care workers, social workers, parole officers, superintendents, judges and our families. We were just trying to find our place in this world, where we were accepted for our own selves. Back then if you "dated" a Black man and you were not Black – it was considered some sort of identity crisis or it supposedly highlighted low self-esteem. My how the times have changed in this global world we live in!

We were not dumb, just not well educated. It was those types of prejudices and viewpoints that made it so difficult for us to make any real transformations in our life. The world was changing so quickly and we were so much more in tune with it, than the ESTABLISHMENT.

Linda was trying so hard to get close, to allow that trust and bond and then staff pushed her away because they were NOT allowed to be close to the youth. I mean, either way you looked at it, it was not the best scenario for either side. Everybody was playing games. The relationships were complicated and it didn't take much for them to unravel. How do you really learn to trust someone when you know they literally hold the keys to your life and livelihood?

It is sad they couldn't have focused more on the gifts and talents that each child held vs. trying to tear us down every step of the way. That was the process, tear you down and rebuild. At least that is how it felt at the time. I believe we have all come a long way in the treatment of incorrigible youth in current times and there is much more freedom of expression and individuality allowed. Linda was one of the lucky ones I dare say. She was a deep thinker and truly wanted to make changes in her life and I hope that she was able to put her valuable personal skills to good use.

Pain-Based Behaviour

All behaviour serves a purpose and rarely involves a random act or gesture. When adults dismiss youthful behaviour as meaningless, they demonstrate how little they know about young people, indeed, their own young people. (Almost) all behaviour is connected with meeting a need. Social workers, like child and youth care workers, spend a lot of time talking about the problematic behaviours of children and young people, often with terms such as challenging, troubling or dysfunctional. Forensic professionals may assign diagnoses to explain problematic behaviours, and suddenly labels appear, such as ADHD (Attention Deficit Hyperactivity Disorder), OCD (Obsessive Compulsive Disorder) or FASD (Fetal Alcohol Syndrome Disorder), to name but a few.

The traditional behavioural focus invites us to consider what might be considered the ABC's of problematic behaviour: First there must be an Antecedent(s) or *What happened before* the Behaviour of interest (usually problematic behaviours), and then what were the Consequences *generated by this youth's behaviour*? Social workers and youth workers often get stuck managing the consequences of youthful behaviour instead of engaging with each youth around personal needs that are being met by his or her behaviour. Intervention Plans are not just about problematic behaviours. Greater successes can be achieved by helping young people develop broader experiences of themselves and others, not just helping to 'eliminate their problem behaviour'. When young people start meeting their needs in different ways, they find it easier to let go of other, less fruitful behaviours from the past. There is much more to young people than their actions labelled as 'problem behaviours'. If we want to help young people change, it is necessary to focus on what's going on inside for this young person. One cannot just attend to the visible, focusing on those outside behaviours experienced by people around them. It is far better to ask *"How do we want this young person to experience herself?"* And *"How do we want her to experience us?"*

Social workers, as do child and youth care workers, talk a lot about the behaviour of young people on their caseloads. But this is only the tip of the iceberg. Children and young people have thoughts and feelings as well. When we focus only on the behaviour, we focus on what Mark Freado and colleagues at Reclaiming Youth International call *'the outside kid'*, but when we include this kid's thoughts and feelings, we focus on 'the inside kid' (Freado, Bussell & McCombie, 2005). In essence, we look beyond problem behaviours to consider the whole kid and the people she or he calls family. When considering each young person as a whole person, then a different set of ABC ground rules might include (Maier, 1978): Affect (Feelings); Behaviour (the Outside & the Inside Kid); and Cognition (Thinking).

How does this kid operate using Maier's ABC approach? Such a question leads me to wonder about how I might connect with this kid and start building a relationship that matters to them, as well as to both of us.

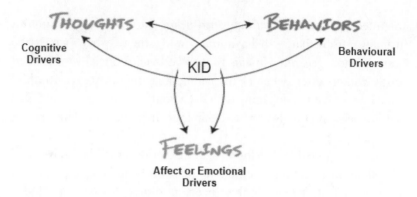

At the end of the twentieth century, British writers Ward and McMahon argued

> "...for children who have experienced the trauma of rejection, neglect or abuse, their inner world is often in a greater turmoil than the "real" world around them. ... The worker who attempts to achieve communication with a child's inner world is therefore operating in highly sensitive territory [where], timing, patience and an ability to demonstrate real empathy are essential" (1998: pp. 13-14).

Reaffirming these sentiments, Anglin (2002) concluded:

> "All children experience a degree of pain and confusion over the course of their development. However, if this pain is the result of abuse, rejection, or neglect, its lingering effects will almost inevitably be re-awakened or magnified when similar experiences are encountered in the intense interaction with youth that characterizes group home life and work. This fact highlights the critical importance of ... worker "anxiety" (pain-based fear). ... It is a disturbing fact that those who have the most complex and demanding role in the care and treatment of traumatized children have ... no specific training for the work. ... Many workers are being hired to work in the midst of this "river of pain" without having engaged in a process to identify, understand, and come to terms with unresolved trauma and pain in their own backgrounds, leaving them vulnerable to defensive reactions when a youth's pain emerges in a variety of often challenging ways" (2002: p. 112-113).

Reviewing the pain identified through the *Sisters of Pain* life stories reaffirms Anglin's (2002) argument that pain-based behaviour requires making connections and relational care that guarantee cultural safety and security whilst building restorative relationships that matter. One must be ever mindful of problematic behaviours whilst working to nurture a relationship that matters for this young person.

Ask the question another way: *Who would want to enter into a relationship with you? Why might they be interested anyway?* It is through a willingness to accept such blunt questions, that helpers locate themselves in the shoes of a child or young person arriving to start receiving out-of-home care or supervision with you. That youth may be thinking: *Who cares? Why should I bother, after all, it's just your job? Why are you trying to connect with me? How are you different from all the others? How can I get away from this?*

Each child or young person who has experienced trauma, neglect and abuse will have learned important lessons from such experiences, often lessons about survival. If there has been repeated trauma, neglect and abuse, then survival behaviours are often relived. ABC kids engage with carers and others wearing their feelings or Affect visible to everyone. Her feeling shapes her behaviour and thinking about what to do next. BCA kids lead with their survival skills (Behaviour), maybe knowing or thinking (Cognition) that by keeping this person at arm's length with my behaviour, I won't be hurt again (Affect) like other adults have hurt me. Try re-arranging Maier's ABC formulation whilst thinking about a specific young person in out-of-home care.

Different social workers or youth workers operate using a range of patterns, perhaps reflecting a 'default response'. Consider the social worker who has a reputation for bursting into tears. What about the social worker who young people say '*she goes official*'? One further example highlights CBA youths: Cognitive functioning informs their Behaviour while there is often dis-connect around Affect or emotional functioning and social norms or conscious reasoning/Cognition. This illustrates the plight of an only child living with Asberger's Syndrome in supported accommodation whilst transitioning towards semi-independent living, away from his family home, managing anxiety through imposing order and organisation in daily living routines. Social workers and youth workers need to actively consider the pain-based behaviours they encounter with every child or young person committed to out-of-home care and supervision. Linda reaffirms how relationships that mattered were those which moved beyond her problematic behaviour to connect with Linda as a whole kid.

Questions for Small Group Discussion or Guided Reflection

1.   Why is it important to look beyond a child's temper tantrum or a young person's problematic behaviour?
2.   What do Linda's narratives share about her "inner kid" that help explain the "outer kid" behaviour that moved her from placement to placement?
3.   How might social workers and youth workers operate more effectively using a "pain-based behaviour" approach to their work with children and young people in out-of-home care?
4.   How might pain experienced by a child or young person in out-of-home care be "lived out" through the relationship with a carer or social worker?
5.   What "buttons" were pushed for you whilst reading through the Linda narratives and what might these buttons say about your "inner kid" and potential default responses with young people?

Room 5
Nicki – *Doing Harm Whilst Doing Good*

Some years before her placement in the Exit Cottage attached to this institution, Nicki had spent a short period of time in the secure unit which accommodated the other young women featured in this book. Nicki was one of the few who had ever escaped.

4 December: Official Letter from the Acting Director of Institutions

Dear [Social Worker]

In order to keep things official, I thought I should write a summary of the meeting held about Nicki where the decision was made to try her in the Exit Cottage.

The meeting was held on 8 November and included representatives from all State institutions that work with girls. All agreed that none of the institutions could accomplish more for Nicki. However, she had to be somewhere while placement plans were made, and there was some feeling that she should leave the State Department of Institutions on a successful note if at all possible.

We felt we could not work with Nicki any more at the Assessment Center for several reasons. It isn't possible to offer therapeutic programming for Nicki while doing assessment work with all the rest of the resident group of girls.

123

This is especially so in view of Nicki's ability to control the peer group. We are further on in the process of changing from a six-week to a four-week assessment stay and could not devote energy to special therapeutic programming. Finally, all staff are exhausted from several months of working with Nicki and we are not productive in our work with her.

We discussed all options available and decided that Exit Cottage would most nearly meet her needs, placing responsibility on her and allowing for a rapid parole. We were aware that the Exit program might not be successful and therefore also recommended that she be discharged at age 18.

Sincerely,

The Superintendent
Service Delivery Division

16 November: Letter to Social Worker (whom she had met previously)

I remember my father disappeared. And we still lived in his house. Then I saw my mother standing in my father's kitchen with Him. I didn't understand what was going on, just that He was in our house and He was kissing my mother.

He was just so brutal and mean and I never understood anything. He'd whip us till we either cried or fell. After awhile, I'd refuse to cry, no matter what, and I'd just tell myself – it don't matter no more. It can't hurt me no more because everything is hopeless. I just deadened myself to all he did. Then I'd never give him the satisfaction of seeing me hurt or cry.

When he'd yell and threaten me, I learned after awhile to just stare at the ground so he couldn't see my eyes – my anger and hate and my fright. And when he came in after me to beat me, I just stood there and closed my eyes and didn't move. I got determined to show no feelings so he wouldn't know how it hurt me.

Instead, I would go to my room afterwards and turn my radio on and just hate him more and more. I wanted to kill him, and I'd just shake all over but I never could cry.

I can't cry over things – personal things that really hurt me. I can cry when I get super pissed. I guess I can't cry because I still feel he's waiting to hear me cry – just waiting for me to break down. And I can't let him get any satisfaction out of my pain.

I used to pick dandelions for my mother and I run in the house and I'd give them to her. But she always got mad and threw them away saying they were dirty weeds.

I used to try to help her with the housework but she told him I was always under her feet and I got beat.

I used to ask her to hold me and I'd cry but she was so cold, she'd just say, "Will you just leave me alone, I'm busy". Always too busy – too busy – except when it came to him.

My school teachers despised me. I had a smart mouth, and mocked or sassed them a lot. They slapped me and spanked me, and dragged me from rooms by my hair or ear. They also made me stand in front of the class while they ridiculed me in front of the other kids.

Every day it was the same shit. It just got worse and worse. I got suspended in Fifth Grade, expelled in Sixth Grade. And I got kicked out of my Kindergarten class too. Oh yeah – I never made it thru Brownies either! My third or fourth meeting I was kicked out. Same with 4-H.

The best things I could do while growing up was beating up the boys, playing baseball, football and basketball. Also dirt-clod fights. And of course I could mouth off quite well.

Academically in school – I was the best student in all my classes – but I always flunked because of my behavior. I know I could have been a straight "A" student and a good, innocent young girl – and everybody's dart board. I chose to become a monster before I'd ever be anyone's doormat.

So I flunked out. I got kicked out of everything. I beat up the boys. I played sports and I read a hell of a lot. Everyone else was reading "Danny the Dinosaur" or the Dr Suess books. I was reading Steinbeck and Laura Ingles Wilder. The teachers just hated that – and so did the kids. But I kept my nose in my books – dreamed up lots of fantasies from different ones. I was also very lonely and scared.

(I wrote the above last night. Right now I'm on my second joint and I'm gonna write some terrible shit that embarrasses me to write, okay?)

My stepbrother was about 3 or 4 years older than me. And as young as I can remember – I remember him always trying to mess with me. First he'd exhibit himself to me and later on he was sticking his hands down my pants. When I was 11 or 12 and he was 16 or 17, he tried to force me to fuck with him.

For as long as I can remember, I was always so frightened of him and felt so guilty cause I knew it wasn't right. I had let him. I had only cried and didn't stick up for myself. And I felt so dirty and ashamed.

I never could tell my mother anything. I was too afraid I'd get beat. Like I never even thought of telling my mother about how the schoolteachers treated me cause then she'd know they had a "reason" so I'd get beat again.

Well, I guess I just began feeling beaten in every way, by everyone and always on the verge of throwing my life in. But hate of Him inside of me – that man who beat me – kept me going. His voice remained in my ears, mocking me.

And all the other "Hims" in the world tried to trick me and hurt me. And I was going crazy because I couldn't trust anyone. God, how I wanted somebody, so fucking badly. It drove my mind crazy and blanketed my heart with a heavy dark cloud. Humiliation, ridiculed and I'm always feeling worthless and no good.

After taking 38 of my Mother's thyroid pills, I woke up two days later, alive and disappointed. I hated myself more because I couldn't even kill myself. Empty all the time inside.

I filled my mind with books, my heart with emptiness and my soul with the rage and bitterness I felt towards everyone – but especially Him.

My stepfather hated cats. One time he was mowing the lawn on his sit-down mower. The neighbor's kitten – Buttercup was her name – was in our yard so he yelled at me to get the cat out of his yard. So I was chasing the cat and the cat got in front of the mower. My stepfather pushed the accelerator and all I remember is running and running and hearing that terrible clunk, clunk as the cat went through the blades.

I couldn't stop the tears.

And hearing Him laughing about running over the cat at supper! That night he bragged about what he'd done and while everyone kind of laughed, I vomited and then got beat for it and sent to me room where I curled up in my favorite spot – by the heater with a blanket and my radio or maybe a book.

Right before I left home, I remember my Mother always telling me, "You were so cute when you were a baby – always smiling and never causing trouble. Now look at you! You're mean and you're always causing us trouble. You're just no good!!"

I just made my face go motionless, clinched my fists and walked to my room. It was always in my room, after the door was closed and I was alone that I'd just collapse. And I let my vulnerability and fright float around the room. I had to release the pain and pressure of storing away all those feeling so I'd run to my room and just let go it all.

Then I'd collect myself – stuff all of me in a box – and go out to face them. I was just a body. That's all. Oh fuck, I feel so bad about all these things that are coming into my mind right now.

Well, I ain't going to write no more. I just wanted to write this to you so you could bring them up when we talk about my family. It will help me to talk to you easier if I can write it to you first.

Nicki

26 November: Handwritten Letter from Social Worker

Dear Nicki

It's been awhile since I've had a chance to talk with you about how things are going since coming to Exit Cottage. Our schedules don't overlap that much but there is still need for some time to sit down for some regular talk about subjects of importance.

I have decided to go through the 12 points in your contract and give you my current assessment of where things stand. I hope you can fill me in on more details.

1: Outside Job: I like the idea of volunteering but hope, for your sake, that it can extend into a paid job.

2. GED (Graduate Equivalency Diploma) Exam: I am still very suspicious of "the System" working. I see that you have sent off your letter and I honestly hope it will be able to happen.

3. The K Family Foster Home: I picked up vibes when I talked with Mrs K on the telephone. To be honest with you, it looked like some sort of "rescue Nicki" effort that they were offering their home. If this is true — are you sure you need that at age 17 and a half? It might make more sense for us to go to the Court and see if we can get you legally emancipated. Another option (but probably inferior) would be to wait until you're 18 and then you can be definitely emancipated.

4. Helping out at Exit Cottage: Be sure that you do you fair share! (This is the authority speaking!).

5. Telephone Calls: You've been cleared for telephone calls to your boyfriend [at a State institution for males located nearby], but not visits at this time.

6. Laws: Watch it!

7. Language: I never did know what this meant. Is your language improving? If so, how? If not, why?

8. Verbal or Physical Abuse: I want you to lay off any of this self-injury shit. If I like the Nicki that I've seen thus far, then let's deal with getting things happening instead of fighting back at the System by doing weird things to yourself or others.

9. Being open and honest: I don't know. I would imagine that there are others who can give you their reading about me. This is also why I want to have some kind of regular conversations.

10. Talking instead of Bottling-Up: Another reason why I want a regular chat. Unless I get to know you better, I won't really know what's happening with you! And maybe you'd just as soon leave it that way!!

11. Involvement: Sounds nice – what's happening?

12. 15 January: I got a lot of work to do for The System if this is to happen! Just another reason why I need to know where your plans are and what you're thinking.

Contingency Plan: Just in case the GED plan doesn't work, I have information about another program for non-high school graduates (preference for women and residents in institutions). It pays all school and educational expenses plus a small living allowance that lets you take a training course through to completion. It can extend up to two years and is designed to help you get job skills that can be translated into earning power. It's open to 17 year-olds. Please let me know what you think.

Social Worker

9 December: Initial Program Plan Written By Social Worker

Nicki has been in the State System for at least four years and has spent time at all institutional programs and group homes for girls administered by the State.

In talking with Nicki, it now appears that primary emotional issues relating to her commitment in the beginning had to do with a long history of physical and sexual abuse in her family. She is not keen to talk about this and it is a very painful area for her, even though it's important that she and staff understand these facts about her past so we can better understand how she has reacted to the institutional system for the past four years she has been in it.

It is appalling to this social worker to reflect on Nicki's claim that during the four years she has been in "The System", very little attention or consistent effort has been directed towards helping Nicki resolve some of the issues from her family life. The pent up hostility, the intense frustration and the deep emotional scars from this period have left Nicki fighting a System which often times did not understand. The System became a symbol of all that her stepfather and family meant to her. At present, Nicki has very limited resources in the community to which she can turn. This, in itself, is frustrating and once again she lashes out at people around her because they haven't helped her sufficiently to get plugged back into the community.

It goes without saying that Nicki is a very intelligent girl but she is not at all pleased to have this thrown at her when she is not handling herself responsibly.

People have responded to Nicki's intelligence and I think that is fine. However, there are often times when she feels on the verge of being crazy when she can't make sense of feelings or use her intelligence to work out the intense feelings she has and carries with her most of the time. Nicki's institutionalized boyfriend seems to be a positive source of support for Nicki at this time. She hopes eventually to live with him in the future.

The principal long-term goal is to get Nicki out of the youth justice system and legally emancipated by the Court. At the same time, we need to help Nicki get her Graduate Equivalency Diploma, work out a place to live and work or school when she returns to her local community. Short-term Goals with Nicki include the following:

1.   Nicki will be seen by the doctor to consider her for knee surgery on her right knee. The surgery was organized while at the other institution but for whatever reason, Nicki broke the cast off of her leg and never had this tended to adequately. This will be a priority while Nicki is at Exit Cottage

2. Counseling with the social worker focused around Nicki's family life and how she hopes to pull herself out of the web that has emotionally entrapped her and leaves her fighting back at anyone who makes her feel threatened.

3. Working on her GED. Contacts have already been initiated with the relevant authorities and verbal assurance has been given towards Nicki taking the exam before her 18th birthday. It is likely that this will occur after knee surgery during recuperation.

4. Nicki's lawyer will be contacted to see whether legal assistance might be forthcoming to help her be legally emancipated before her 18th birthday.

5. Pursuing an outside job as soon as she is able to start. It is unlikely that this will occur until after knee surgery.

6. Telephone calls with her institutionalized boyfriend, with future visits if approved.

7. Taking leaves from Exit Cottage as they can be arranged. Mr and Mrs K have offered their home although there seems to be some question as to the kind of involvement that Nicki wishes to have with them or of their expectation of Nicki. Mrs S has also offered to have Nicki come to her home occasionally on leave and this will be pursued.

8. See if we can locate Nicki's brother, the person who is perhaps the only other natural family member who Nicki has ever felt she could talk with, about things in the chaos that existed in her family. She has lost contact with her brother and attempts will be made to locate him.

9. Obeying and fulfilling all responsibilities and abide by the rules of the Exit Cottage program. This will be very important for Nicki as she must understand that some responsibility must be placed on her if she is to have a chance to finally break herself out of the legal system.

> The most difficult thing for Nicki to do will be to overcome her own paranoia about how people are coming across to her. It will be important that all Exit Cottage staff deal with Nicki directly and honestly, and to expect the same in return.
>
> 10   The long range target date for leaving the institution has been set as 23 May – Nicki's 18th Birthday. However, attempts will be made from the beginning to achieve legal emancipation through the court earlier if possible.
>
> 11.   There will be a built in review of the Exit Cottage program with Nicki and her performance in the Exit Cottage program – and at 3 month intervals.

Christmas Break: Letter to Social Worker Received on Return from Holiday

Hi

I don't know why I'm writing or exactly what I'm going to write.

I guess I've just been feeling bottomless and empty. And I feel like I've lost all the goals I was striving for. It always seems I lose before I gain, in every situation that comes up.

It's always so lonely around here in the night times. I hate loneliness. Yet I hate aloneness much worse. And I feel a tremendous amount of aloneness. So alienated.

We had a few difficulties while you were gone. A pretty major disaster as defined by everyone. Yet I don't feel it is as big as they are blowing it up to be.

Well, at this present time, I find myself very confused. So before I rattle on into eternity, I'll put down this pen. See you in my "Contract Review Board".

Nicki

27 December: Formal Institutional Incident Report Recorded at 2:55 p.m.

A fire started in Nicki's Room after she left a candle burning. It set fire to her books and the shelf. Smouldering books were removed. Exit Cottage residents were told there would be no burning of candles in their rooms.

27 December: Formal Institutional Incident Report Recorded at 10:30 pm

Nicki cut on her arm with a razor blade. We talked with Nicki and after a short while, she accepted the suggestion of cleaning up and having her arm taken care of. Shift Supervisor was called and the nurse was called back to campus to go with Nicki to the hospital and have her arm attended to.

28 December

It may sound stupid, perhaps even childish. Sorry to say it but I need a family – somewhere to belong. I cannot take any more of this aloneness.

I would like a Mother and a Father, but knowing this to be an impossibility that I cannot handle anymore, I have decided that my life is no longer worthwhile.

Of course there are many other things that interfere with my life. But I do not feel like going through it.

I don't have anything left to fight for. That's why I am leaving the way I am.

Imagine, this place has my mind and soul. And now they'll have my body too! Ironic enough.

Not much more to say.

Nicki

28 December: Formal Institutional Incident Report Recorded at 8:30 p.m.

Nicki threatening to commit suicide by jumping off the institution water tower at approximately 8:30 p.m.

Nicki handed in a suicide note to staff on duty and then left the Exit Cottage at about 8:30 p.m. Mr J read the note and immediately contacted Security at the Post Phone. Mr J had earlier tried to delay Nicki's departure but was unsuccessful. Security followed Nicki and observed her climbing the water tower and insisting she would jump. Mr K eventually succeeded in talking Nicki into climbing back down the tower and returning to Exit Cottage. Nicki later reported that she was feeling dejected and alone due to being alienated from her family and to a series of recent incidents with separation problems. Nicki was left in the Exit Cottage for the night, with regular half hour checks made by night staff after Nicki retired to her room. This was done in the interests of her safety. She appeared in reasonably good emotional condition after returning to the cottage. Nicki is to meet with her social worker the following day to discuss what type of help she needs.

3 January: Youth Mental Health Service Admission Note

Presenting Problem: Nicki has been asking for several weeks to talk to a psychiatrist and in the last week has made three suicidal gestures: (1) Cutting her arms; (2) Overdosing on Valium; and (3) Climbing the water tower and threatening to jump. Nicki says quite frankly that those were only gestures and that she does not really want to die.

History of Presenting Problem: Two years after Nicki's parents divorced, her mother married her stepfather. Nicki was reportedly beaten by both her father and stepfather from eighteen months of age until she sought refuge with Youth Services at the age of thirteen. Nicki admitted to purposely provoking her parents to get angry reactions. Nicki was screened by child mental health service but she was transferred to youth justice services where she was placed in the secure unit. She eventually managed to escape from there through an historic breakout involving a group incident which distracted staff so that Nicki and another girl could get out onto the patio, use the trampoline to jump onto the roof, and out over the roof to the highway.

Such were Nicki's emotional strengths that she induced one of the institution staff to quit her job with the State and take her as a foster child. This placement apparently worked well for a period of time until Nicki stole the foster parent's car. She was then placed at an institution for younger teenagers but began cutting on herself so badly that she was returned for re-assessment.

Her next placement was in an independent cottage where she remained for three months. Apparently she spent the entire three months using and selling amphetamines. Eventually, some people whom she had sold some bad drugs came in and wrecked the place so the independence program was closed down. After spending a few weeks at another group home, Nicki ended up at the Exit Cottage and now with the mental health service where she started.

Current Family Situation: Nicki's mother and stepfather want nothing more to do with her and are presently making it impossible for Nicki to have contact with her youngest sister. Nicki is the twelfth of her mother's thirteen children, all of whom live out of the home.

Mental Status: Nicki is a well-developed, well-nourished seventeen and one-half year old Caucasian girl who came to the interview dressed in a boyish manner with workman boots, jeans and a boy's crew neck white sweater with black and red stripes down the arms. She wears no make-up but her hair is long and free flowing. She displays little overt anxiety but tends to be quite constricted and tense. Her mood is depressed. Her affect is a cool facade of bravado and/or "knowing all the answers". She speaks in the language of today's youth. Her speech is totally coherent and relevant. Her main preoccupations center around her feeling the need for "a family – whoever wants me", her dislike for institutions and authority figures and, on the other hand, her fear of her approaching eighteenth birthday. She feels totally inadequate at the prospect of being on her own. She blames all of her problems on others. Nicki is oriented in all areas. Her memory is intact. Intellectually she is within the average range. Her insight and judgment are poor. She is easily frustrated and has poor impulse control.

Tentative Diagnosis: Unsocialised Aggressive Reaction of Adolescence manifested by impulsivity, drug abuse, problems with authority figures, blaming others for all her problems, etc.

Recommendation: Nicki is formally admitted to State Mental Health Services

Addendum

Nicki remained on this social worker's caseload for little more than six weeks. Her legend well and truly preceded her, and was reinforced during her brief stay at Exit Cottage. It is important to recognize that this short term placement in Exit Cottage involved a decision made by the three senior managers of youth services in the State, and the assignment of this social worker to Nicki's case.

This was a decision taken on high, not a carefully considered professional decision made with family members and significant others.

During the more than four years she spent in State Child Welfare and Youth Justice services, Nicki ended up spending time at every placement available for girls in that State System.

Nicki herself had sought help from local child welfare services as the twelfth of her Mother's thirteen children. Help was sought after a long history of physical and sexual abuse perpetrated by her stepfather and stepbrother.

Wherever Nicki went around the System, professionals working with her tried everything, and failed. The System also failed Nicki. Her first placement at the secure unit and a subsequent high profile escape resulted in Nicki being labelled a hard core delinquent.

As a very bright young woman, Nicki used intellectual games with everyone assigned to help her. She succeeded in getting one State employee to give up her employment and become Nicki's foster parent. Then Nicki stole this foster parent's car. The Directors of all State institutions for children and young people met to consider what could be done with Nicki.

Directors of the State Child Welfare and Youth Justice System stated that the goal was to emancipate Nicki legally from the State system, thereby placing responsibilities for decision-making squarely on Nicki's shoulders.

The closer this emancipation plan came to becoming a reality, the more Nicki's coping skills were tested and crumbled. All the emotional turmoil that had not been addressed by professionals in the Child Welfare and Youth Justice systems for more than four years now overwhelmed her. Instead of legal emancipation from the Youth Justice System, Nicki was transferred to adolescent mental health services.

Nicki thus continued her "career" in the "State Care System", as a registered mental health patient instead of being a young person in out-of-home care. We believe that after a lengthy period in prison, Nicki died.

Aliese's Reflections

This story ends tragically and she was one of my closest friends. She was tough, like me, and she was smart, like me. I trusted her. She said what she meant and meant what she said.

School. Yeah, they always hated us. It was just another system where we never fit. I remember once in 7th grade when I was expelled after being in the school one day – I did not even do anything. But, the school was afraid of me being a bad influence on their ideal little citizens. We were the smart ones, who got bored with all of them and their curriculum. They tried to teach us so much useless information, and nothing that we could truly relate to, in our real world. We were a generation that questioned everything and for good cause as it turned out.

We were intelligent and had the ability to learn, we simply got bored with their itinerary and became class clowns, the voices for others, or simply chose not to attend. Besides, what real chance did you have when every report card followed you from school to school? We challenged their ability to teach, the slanted lies of history, and grammar rules that still befuddle me to this day. Back in those days, the teachers did hit you, did ridicule you, and God forbid IF anything bad ever happened on the campus, you were automatically to blame and no questions asked. It was so difficult. We did not fit in anywhere. Not at home, not at school, and certainly most of us did not deserve to be locked up and mistreated so badly.

They were trying to conform us into their images of what little girls should be like. It was the most bizarre concept ever. I mean how do you take someone who has been beaten daily, raped like a savage dog and now try to teach them English? Like any of that really mattered in our world. What a joke!

We were not the problem, but rather, the by-product of the problem. That is one of the most important things I feel they didn't know or understand as carers or jailers. We were lucky when an honest and knowledgeable person came in contact with us. In this case, it was our social worker. As noted on December 9th of the social worker notes, "it is appalling"… Point made. The system saw us as the problem and the causes of the problems, rather than looking at the real issues.

But then again, we were here, locked up, to work on our issues and NOT that of the system. It was so hard for us to distinguish the difference between the two. Meaning to say, our problems vs the system, when most of our problems were the aftermath of a failed system, failed marriages, abuse caused by others to us, and a society that was rapidly changing view points on everything! Many of the caregivers over the years looked at us with disgust, or the other kind, the worse ones. Those were the ones who seemed to enjoy discussing our physical rape and abuse. I mean, it happens. It freaked us out and creeped us out. Those kinds of ugly things made it very difficult to reach out in any true depth or honesty. So by the time you got to this high security unit, man, you had pretty much seen it all and it was the end of the line. So much damage had been done to us over the years. This is what had happened to Nicki.

Nicki's wisdom shines through in her letter to her social worker around Christmas break. I love where she says "It always seems I lose before I gain …" That is so profound and it is the way life works, or that has been my experience. There is always a set-back of sorts before some breakthrough. And also, that she recognizes the difference between loneliness and being alone. Many educated adults to this day have a hard time coping or understanding that there is a difference between them.

Nicki was my friend and my confidante although we did not get to spend much time together. Loneliness is such a hard emotion to have. I don't think we are really equipped to handle that at a young age, even through the course of natural development in a healthy and thriving environment. That is why we had the family unit, like the wolf pack – in part, being a part of a family unit. The balanced inter-relationships are central to the fundamentals … like Stevie Wonder sang in *The Keys of Life*… there must be a sense of belonging and duty that comes naturally.

One huge part of Nicki's life is when she was in a state mental hospital and they used 'electroshock treatment' on her. This went on for months. It was something right out of Ken Kesey's, *One Flew Over the Cuckoo's Nest*. I don't think she ever really recovered from those sessions. The effects of so many years of abuse had simply taken over and it makes me mad and sad to have lost a good friend just because she was born into a dysfunctional family.

How do you ever truly recover from that sort of abuse? I later learned that she got hooked up with some girl on a joy ride. The other girl had stolen a car and drove to somewhere in the Midwest – some very back woods thinking in that day. The girl had a handgun and she robbed some local-yokel gas station. I don't have all the details. I do know that she was incarcerated for many years, raped in jail by one of the guards and had the baby while in jail. At some point in time, one of her old probation officers had her transferred to another state, closer to home. The child was put up for adoption. Nicki later died but I don't have the details. I cry tears for my sister now and feel that I somehow let her down.

Doing Harm While Doing Good

We are indebted to Australian scholars Ainsworth and Hansen (2012) for articulating *The Child Protection Paradox* that confronts each social worker or child and youth care worker engaging with children or young people placed in out-of-home care. We think the same principles apply when working with young people who may have started off as child protection 'at-risk' kids, but their pain-based behaviour increasingly drew them into youth justice networks. In some places, as in Scotland, child protection and youth justice services are more integrated and mediated through the Children's Hearings system until such time as a referral is made to the adult courts. In New Zealand, the distinction between child protection and youth justice is more clearly defined. We think the following principles apply for all children and young people in out-of-home care.

Children's rights and parents' rights are both central to this paradox.

"Child protection authorities appear to be reluctant to acknowledge that removing a child from parental care causes trauma for the child and the parents. While it may be in the long-term interests of the child to be removed, the fact is that at the point of removal the child is trauma-tized and this should not be ignored. Equally, parental distress and grief is profound (Burgheim, 2005; Davies, 2011; Schofield et al., 2010) and neither should this be ignored. … Such denial of parental distress and grief may of course allow child protection caseworkers to rationalize their action(s) in terms of "doing good". Moreover, focusing on the good and ignoring the harm may be one way caseworkers manage the stress of child protection work and in turn justify their actions which are some-times wrong. … But this hardly seems humane" (2012: p. 149).

Regardless of any potential harm, it is important to acknowledge that child protection workers do help by removing children from seriously abusive parents. Everyone agrees with this. However, little attention is given to the increasing number of children who are removed from parental care and lose contact with extended family members. Moreover, many of these children are not restored to parental care, regardless of what child protection policy statements might claim. In her review of child protection services in England and Wales, Munro (2011) called for a return to relationship-based supportive practices that encourage and reward parental efforts to alter their lifestyles and parenting practices whilst attending to fundamental child protection concerns. Scott *et al* (2010) argue for a more humane practice where empathy, respect, genuineness and optimism are the cornerstones of practice.

Nikki was a young woman who came into the Child Welfare system under child protection legislation. She had experienced physical and emotional abuse and neglect for a long time before the system really did anything. As Nicki got more and more angry about what was happening in her life, she got into more fights and started running away. At this stage, the system gave her the label of "incorrigible" youth in need of supervision, not simply a child in need of care and protection because of historic abuse. The more caseworkers in the system responded to Nicki's "incorrigible" behaviour – the outer kid – the more Nicki bounced around the system. At the age of 17, Nicki held the record for having been placed in every State programme available. She left a couple of these placements in disarray before moving on.

As Nicki approached the age of 18 years – adult status – all State Child Welfare managers gathered together to plan Nicki's systematic transition to "independent status" and leave the Child Welfare System. After nearly 3 years fighting her way around the Child Welfare and Youth Justice systems, Nicki transitioned to the Child and Adolescent Mental Health Service. Earlier in her Child Welfare placements, Nicki was rejected by this service because she presented as a 'character disordered' youth instead of someone with mental illness. As she approached age 18, Nicki presented with mental illness symptoms, heightened no doubt through having had these "symptoms" ignored throughout three years of child welfare placements.

Aliese drew comparisons between Nicki's tragic experiences in the mental health system with those highlighted in Kesey's *One Flew Over the Cuckoo's Nest*. Nicki became and remained a victim of the State child welfare system. Nicki gave us plenty that told of her pain-based behaviour. Doing harm? Nicki had plenty of reasons to be angry that the system had done her wrong. When the anger and nightmares left her exhausted, Nicki entered a black emotional abyss that enticed her towards suicide. Nicki was bright enough to out-fox group life counselors and social workers. Nicki learned from every child welfare placement, even how to distribute cannabis or sexual services. Were the State-employed caseworkers doing good while doing harm? Or were they doing harm while doing good? The paradox remains. When working with young people like Nicki and her Sisters of Pain, inexperienced social workers and youth workers must grapple with the *Doing Harm While Doing Good Paradox* underpinning care work with children and young people in out-of-home care.

Ainsworth and Hansen (2012) argue that the forensic model of child protection practice has failed because it focuses solely on the child, not the child in the context of his or her family. A child cannot be removed from his or her family and immediately offered a brighter future by the State. The research on successful foster care placements is not altogether encouraging, especially in the USA, in the world's biggest economy where there are more gun-related killings than in any other OECD state. Nicki's life ended with drama, underscoring how doing harm while doing good resonates through the *Sisters of Pain* life stories. Though rarely discussed in the social work or child and youth care literature, *The Child Protection Paradox* remains a contemporary challenge for the social work and child and youth care fields.

Questions for Small Group Discussion or Guided Reflection

1. How does *The Doing Harm While Doing Good Paradox* operate in Child Protection work with children and young people in out-of-home care?

2. What competencies and resilience skills were evident in the fragments of Nicki's life story?

3. What *good* did a Personal Care Plan offer Nicki through administratively 'kicking her out' of the system?

4. What *potential harm* was threatened with Nicki's new Personal Care Plan as she 'aged out' of Child Protection and Youth Justice services, and Health and Welfare professionals moved her into the State Mental Health system?

5. What example(s) can you identify where the *Doing Harm Whilst Doing Good Paradox* was operating in practice with particular children and young people living in out-of-home care?

Room 6
Carlita – *Rhythms of Daily Living*

22 August: Social Work Notes

Carlita is nearly 17 years of age, a girl of mixed Native American and Caucasian ancestry who was committed by the Juvenile Court for persistent running away from the family home, incorrigibility and involvement with prostitution. She is the only member of her family to have been in trouble.

Virtually all areas of Carlita's life are wrapped up in avoiding problems that have occurred during the past two to three years. There is considerable depression which is compounded by feelings of persecution from those around her and little perceived support from family or friends. The result is a young woman who is nearly immobilized at the present time – at least in the positive sense – and she is a ready candidate for use and abuse by pimps and people who wish to use Carlita for their own ends. She covers her fears with anger and hostility, and avoiding issues through involvement in prostitution and drugs. It is possible that Carlita has more going for her by way of back-up support from family than she herself recognizes.

After a slow start, Carlita made 16 "I-Statements" that reflect how she views her life at the beginning of her stay in the secure unit:

1. I started getting into trouble when I was 13.

2. My parents were away from home visiting family

when I got picked up after my paper round by a guy who took me drinking and tried to rape me.

3. I got away from him, called the police and they took me to detention.

4. I had to stay in detention for 2 weeks until my parents got home.

5. I stayed good for 3 or 4 months before starting to run away from home again.

6. I was looking for someone who would understand me.

7. I met some Black guys through my cousin and that's how I got into prostitution and also how I started using drugs.

8. I thought the excitement and the people I was with were fun.

9. When my parents found out they pretty much disowned me.

10. I am the only person in the family who has gotten into trouble.

11. I don't think my Mom cares about me. My Dad is the only one who does. My Mom doesn't want me home and my brothers and sisters don't care. They just call me names.

12. I haven't been to school for almost a year, ever since I left Junior High because of the prejudice there.

13. I used to do good in school but now it is hard to keep my mind on it because I keep thinking about all of the problems I've got.

14. I don't know what to do except just die.

15. It's hard for me to be around other people because of the way they act toward me.

16. I feel lost.

Carlita

Carlita is said to be a moody young woman and her involvement in the program may be influenced by her moods day to day. She has a lot of potential for pro-social behavior and her intellectual capabilities seem greater than she leads people to believe. With nurture and support, Carlita can achieve. Her delinquencies, running away and involvement in Street Life may have been about avoiding feelings of loneliness, inadequacy, dependency and rejection. Placement in the secure unit will hopefully give Carlita time to develop relationships with patient, caring adults who will not let her reject them. The primary goal is to minimize continuing involvement in self-destructive acting out. Among Carlita's personal strengths are her abilities with Arts and Crafts. Use activities as a means to talk.

1 September: Care Worker Notes

Carlita and I talked for about an hour and a half tonight, starting in the living room but moved to the school room due to the noise. Once in the school room, Carlita just started talking. I asked her why she was in the secure unit. She said it's because she runs away a lot and has been unable to live at home.

She told me of her running away a lot due to her mother's drinking and picking only on her and not the other kids. In April Carlita was coming home from a fair and was waiting for a bus when this guy came up to her and asked her if she wanted a ride. She told him that she was waiting for a guy and the guy told her the buses had stopped running 30 minutes earlier. So he offered her a ride again and she refused.

He left but returned, following her. She got scared and ran and hid, then went to a gas station. The guy caught up to Carlita there and propositioned her again. His offer was made tempting so she took him up on it. They drove out by a lake where he took off his clothes and tried to rape her. She managed to get away but got lost. After finding the main road, she then bumped into a Highway Patrol car.

They took Carlita to the station where they tried to contact relatives without success. When asked why she had so much money in her purse, she explained it was paper collection money that she had collected that night from her paper round. The police said she was lying and must be a prostitute. They took her to Juve where she was held for 10 days and before being sent back home. Within hours, relations with Carlita's mother had deteriorated further.

The family sent Carlita to live with her brother and sister-in-law in the Midwest. They tried to help her through buying her nice clothes and sending her to an all Indian School. Carlita had a hard time at the all Indian School because she didn't fit in. She wore the wrong kind of clothes, dresses instead of jeans and sneakers, and everyone picked on her. She started skipping school after she was beat up by some of the girls there.

This started troubles with her brother. She started running away by being distracted by guys and offers of having fun. When living with her brother they would always have big booze parties and do Indian dancing, play the drums and smoke the pipe. When the drinking got pretty heavy, her brother would send her to her room. The brother's friends would ask her out but the brother wouldn't let her go. So Carlita started running around, being gone from the home for weeks without letting them know where she was or that she was alright.

One night she took off for about 12 days and on returning, she and her brother got in a big fight. Then her sister-in-law and she started fighting. In the end, Carlita was kicked out of the house and ended up turning herself in to the Juvenile Hall.

Then, when everything was arranged for Carlita to be returned home, and while waiting for the airplane, she and the escorts sat in the lounge and got drunk waiting for the airplane to depart. Once on the airplane, she discovered it was going to the wrong city. She ended up staying with some Black guy for a couple of weeks. The guy took her home with him where she stayed with his sister.

I asked why she didn't call her parents and she said that she didn't know, maybe because she would get in trouble. Anyway, she finally did call them and took the bus home. After returning, she was there only a few hours when she and her mother got into a fight and Carlita ran away again.

On one occasion while on the run with her cousin, they were having dinner downtown when two Black guys approached them to go to a party. After a long discussion, she finally said yes. They took a taxi to an apartment where Carlita walked in on a card game with about a dozen Black guys. One asked her, "Is there going to be a party"? and she said, "I guess so".

They all started drinking and taking dope. Carlita got really high and one guy told her to go up stairs because he wanted to sleep with her. She said no but he threatened her. So she went. She finally reached the room with a lot of difficulty due to the drugs and booze. Then she got to the room, the guy told her to undress and she did.

He turned the light on and she discovered that there were a whole lot of guys up there. They tied her hands to the bed and each took turns violating her. One tried to have her do other things but she refused. For refusing she got beat up pretty bad.

She said they hung her out a window about three flights up because she wouldn't let them have her anymore. She finally agreed and they let her back in, and they all took their turns again. Carlita said that her cousin had gone through the same ordeal but that they beat her up a lot more. One guy beat the cousin with a coat hanger really bad.

Carlita could hear her cousin yelling for her and she yelled back. This went on all night and the next day, Carlita said that she passed out. When she woke up, one of the guys told her to get dressed. She dressed and then came out of the room where she saw her cousin for the first time and was totally shocked by her appearance.

The girls were told not to say a word about what went on or else they'd find them and kill them. They were each given $20 which Carlita initially refused and then both of them were dropped in an alley off Main Street. They could hardly walk but Carlita and her cousin got to the street where they found a police car and collapsed in front of it. Both were taken to hospital where they were kept for nearly two weeks.

The girls made statements to the police about this event but they finally accused them of lying. The police probably believed that they got beat up by their pimps because they didn't bring home enough money. So the whole thing was dropped. Carlita's Mother told her she was lying and she wouldn't believe her anymore. She told her brothers what happened but they agreed with their Mother. Carlita says that she has tried to talk with her Mother but she just kept calling her a "hoe" and a "no good".

At Juvenile Court, Carlita told them she didn't want to go home. She wanted a foster home. Instead they sent her here to the secure unit. She hopes this placement will "make me quit running away and have me understand my parents better and them me".

6 October: Social Worker Notes

I met with Carlita's parents today. Father confirmed that he hadn't called, and that he wanted all calls stopped from Carlita for the time being. Mother was not talkative and may feel – because of culture – that she should remain silent and let her husband speak for them. At this time, there is some question about whether the family home is still a potential option for longer-term placement.

6 November: Summary of the Planning Board Meeting

Carlita has stabilized considerably since arriving ten weeks ago. She is more open and relaxed in both her body language and also in her manner of interaction with staff and peers. She has had two visits with her parents and in one of these, her social worker was involved and noted that there appeared to be much better communication now between Carlita and her parents. She now feels that they care about her. Their attempts to stop her doing some of the things she was doing in the community was not because they didn't like her but because they cared about her and didn't want her to hurt herself. Carlita is looking much more now at what she, herself, does in her interactions with both staff and peers. She now sees that some of the things she did in the community – like running around and doing just anything she felt like – were pretty dumb. We now see more honesty in Carlita's interactions with staff and peers, although she still has some difficulty standing up to the stronger group. In such situations, she has difficulty controlling her anger but now knows this to be an area for further work on her part. In all areas of school, Carlita has shown improvement in attitude and effort. Is less resentful than before and seems more relaxed. Is motivated in school.

3 December

Dear Social Worker

Hi. What it is? Tell me about it!

Well, as "you" can see, I'm going through a lot of changes and I do mean changes! (You know. I'm sure you know!)

I'm just going to sit here for a minute or so to try and at least express my thoughts, feelings and my understandings. So read for what I am about to run down to you.

I know I am here in this locked up place because I run too much. I do realize that I fit in this program. You and all the staff I talked to think I fit right on into this place.

I guess my feelings I once kept to myself have finally come to a point where I need to let people and "my Parents" know how I feel, how I talk, how I write, and what I feel within my mind.

I guess you could say I'm very understanding. I got a good peace of mind (that's when I set it to the right point of view). Now I find myself talking to staff. While talking, I (myself) get to a better understanding point. Same with the staff I been talking to.

I guess I've come a long way to accomplishing what I have at the time being. I'll keep on keeping on to a better understanding with the staff I've been talking to. Same with "My Parents" and with "you".

I know I have misunderstandings here but I'm going to change that, you'll see!

I know you know, the staff know and my Parents know that I've been so depressed at times but we all know, and I know especially, that there is an answer to that depression I have when I feel so down and out.

But we all know that there's an answer just waiting to slip out of my mouth to lift that problem out of my reach. So I'll find those words soon as possible (you'll see!). I'll just set my mind into my problems and try to work my damn ass out of this locked up place and get on campus.

I'll show you, my parents and everyone else that I can reach the point I've missed in the past (you know?). I swear, I'll make it to the top and face all of my problems. I mean I'm going to make it. Yes, I am!

I'm serious. I know I can talk to my parents and get a better understanding, both from my Mother and my Father. I do think they love me a hell of a lot and I do feel the same towards the both of them. And I'm going to keep that understanding between us.

I'm so damn serious about it going to be that way with my parents, and it should have been that way in the first place. Huh? Say al right! (all right!)

Carlita

8 December: Social Worker Notes

I met with Carlita and her parents today and confirmed with all sides that as of now, we are very much looking towards her future return to the family home. I encouraged Carlita to start talking with her parents about what will be expected of her when she returns home. They might also spend time talking about how Carlita handles her feelings and attitude when she isn't doing well. Like on the day she got a C-grade on a Health test because she didn't study much.

Things seem to be moving along quite well for Carlita. I think that unless something drastic comes up in the next few weeks, we should be looking towards a move onto campus after the New Year.

17 December: Social Worker Notes

I encouraged Carlita to watch out about getting sucked in to other people's hassles. We then talked about how she feels that she has been getting double messages from staff —

some say she has been making progress while others indicate she's made no progress. I said that I thought she had made gains, particularly in thawing out, looking at what has been going on at home, and being able to look again at some of the dumb shit she did.

Once again, we have all to be clear about our expectations for Carlita. It may help if everyone re-reads Carlita's initial care plan. It's important to draw this kid out. That means listening more and not throwing messages back at her that she isn't doing anything. When under pressure, staff might say anything. And it's also when its easy to say things without knowing why or knowing what the reasons are.

This came out because Carlita feels she is being given two messages by staff. The message I am giving is: (1) we have made gains (2) we have a way to go but need to spell out specifics so she knows what we're asking her to do; and (3) it's our job to sift through and sort out what is and isn't true about Carlita. That mean now what's in her personal file in the office and what her care plan has involved from the start!

21 December

Dear Mrs M

Hi. Well, for the past 2-3 weeks all the staff have been jumping on my case because I'm falling down and losing what I've accomplished since being here in this place. There is no way to change it except "me".

I really can't do anything anymore. I find myself sitting here in my room, thinking to myself that I'll never be able to face my problems. It seems like when I try to be serious, everyone is just taking a glance at me then turning around and walking away, laughing at me. So I stand like a fool.

I'll change all this game playing around. Think for myself and know that there is a "me" just waiting, waiting, waiting. But now I'm hurting that "me" so much.

I'll find a way out of all these troubles that have made me "so down and out". So I promise you, I'll do the best I can so be by my side to try and help me please.

Give me one more chance so I can make it up to you! Think about it. I'll do the same, ok? Sorry about what I said at the table!

Carlita

4 January

Dear [Social Worker]

Please read this when you have a minute or so. Thank you!

Well, well, well what you been doing? It's about time to sit down and drop a line or so to "you". "I" might as well tell you what I've been thinking about since my last Board.

1. First of all, "My Parents" understand "me" more and more each time they come to visit "me". And I (myself) understand them more and more. So I wish I will keep stepping in the right directions (you know?) I'm sure you do!

2. I've been doing a lot of thinking about my goals for home like you told me to do. There's some good advice!

3. About my boyfriend in that other institution. I've known him for a year and three months today and I think he and I are just going to be friends (you know?). Because I know how he feels towards "me" and vice-versa! So we are just friends but how can I convince my Parents? Or I could leave him at this moment until I get out of here?

4. And me getting out of this locked up place. I think I'm just about ready to move on campus. I think I have come a long, long, long way from the "me" I used to be. And I'm sure you do agree with me!

I know I had a lot of ups and downs with myself. But when I'm in my room (honest) I do a lot of hard, hard thinking about just everything!!!!!!!!
I think I could handle it on campus (honest I really think I can!). You probably have in mind that I'll run when I get out on campus. But why should I? There's really no reason to. Because if I do, I'd lose everything I've worked for.

So I think that there's really no reason to run from here. I really am serious!!! I wish I could have started thinking like this before I did it! You know? I'm sure you do! I'm ready when you're ready to talk. See you as soon as possible.

Carlita

15 January

Dear [Social Worker]

I feel so down and out about what I'm facing at the present time. No freedom nowhere, somewhere, anywhere. With all the disappointments, despair, anxiety, frustrations, defeats, loneliness, I don't know if I have the strength to continue the ever evolving and adjusting struggle.

I can't "give up".

Sometimes I feel a face of everlasting happiness and there is really only sadness.

My face shows "no fear" but look closer to see the tears.

A face with eyes that I wonder what they really see.

A face showing hope for tomorrow knowing there will be nothing but sorrow.

A face giving the impression of gladness when it feels more like madness.

A face that looks so sweet but also a face of strength, power, fortune, fame, courage and integrity.

Carlita

Well, well, well here's what you want, so get ready, here I come. My "What ifs?"

1. *What if I get involved in drugs once again?*
2. *What if I'm down town at a time I shouldn't be?*
3. *What if I'm not in school when I should be?*
4. *What if I get picked up when I wasn't doing anything?*
5. *What if I have a fight with my family?*
6. *What if I get the impression I need to run away?*
7. *What if I feel so down and out?*
8. *What if I hang around the wrong people?*
9. *What if I take a ride while walking down the street?*
10. *What if I get raped?*
11. *What if I go out and don't come back for 2-3 days?*
12. *What if I get set up for drugs?*
13. *What if I get picked up for being drunk in public?*
14. *What if I hang around the Central District of the city?*
15. *What if I shoplift?*
16. *What if I lie?*
17. *What if I'm so depressed?*
18. *What if I spend most of my time calling this dude and that dude?*
19. *What if I walked around when I should be at home?*
20. *What if I go to Court?*
21. *What if everything is going so well and I fall down to the ground?*
22. *What if I write to the wrong people?*
23. *What if I run into J and his so-called friends?*
24. *And last but not least, what if I go to prison?*

This is what I want to do for my future:

1. *Most important is to finish school.*
2. *Get a job so I'll be able to go on to college.*
3. *Be with my family.*
4. *Meet understanding people.*
5. *Meet people who would like to share what's happing in this world.*

6.   *Be able to look forward to a happy life.*
7.   *Be able to see things as they really are.*
8.   *Be able to travel around.*
9.   *Be able to watch changes in my family and also in me.*
10. *Give a helping hand.*
11. *Become a secretary in some income tax business.*
12. *Enjoy outdoor sports.*
13. *Look forward to things of my own enjoyment!*

Carlita

---

19 March: Institution Review Board

When Carlita arrived almost 9 months ago, she was highly moody as well as being extremely dependent. There have been improvements in both areas. She continues to play the role of poor, dumb me to elicit an overprotective response from staff and teachers alike. Mood swings are quite apparent, fluctuating from being very mature and pleasant on the one hand, and immature and hostile on the other. Carlita is a fairly bright and engaging young woman who has an ability to charm the birds out of the trees. While this is an asset, it has also been known to cause her considerable difficulty. She knows that she has the ability to succeed with her family's backing. Recommendation was to move Carlita to an open campus program.

Addendum

Carlita continued to do well on campus, with improving performance in the campus school and life in the open living unit going smoothly. She didn't run away as she once feared. Furloughs back to her family home were initiated and parole with a condition of residence in the family home was eventually approved. Nothing further is known about Carlita or what happened to her.

Aliese's Reflections

So typical of the police to assume Carlita was a prostitute, just because she has some money on her. They would never believe she had a job. Those were the times. I was surprised to read that Carlita had turned to the cops for help as she should have known better and that she would get no help from them. But after experiencing a night of gang rape, I am sure she was desperate. Oh how my heart cries. Typical of the System to just lock her up instead of sending her to a nice foster home.

She had a good home to go to and that was a very rare situation. From reading her letters I can sense how willing she was to make an effort and how she wanted to get back home. Those are sides of her I never knew, sides she never really showed me. It was much cooler to be tough and anti-establishment on all levels.

I remember feeling so crushed when we let ourselves or the staff down, or the staff thought we had let them down. Everyone had different expectations and what everything meant to them and how they applied their views and opinions on us. Carlita did not have years and years of abuse like so many of us did and while she learned a lot there, she probably never needed to be confined like that. You can sense the softness in her and the vulnerability, or at least I can.

The pain that we felt was tremendous when we were at our lowest of lows. Many of us who had been physically beaten and raped so many times lost track and lost count, lost our families, lost our friends and loved ones and we had become just lost souls. We had been abandoned, betrayed and lied to by just about everyone we had ever known and now we were being forced to deal with our issues. Oh my God, where would you begin?

Sometimes the loneliness and desperation just overcame us. Remember, we were children! Sometimes the pain was just unbearable and you wanted to die right on the spot. The feeling of hopelessness was always just around the corner. I can feel Carlita's feelings in reading her letter of despair. When you are locked up in a concrete room, with concrete walls, a metal door and bed, and bars on your window, and then you are confined in your cell to think about things and to find any meaning in life, any essence of hope and how you can change all that is wrong with you. Good grief ... it is a wonder we survived any of this at all. Here you are feeling low down, like crap and all used up, so let's put you in this happy setting so you can remember all you should be thankful for, remembering what your game plan is ... it was ALL on us! ALL the time! Just read the kid's list of what if's ... so much fear, fear of failure, fear of being locked up forever, fear of not doing the right thing, fear, fear, fear!!!

I have a good feeling that Carlita made it okay on the outs. She had a good family, maybe they weren't perfect and had some struggles – but they loved her and she wasn't abused. That in itself is a miracle. The Native American has a different culture too. We always try to salvage the family unit, even if it means a temporary separation. The "System" had no sense of family and no way to conceive what Family was.

Rhythms of Daily Living

The quality of relational care – regardless of age – is directly linked to the daily management and oversight of basic bodily comforts and personal safety needs. Because of risks associated with physical safety and security, some children and young people are required to live temporarily in out-of-home care while life plans are being reshaped and implemented. No matter how many developmental milestones are evaluated, remember: all clients are different, each in their own special ways. Relational care is engaged through personal rhythms and opportunity events with young people. Engagement in caring relationships promotes personal development and social maturation with children and young people through relational rhythms that are, in many ways, auto-therapeutic. These relational rhythms between a young person and their caregivers are fundamental to that young person achieving developmental outcomes that matter while in out-of-home care.

To examine this further, we consider five important rhythms that frame responsive social work and youth work practices with young people in out-of-home care. Understanding (and heeding) the importance of these rhythms is fundamental to successful interventions. The first *Rhythm of Daily Living* involves *family and extended family members*. These rhythms connect with kinship networks that exist for each child or young person received into care

(Ainsworth, 1997; Burford & Casson, 1989; Pennell & Burford, 1995). Family rhythms are closely associated with circumstances that resulted in each child or young person requiring child welfare services or being admitted to a foster home, a residential school or assessment centre. Family rhythms contribute to the socialisation and behavioural training each young person has received before coming to the attention of child and youth care professionals. For all these reasons, it is essential that planned care and treatment give priority to the active participation of family and extended family members. It is difficult to ignore research evidence showing how, despite what child welfare professionals may wish or think, after leaving care children and young people resume contact and retain some involvement with family and extended family members (Fanshel *et al* 1990).

The next rhythm requires us to identify each child's *education, recreation and learning rhythms.* These include both formal and informal rhythms associated with a child's capacity for learning, their formal educational activities and achievements, and recreational pursuits that contribute to large muscle and cardio-vascular development, eye-hand coordination and time-structuring through leisure activities (Small & Fulcher, 1985). The educational, recreational and learning rhythms will have been severely disrupted for many children and young people placed in foster homes or residential care, such that these rhythms are under-developed, as noted in Kendrick's (1999) study of Scottish children, a finding reinforced through subsequent research (2012). Paradoxically, these are the very *rhythms that connect* children and young people to a peer group, giving opportunities for behavioural, social and cultural learning so important to long-term future development and achievement (Maier 1975; 1987). These educational, recreational and learning rhythms are influenced through the purposeful use of activities at home as well as in day or residential schools and centres (VanderVen 1985).

Rhythms associated with group living also need to be identified, whether at home, in a foster home, attending a summer camp or living in a residential school, a group homes or other institution (Beker & Eisikovitz 1991). When examining the daily and weekly activities of children and young people, one finds that each day follows particular rhythms associated with food, sleep, work and play times – all requiring sensitive daily management (Fulcher 1996). Rhythms of group living are concerned with weekday routines and activities, as well as events that occur on weeknights and weekends. Weekly and monthly rhythms can be discerned, depending on whether a service provides short-term respite care, crisis care, or services offering longer-term supportive care involving education or residential supervision. Monthly and seasonal rhythms are also commonly associated with school, work and holiday periods. Residential schools and care centres sponsored by religious organisations frequently employ weekly, monthly and seasonal rituals in the delivery of child and youth care, or, as in Malaysia and other parts of the Islamic world, the offering of prayers five times a day. Annual reports demonstrate how yearly rhythms of care are important, most graphically seen when a child is re-classified an adult at the age of 18. At such times, support services upon which young people and families rely are often withdrawn, or as with a youth with developmental disabilities moving from welfare services to health and disability services.

Rhythms of daily living need also to engage with a fourth set of rhythms associated with *community and peer group activities*. Responsive practice requires that each child or young person is provided with opportunities to engage in social experiences that help connect them to normative peer group activities (Fahlberg 1990; 1991; Halverson 1995). Children and young people in care, wherever they live, have frequently had their community and peer group rhythms disrupted as placement decisions are made without careful consideration of the unintended consequences in decision-making. As young people are moved from one setting to another, or change schools, it follows that they are also moved from their friends and important relationships severed. Young people in care quite often become involved with other young people in care or engage in peer group activities that have a deleterious effect on health and wellbeing, whether through alcohol and drug abuse, sexual abuse and neglect, or physical abuse. Unless new relationships are formed through the management of purposeful activities with alternative peers, then children and young people in care have little choice but to return to old friends and activities. These old relationships and patterns of behaviour have all too often resulted in the untimely deaths of young people in care, or her-stories of struggle for survival in abusive relationships. Responsive practices need fundamentally to build from recognition of how these rhythms impact on children and young people, and how pro-active engagement in community and peer group rhythms can benefit children, young people and their families (Maier 1981).

Finally, one must not ignore *cultural and spiritual rhythms of caring* that operate in the delivery of responsive child and youth services. Elsewhere (Fulcher 1998; Tait-Rolleston *et al* 1997; Cairns *et al* 1996) it was shown how cultural rituals of exchange are commonly overlooked in the delivery of social work or child and youth services (Stewart 1997; Wilcox *et al* 1991; Simon & Smith, 2001). Images, sounds and smells of childhood spring to mind that reflect cultural and spiritual rhythms of caring. These operate in any family or foster home, as well as in residential schools or group homes. One quickly works out why minimal cross-cultural competencies are required if social workers or child and youth care workers are to avoid significant gaffs that leave some children and carers feeling culturally unsafe (Rangihau 1986; 1987; Shook 1985; Leigh 1998). Rudolph Steiner centres have taught the world a great deal about spiritual rhythms of caring and learning, seeking ways in which these rhythms can be carefully balanced for each child, or for living and learning groups of young people.

Questions for Small Group Discussion or Guided Reflection

1. What are the five basic rhythms of daily living that require attention in work with children and young people like Carlita in out-of-home care, and what other rhythms might be considered?
2. How do the five basic rhythms of daily living help you to examine Carlita's historic trauma and potential restoration from the trauma of gang rape and being labeled a prostitute by the police?
3. What cultural or spiritual rhythms of daily living might have been influential in Carlita's life and needed to be given more attention in her personal care plan?
4. What education, recreation and learning rhythms were identified as important in Carlita's narratives?

5. What restorative rhythms of family and extended family living are important when thinking of Carlita's future, when she eventually leaves the secure unit?

Room 7
Teri – *Meaning-Making*

6 December: Social Worker Admission Interview Notes

A personal interview was initiated within 24 hours of Teri's arrival in the secure unit. A tone of uncertainty prevailed throughout the interview but Teri increasingly involved herself as the interview process continued. Near the conclusion of the interview, there was a lull in the conversation followed by Teri's exclamation:

"I don't know why I've been honest with you. I'm not usually, but I guess I've just got nothing more to lose."

18 December: Summary of the Initial Planning Board Meeting

Teri is a 16 and a half year-old young parole violator. She was committed after several unsuccessful placements in foster homes and with relatives, a history of school problems, runaways and drug use. After 6 months in an institution for younger teenagers, Teri was paroled to her mother who lives out of State, a placement considered very risky at the time. When Teri arrived, her mother was in a psychiatric hospital. Nonetheless, Teri remained in that placement until earlier this year when she returned to live with her aunt and uncle.

Teri has admitted to having been extensively involved in the use of drugs during her time away. She also admitted to having been promiscuous, having been involved in numerous runaways, and to having had serious problems adjusting to school.

Teri has a history of long-standing communication problems in her family. She may have more difficulties communicating with female staff, both in a counselling role and also in setting limits on any inappropriate behaviour. Teri admits that she carries a lot of anger and can further describe frightening dreams which occur quite frequently. Our primary objectives would appear to be (1) helping Teri to begin the emancipation process away from her mother through encouraging Teri to talk about past events that have fuelled long-standing feelings of anger in that relationship; (2) help Teri find more successful ways of handling her anger in relationships with both adults and peers; and (3) support and encourage her in all areas where Teri demonstrates responsible behavior.

Teri last attended school as a 9th Grader. According to her age, she should be in the 11th Grade, so is roughly two years behind in school. Writing skills and improving her vocabulary and spelling were seen as important areas of focus. Her Assessment Center teacher felt that, although Teri has the potential to work in a regular school setting, she cannot accept the effort it would take to complete her high school education as a realistic or worthwhile goal. Here, she is quiet in class, making no waves or ripples whatsoever. Asks questions when she needs to. Seems to be concerned about her school work.

24 March: Care Worker Notes

We had quite a long, involved and occasionally hectic session today. Teri has many unanswered questions she is hashing over in her mind. The major area of uncertainty and of utmost interest to her at the present time is where she will go when she leaves here. She has many feelings (some quite acute) concerning each possible option available to Teri. She tried very hard to convince me today that going to her mother was the best possible choice available. She bases this conclusion almost solely on the recent letter she received from mother which was both lucid and uncharacteristically understanding and compassionate. Teri bristled when I noted how here was one fairly good letter, but did that necessarily offset all the others which had been drifty, vague and self-serving?

After she calmed down, Teri admitted that perhaps she had been a little bit premature in her judgment. I asked what had happened to all the good feelings she displayed around the possibility of going to live with her father. Teri confessed that she had not really felt all that optimistic about it but at the time it seemed a much better choice that her Aunt and Uncle. In the interim, many of the fears she has towards her father came surging back to the fore, and she isn't sure she could cope with that situation.

Teri stated rather strongly that some staff had accused her of "going around in a circle". She said "If they only knew the truth about it, I have gone around that circle more than once!" Teri was a bit astonished when I told her that it's probably that she may travel that entire circular route several more times before she could make a final decision.

Teri expresses much apprehension over father's frequent acts of violence. As far as she knows, this can occur whether he has been drinking or not.

She told of him ripping the phone off the wall one time when he was bugged because the kids were getting too many phone calls. On several occasions he has made some wild and violent threats to and against other people, including both her mother and stepmother. Some of these threats were carried out against both women in the form of physical beatings. I asked Teri if she had ever discussed her feelings with her father. She replied that she never had, and furthermore didn't intend to, since it might jeopardize the relationship she presently had with her father. "I love him and he's a neat guy. I don't want him to get mad at me!"

Teri was very thoughtful after I told her I was very concerned about one area in particular. She showed little tendency to put staff on but that she was occasionally guilty of bull-shitting herself and this was a real danger. It was of much greater importance to be honest at all times with herself, since she would only be associated with us for a relatively short period. She has to live with herself for her entire lifetime.

I'm not sure how much of this will be retained but Teri welcomed the opportunity to vent some feelings and test out some of her ideas.

29 March: Social Worker Notes

The frequency of Teri's flashbacks and headaches are said to be increasing. This may be associated with her fears about becoming like her mother and need psychiatric care. Teri's fear of what's happening makes the whole thing worse. I've urged her to try and accept these as something that does happen to her instead of trying desperately to find out why, or what's wrong. Be very supportive and ready to move in as needed. I will contact the doctor to see if we can get a consultant in for a specialist opinion. Until then, play it low-keyed, give support and encourage acceptance as a part of her life just now. It can be overcome!

30 March

Mr [Social Worker]

High

I guess I have some stuff to ask you so will write down a few so the time I talk to you, I won't forget! Okay?

Subjects

1. *My terrible weekend*
2. *What you meant by a doctor*
3. *Some thing that will come up.*
4. *About my visitor!*
5. *About ....*
6. *Where my head is at!*
7. *Some important questions.*
8. *Something I didn't mean to say.*

Well, that's about it, except I want to explain my flashing to someone you selected.

Hang on to this!

Talk to ya soon, okay?

Teri

19 April: Social Worker Notes

Teri is talking about wanting to start school on open campus. She feels ready and wants to start working herself towards an open campus cottage, asking where? I just don't know. I told her I needed more time to think about it before Board and we'd talk about it again on Tuesday. My first reaction was that it's too early but given that Teri has not been in a public school since 6th Grade, it might be a good move. What do others think?

24 April: Summary of the Planning Board Meeting

After a stormy period which almost overwhelmed Teri with the "what ifs?" in her life, Teri now seems to be back on the upswing. Intervention of care workers in conference with Teri and her aunt and uncle has opened up communication significantly. The success of being able to converse seriously with her aunt and uncle compensates for the complete lack of contact with father. Mood swings are almost daily tied to contact with family. Teri is to be enrolled half day in the campus school. She asked the Board for this step and feels the time is right. Further conferencing with aunt and uncle will be organized as their relationships with Teri strengthen.

1 May: Letter from Mother

Dear Mr [Social Worker]

Thank you for your letter. Needless to say we are very proud of Teri and realize a lot of the hurdles she has had to overcome. We thank you very much for everything you have done to help her. My brother and wife are *here now with their daughter. They speak very highly of you and of your school. Needless to say, I was cautious after all the earlier experiences.*

I knew Teri needed help and in my own way, I tried but was not in any condition to help myself. I blame myself a lot. On the other hand, my husband feels that he's to blame because if he really laid down the law, Teri would listen. But he's a cross-country truck driver and that creates problems. Also he felt sorry for Teri and the hardships she had encountered. He loves her as much as a real dad could. So we both feel we failed her.

I pray Teri can understand there's not a person who hasn't done something wrong in their life. Who are we to say she did the worst wrong to us? It's like the pot calling the kettle black. No, Teri is not and never will be the black sheep. Never! She's our darling daughter who we love dearly.

Mother

22 May: Care Worker Notes

Teri is loaded with some heavy feelings about the probability of a move to campus in the near future. I gotta admit that I was not ready for that piece of news either, and had to quickly resolve some of my own feelings about it. I finally levelled with her and told her that I could not honestly agree with the decision to move her just yet. I could see advantages gained by open campus and also disadvantages. Where these balanced out was my own personal uncertainty.

I was at a loss for words when Teri asked "you have really been in an uncomfortable position all the time we've been talking haven't you?" When I recovered, I told her that she was right — it's never easy when you are torn between loyalty to your fellow team members and your own personal feelings. That seemed to set the stage for some really down to earth straight and honest talk.

This girl has got feelings that I never even suspected existed. Some are fairly simple and others highly complicated – too complex perhaps for my unenlightened brain to unravel. Name an area, Teri has some feelings – sometimes very deep feelings – about it. I thought I knew Teri fairly well but I must admit to seeing depths here I've never seen before.

Teri is scared shitless about leaving the security here for one thing. Not the place so much as the people here. Her immediate reaction to the news that she might be leaving soon was that we were rejecting her, with out and out abandonment! Teri doesn't fear the move to campus nearly as much as she fears leaving here.

Teri was able to vent some feelings and discuss some matters of real importance to her. We agreed to talk again, perhaps on Sunday, after we've both had an opportunity to work some things out in our own minds.

26 May

Mr [Social Worker]

First off allow me to introduce myself. I'm Teri, age 17. I am writing about the changes I have made and about the cottage that I want to go to.

OK, the changes? I have slowed down tremendously. I have become close to some staff. If you think back I said I could never get close to staff because they were all the same. Well they aren't! For sure!

I can now talk about my past without getting all out of shape. I just have a little problem with starting a talk. I've gained some confidence which is better than none, true?

When I have a problem that I can't handle, I go seek further help or advice. If the help or advice isn't around, I think the problem through and then try to handle it the best I can. Which may not be the best but if it isn't okay the first time. But if it isn't okay the first time, I have learned it isn't too late to go ask for help again.

I feel I am ready to leave this secure unit place and believe I need a place that is run on an individual basis. I don't think I need strong supervision or a lock-up cottage. I feel I now need some place I can go to on leaves and work out my family problems.

Letters and talks won't solve my problems. Going out on leave and getting a feel of what is happening so we can work from there. That is what I need now.

I don't think school should be held against me like in case I wanted to leave school. I am going to quit anyway, so why hold it against me now? I have not one problem with the kids at school. I can joke around or be serious and people like me for what I am. Yes, for what I am, not because of what I was or will be. I can now talk to my teachers about problems of any kind. Yep, school has really helped me, not learning wise but in relating to all age groups.

Okay, the place I want, or that I feel they can offer me the most is Exit Cottage. It is going to run on an individual thing, and that's the number one reason I would want it. My reason might not be the best because I don't know nothing but what I have heard.

Another reason is because I could carry on from where I am leaving off here, go work on living at my aunt's. The reason I didn't want it before was because everyone else did. Now, at last I feel that if I don't say what I truly think, you guys will never know. Also, I wouldn't have to go through the hassles to get a leave. I could start off right away working on getting things sorted out with my aunt and uncle.

I hope you can understand what I am saying. I'm not just saying No, No, No. True, when you people first told me about going out on campus, it hurt me, scared me and tore me apart. I thought you guys let me down and also myself, for not talking about what I really want, out of fear that I would get let down. I feel I handled it real well, at least I didn't do too much bad, just talked and cried. Thankfully, I now have some sense in me to report on what I have thought about and I as a person think is best for me.

Mr [Social Worker]. You know that thing about me always hating you? You are a righteous person but sometimes you come on too strong. Did you know you have a heart?

Until two nickels don't make a dime, shit you must be the best social worker I have ever had. But don't forget, I will still hate you at times, okay?

Teri

21 June: Youth Parole Contract (Pre-Release)

Certain conditions of my release have been discussed with me and I am aware of the specific regulations restricting some of my activities during this period. In accordance with this Agreement, I will:

1.   *Obey all federal and state laws and all county or city ordinances defining crime.*
2.   *Obtain prior approval before changing my residence.*
3.   *Obtain prior approval before leaving the State.*

Move to Exit Cottage to complete the following:

1.   *Assume personal responsibility for all my actions, respecting the rights, privileges and property of others.*
2.   *Complete Summer School.*
3.   *Maintain regular contact with my Aunt and Uncle as much as can be arranged.*
4.   *Get used to working in part-time job every Saturday where my Aunt and Uncle live.*
5.   *Get help learning how to manage my money at the bank, and find out about budgeting.*

Teri

12 July: Institutional Incident Report – 8 pm

Teri did not return to the cottage at the appointed time. It was reported that Teri was last seen leaving the local bowling alley riding on the back of a motorcycle with an unidentified male driver.

Police alerted and Teri was formally placed on AWOL status.

Addendum

The authors know nothing further about what happened with Teri but she is remembered with fondness. We think she returned to live with her aunt and uncle but this didn't last long. She was discharged out of the State System at age 18.

Aliese's Reflections

As I start to read the evaluations of Teri, the memories flood my mind. I find the constant common threads. We simply never fitted into society, we never were accepted and one false move by us while being detained or trying out a new foster home – we would be kicked to the curb again. With all the training and all the talking through things in our own personal life, and trying to learn to cope with society....no one was taking the time to train the parents. By the time we had reached this high security abode, so much damage had already been done to us and we were just knee-jerk reacting to the world that surrounded us, the dysfunction that had raised us and then abandoned us to our own wiles.

Teri and I were close. She was small in stature but had great heart and she and I became sisters instantly. Her spirit was connected to me in a way unexplained – as I don't know whether she was Indian or not ... but that is a spiritual level on which we connected happily. She understood about travelling in circles ... as one can never reach the next level, the next steps in a better direction, until we have learned the coping skills and to have some sort of clarity about the situation, hence, walking in circles. The anger, the "bullshitting" staff and herself – that was part of that whole walking around in circles. Not really knowing how to cope. I think I still do this today, even with all the coping skills, experience, healing and forgiveness. It is in part, the natural way in life and we all do that – on some level in our decision making process. Learning to live with one's self.

I do wonder how many of us can really say what we have accomplished. I am in my mid-fifties and have 'almost' conquered being content. With that being said, on the downward cycles, I have to remind myself about contentment throughout the day. Being content and just breathing. Perhaps that is as far as I will ever get, and unfortunately it is further than many of my sisters will ever be able to travel; at least in this world as we know it. Accepting one's self. Teri was a very insightful young lady, and the flashbacks, the headaches were obviously her inner struggle with her spirit – accepting and finding contentment instead of focusing on the fears and pain. That is a huge accomplishment for any young person, let alone someone whose background was so wretched.

I see Teri's bravery in wanting to attend open campus – ready to leave her safety zone, regain more control of her future and recognizing the disadvantages facing someone like her, behind in her education. Marvellous! Overcoming the ups and downs of her family is a huge hurdle, as her mother mentions in a letter. She had either the love of her parents OR love from her parents, but as adults and people; they had their own set of problems. Who knows, the mom may have been bi-polar, and that goes back to what I said earlier. It was not, and is not, just the children who needed guidance, help, and counselling, but also their parents.

I love it when I read what she told the social worker – again, such insight – regarding him being in an uncomfortable position. It is ALWAYS the toughest job on the team, being the social worker. You are tied to the emotional set of problems, and also, all the physical needs and working all of that, through this system of rigid rules and performance evaluations. What a task. I'm proud of the groundwork here, the foundation of trust being formed and built upon.

It is what I said at the beginning of my reflections. She made such great strides! As I read through her notes, I can see why Teri and I were close. She traversed through her mind, making her own evaluations and coming to terms, trying desperately to regain control of her life. That takes so much inner strength. I like where she tells the social worker straight up, that sometimes she still hates him. It made me laugh. I mean, she's a kid after all and being able to shoot straight from the hip, means she totally trusted him and loved him.

Somewhere through this process – Teri just got lost again. It is sad not to know her whereabouts or whatever became of her. I would like to believe that she, like me, made it through to the other side of life. Teri learned a lot and felt confident about taking this new-found knowledge and inner strength and apply it to the life that she knew best. I see her on the back of a Harley, riding off to freedom – I hope.

Meaning-Making

Meaning Making refers to the processes we go through in making sense of our experiences. An action occurs, we interpret it according to our own way of making sense of things, and then we act according to that perception. Meaning-making is closely embedded in cultural learning that begins from infancy. Thus different young people may respond very differently to a simple gesture because of what that gesture means to them. A handshake offers one good example of how meaning-making is grounded in cultural learning. In places like North America and Northern Europe, children learn to greet people with the shake of a hand, a reciprocal gesture normally involving right hands. However amongst the more than 1 billion peoples of Islam around the world, shaking hands is an exchange carried out only amongst participants of the same sex, adhering to cultural prescriptions about touching someone of the opposite sex.

It is not 'what we mean to say' with gestures or words but how what we say (or do) through gestures or words is interpreted by a young person or her/his family members with whom we engage. Did any particular thoughts cross our mind upon learning that Teri was last seen by anyone in the juvenile justice system riding off into the sunset on the back of a motorcycle with an unidentified male? If rehabilitation care or treatment involves parallel meaning-making processes, then Teri clearly learned from the secure unit culture and adult-youth relationships to ensure that having gone AWOL (absent without leave) she was never involved with police or the court system again. It might be said that Teri took meaning-making to a new level by "*doing it her way!*"

Social workers and youth workers play specific roles with each young person we are asked to 'look after', or they are assigned to us and become our responsibility – whatever meaning we give to the court order. Some workers deliver direct services day to day with a young person, be that in foster care or a group home. Others provide indirect support and supervision for front-line carers. Some carry responsibilities for agency protocols and procedures that support helping and healing whilst others enact helping and healing processes with particular young people and family members. With meaning-making, it is not so important 'what we do' but that *we do it together with a common focus and a shared care plan – with goals identified through the participation of each child or young person and a key family member.*

Shared parenting or multi-disciplinary teamwork includes participation with the young person and sometimes key family members so that all agree on what we are doing and our overall approach. The goal of a team parenting approach is how best to 'be with' this child or young person in a meaningful way whilst she or he is under our supervision in out-of-home care. This does not mean that all of our interactions with this young person will be the same, or even need to be. Relational care doesn't work that way. It means that all of our relationships with this young person are working from 'the same page' of our plan and overall approach. That way, each person focuses on building working relationships with this child or young person and family members – relationships that have meaning for them. From Day 1 we are seeking to build shared meaning about what we are doing and where we are going with this particular young person throughout their involvement in our out-of-home care. We recognise that meaning-making processes are embedded in cultural and social interactions. Social worker and carer(s) are continually making meaning of what is going on with this young person and together, building up a shared understanding about our "team parenting" and what is happening across all the parties in this relational care team. Consistency in our overall approach, while the unique personalities of relational care blossom, means that team parenting or caring activities nurture and support personal growth and the development of resilience with this young person in our out-of-home care.

Relational Care begins with meaning-making around *Bodily Comforts* which – at a very sensory level – is where out-of-home care of any sort begins. Bodily comforts range across many somatic complaints – headaches, menstrual or tummy aches, hunger, thirst, warmth and indigestion. Attending behaviours and the focusing of motor neurons behind the eyes are shaped through Bodily Comforts and meaning-making associated with making connections with others. Fear and early trauma shape the *Rhythms of Interaction* which follow, and the forming of and meaning given to caring relationships. Maier (1987) reminded how "before any word is spoken, a whole stage of cognitive development has been traversed" thus showing how the brain interprets and gives meaning to events in the hours and days following admission to out-of-home care. Communication through actions that promote bodily comforts speak louder than words!

Relational Care is ever mindful of how *different children ARE DIFFERENT*, even within family groups. Meaning must be given to differences such as these when planning relational care for any child or young person. Such differences are often demonstrated through the quality of *rhythms and interactions* that can be observed between a child or young person and their carers and others – whether family or extended family members, foster carers, residential workers, teachers or peers. Meaning-making about the overall direction of relational care is monitored through a young person's achievements week to week, seeking ongoing feedback about questions like *"where is all this going"*? Meaning-making such as this builds from a young person's capacities to experience *predictability* or knowing in their world. At what point does a child or young person KNOW she or he can make personal achievements and celebrate these achievements in daily living with others? Team parenting focuses attention on how this child views the world around them and what meaning she or he gives to being in their place in that world. Predictability is also concerned with time orientation and meaning-making about time. Some children, even young people spend a lot of time operating in the NOW! Significant cognitive development takes place as a child or young person moves from managing NOW-NOT NOW distinctions, before starting to make Tonight-Tomorrow distinctions, or more complicated temporal distinctions between weekdays and the weekend. Meaning-making around time-structuring is learned through daily living in a particular social and cultural context, this week, this month, this season, this semester, and this year.

Dependability or emotional trust gains meaning as relational care progresses. Emotional intelligence follows its own developmental trajectory and is shaped by early life experiences, trauma, crisis events and significant times of transition. Unless relational care monitors this emotional dimension, it ignores the ways in which emotions shape each different child or young person's thoughts and behaviour, and the meaning she or he gives to emotional exchanges with others. *Life skills* are best learned in relational care when a child or young person's bodily comforts and personal differences are recognised, and when that child or young person is connected *in rhythm with* another or others who affirm and nurture her or his knowing that they are engaged and feeling purposefully engaged with another or others. *Specialised behaviour training* is best learned through relationships that matter. *Care for the caregiver(s)* is essential to relational care provided for any child or young person in out-of-home care. Supervision helps carers and social workers to make meaning of their out-of-home care experiences, helping to ensure that worker issues do not distract from team parenting efforts.

Questions for Small Group Discussion or Guided Reflection

1. What factors need to be taken into account when engaging in meaning-making reflections about our work with a child or young person in out-of-home care?
2. What meaning-making process might Teri have started making about being a kid in secure care without educational qualifications?
3. How does culture influence meaning-making for young people, their carers and social workers, such as might be encountered with a young asylum seeker escaping warfare, a youth whose parents were killed in his presence?
4. What elements of relational care are involved in a young person coming to know – or give meaning to knowing and trusting – their carer or social worker?
5. How might youth participation – as well as family participation – in decision-making about their care give special meaning to the relational out-of-home care offered and the kind of relationship(s) that blossom?

Room 8
Leanne – *Noticing Out There and In Here*

4 June: Social Worker Notes

I just met with what seemed a very flaky kid today on her arrival at the secure unit. Several times she faded in and out, and admitted it's a problem for her. She is generally a very depressed kid, mostly about family. I told her we would begin by giving her time to tell about her past so that we could – together – start looking at where we go from here. Going home with mother looks like a possibility.

12 June: Summary of the Initial Planning Board Meeting

Leanne is a 16 year old girl who was returned to the Assessment Center as a parole violator. She was first committed at the age of 14 for truancy, incorrigibility, running away and drug use. She was sent to an institution for younger teenagers where her mother and stepfather were involved in family conferences for six months. In the end, Leanne chose not to return home and paroled to a group home. At the group home Leanne had numerous problems, including running away, school misbehavior and drug use. After four weeks, Leanne was returned to the Assessment Center and after re-evaluation was returned to the group home with recommendations about clear boundaries and limit setting coupled with regular counseling sessions focused on her anger and depression.

Leanne continued her drug use and extreme incorrigibility in the group home and at school resulting in parole revocation. The only public school records available indicated that at the school Leanne attended while at the group home, the principal described her "as the most disruptive child we have ever had here". She is capable enough but not motivated.

6 August: Social Worker Notes

I explained to Leanne why I was restricting her mother's visits to every other week. Leanne tried her best to point out why I was wrong with this decision. I explained that I thought most of her problems related to how she interacted with her peer group. I assured Leanne that I was not meaning that she was messing up. The truth is, I don't know exactly how she interacts in the group. We will start looking more closely and she should do the same.

She reminded me that I had told her this might happen when I first talked to her on the day she arrived. I explained that too many people have let her call the shots and that, while I understand what her reasons were, I disagreed with those reasons. I would stick to the decision and she could either look at what I was saying or she could fight me. Either way, I would stick to the decision! She said "I won't pout" but she was none too pleased.

11 September: Summary of the Planning Board Meeting

Leanne has improved considerably in her school performance. She still sets other girls up in her relationships in the cottage and comes on as though she is a very innocent party. Her stubbornness is still the greatest problem she has to face with peers, always getting the last word in. Leanne is a very perceptive girl who gets others to do her bidding. At school, typing is a strong point but she has shown improvement in all areas. She is gaining confidence in herself that she is doing what is expected of her – although at times she still needs reassurance. In the areas of temper control and peaceful conflict resolution, Leanne's gains are minimal. She does an excellent detail and her room care is usually well done. Leanne excels in recreation activities – skating, swimming and any other active sports. She displays poor sportsmanship if not winning or not being first to play. This also applies to card games and other table games. She is very competitive and generally a poor loser. Personal grooming ranges from poor to fair. She bathes often but usually has the sloppy, unkempt look.

16 September

Dear [Social Worker]

Well hello there! How have ya been doing? I'm doing okay.

I've been having a few mixed feelings lately because one person will say something to make me feel good then what do you know, someone else comes along and makes me feel like I'm never going to get out of here.

The reason I'm writing is because I told you a few weeks ago that I wouldn't ask you to talk to me anymore and I keep my word.

You know, it's kind of hard to do good here because I have the impression that everyone thinks that there isn't any good in me.

I'm in my room right now and when I get stuck in my room, I write to someone and get my feelings out. That's how I decided to tell you.

It hurt me a lot when they told me at my Board that I was using my parents because I'm not using my parents. Believe it or not, I love my parents and I'll do anything for them. I don't know in which way I can be using them. For one, they ask me if I want clothes but I tell them that there's no sense in getting clothes while I'm in here. I think I can live with the clothes I have.

I don't use them as a crutch. Sure, it makes me feel wanted when they come here to visit me.

I'm not using them as a place to go for when I get out. You know what I mean by that? Well, I'm not saying I want to go home just so I don't have to wait for a foster home, or a group home.

I have a lot of people on the outside that want me. Every single one of those people will let me be anyone, or anything I please. No rules, no nothing. I mean nothing!

Since my Board, I've been handling my mouth and actions. Maybe staff haven't noticed that because they may think that I'm not going to change for awhile. I've come a long way in the past two year and I sure can do it some more.

The first time I was locked up I swore never again. Three times in the Assessment Center, two times at the group home, once in the other institution and now here: I guess I lied to myself.

School is coming along nicely. I have five more chapters in History to do then go on to US History. About seven more chapter in Biology then I'll be finished with the book. Mr H, the teacher, said that when I'm done with Biology, I'll probably take Math. I don't think it's a good idea because I have all my credits in Math and I'd rather work on something that would help me get credits.

The keyboarding teacher said that if I get up to typing 40 words a minute she's going to see if I can take the State exam. I can type 35 words a minute now so I can get to 40 words a minute soon.

I'm still going to try for a parole from here. So don't be surprised by how hard I'm working. I mean really!

Leanne

15 October: Social Worker Notes

I was very impressed with how Leanne is now looking at what she does and how she is trying to make some changes in her relationships with others. A high point looks to be the new relationships that she is finding with her mother as she tries to see mother's point of view. Leanne's feeling that she is ready for a lift and wants a lift to signal to her family that she is getting somewhere. I agree.

16 October: Summary of the Planning Board Meeting

Leanne is doing quite well in her program at the present time. She has made consistent growth in the relationship with her mother and it's felt there is more give and take in this relationship than ever before. Leanne is discovering that her mother does care about her but she has difficulties in setting the necessary limits with her daughter. Leanne has found that as her own love for her mother has begun to have a firmer foundation, Leanne has begun to gain a broader understanding of her mother and what she has sought for Leanne in the past few years. This has strengthened her motivation to return home. At present there is more focus on Leanne's actions in the living unit and she seems less concerned with her peers and peer group dynamics. Leanne seems more relaxed than we have seen her since she has been here and she is able to carry herself now rather than having to seek constant assurance from staff that she is doing well.

We will now enrol Leanne in a half-day school in the open campus program as we feel it is now time to expand her program and start preparing her for a move to open campus.

Visits in the Ad Building with family members have also been granted which will give Leanne opportunities to meet with more family members in a less-structured situation.

In school, Leanne's written work is good and she takes part in class discussions. She relates to everyone and generally handles school well. In English she has been blossoming lately, doing a good job in written work and with oral participation. She is academically capable but has a lot of weak spots in general knowledge. She's moving ahead and minding her own business. She is making steady progress and improving some each week.

Leanne has made gains in all areas. Peer relations have improved – doesn't use peer group for her own gains now. Staff relations have improved. She spends less time talking a good game. Seeing more action on problem-solving (her's as opposed to everyone else's). She's more relaxed. Appearance has improved. Happiness shows.

---

27 October: Placement Board Cancellation

Due to Leanne's recent involvement in helping to organize a riot in the secure unit, we would like to re-schedule her Placement Board meeting until further notice.

---

26 November

Things I need to work on –

1. *I still need to get better in my relationships with both adults and kids my own age.*
2. *Lately I have been sitting on the sidelines looking in at what is going on. I think I need to get to know people more.*
3. *I still have troubles talking about my feelings.*
4. *I have been able to really get to know and be honest with my parents*

185

while I've been here. They want me home. I want to go home and I want to get there as soon as possible.

5. *I've got to look at the bright side of things. When I don't, I get fed up and feel like not trying.*

6. *I feel that I should be about ready to leave this institution sometime in late March or April – that is unless I get myself into some kind of hassle between now and then.*

7. *I think I should be out of here by the end of the school term at the very latest.*

Leanne

26 November: Summary of the 6-Month Review Board Meeting

The first three months of Leanne's involvement in the program she had a continuous "snow storm" going, assuring everyone that she did not want to get out of this institution, the same method used at her earlier institutional placement.

During this period, Leanne became a very negative leader who used threats to keep peers in line, and was also verbal in an inappropriate manner towards staff when confronted on her actions and behaviors. Until the past few weeks, Leanne has found it difficult to own up about the negative behavior she has been demonstrating. She has commonly projected blame onto her peers and staff.

Leanne finally arrived at the place where she realized that a continuation of the games would only lengthen her stay here. Nobody here accepts them and we know she can do better. We expect more from her. Slowly, Leanne has begun to show some signs of interest in others, and starting to realize that others may be interesting people in their own rights.

26 November

A Review of My Life Here

As I came into this place, I was determined to get the people here to think that I didn't have any problems so I took all my problems and stacked them away. (I tried to anyway). I wouldn't show my anger when somebody made me mad. I would just sit down and show no expression whatsoever on my face. It was really hard but I managed to do it.

When I talked to the staff I would agree on almost everything they said. I felt that I should say what I feel but I didn't.

As the weeks went by, there were girls coming up to me and telling me what so and so did to her. I would get up off my chair and go yell at so and so, go sit back down and again, no expression on my face. As this went on, I decided to start taking advantage of the girls by projecting all the blame on to them. If staff came up to me and asked me why I did this or that, I wouldn't admit to it.

Whenever the girls would be telling me about their feelings on a subject and I disagreed with them, I would get angry. You see, I had my feelings and nobody was going to change them. I wouldn't want anyone to tell me what I was doing wrong. I didn't want to accept the fact that I have faults.

I felt bad vibes from my peers and staff. The girls wouldn't admit to me if they were angry at me because they knew if they did, they sure would hear it from me.

Staff were constantly getting on my case about my behaviors. I got tired of it so I went to my room to think about it and ended up coming to the conclusion that is was just their point of view. So I would keep on as I was before. I didn't want people to think that I was a bad ass.

More days passed by and the same things were happening so again I went to my room to think. I made up my mind that I would try it their way. First of all, I started talking to the girls and really got to know the good parts in them. I was able to sit down and talk and listen to them and their feelings. I realized that they sure got some good points on things. I started to talk to the staff and they told me what they feel about how I was doing. It was pretty good too.

I feel that finally I'm getting up there. It's a great feeling. I don't have to have the last word in anymore. I can sit here and watch some girls arguing and trying to get the last word in. I think back and picture myself about two months ago. I think about others' feelings before I do something. I feel that I should get into the group more and also build more of a relationship with staff.

I think that one of the most important things I've progressed in is my relationship with my parents. We can talk about my problems and theirs' too. We have been making plans for my future. We know that it isn't going to be easy when I get out but we are willing to put forth some effort towards our lives when I get home.

I have come a long way during my stay here. I feel that I don't need to be here much longer but I also feel that I do need to stay long enough to strengthen my relationships with staff more. I'm starting to feel pretty secure around staff. I can trust them more.

Leanne

26 November: Summary of the 6-Month Review Board Meeting (continued)

Leanne is a capable girl. Her room care is well above average. Peer relations are only fair and adult relationships have been strained until recently when Leanne began to invest herself in developing relationships with staff. It is very apparent that this was probably the most difficult task that Leanne has undertaken during her stay.

Leanne seems to have developed a closer relationship with her mother and stepfather and is dealing with the issues that caused failures while she was living at home. Leanne still presents as a very lonely and unhappy girl, but she does have a steady disposition.

ACTION TAKEN

1. Leanne is to be enrolled in a full day in school in the open campus program.

2. She will be given a chance to visit and tour around each of the open cottages as a way for Leanne to evaluate which would be the best possible placement for her future next steps.

12 December: Care Worker Notes

We may have a problem and then we may not have. It all depends on whether what came out tonight is new business or old business which has been addressed already during Leanne's stay here. Hopefully somebody will be able to remember because I don't remember anything about it.

Anyhow.... Leanne was once again in a depressed mood and spent quite some time speaking of everything else except that which was on her mind. I felt that what was troubling her must in some way be connected to her furlough home, or at least with the failure to have one granted. As it turned out I was partly right, but not in the respect I thought.

As our discussion progressed, Leanne's comments about her parents became more and more derogatory and at first I thought she was in a way trying to blame them for not being home for Christmas. This was far from an accurate diagnosis.

Since we were getting nowhere, we set up a court trial were I would toss questions at her and she would answer each one honestly and truthfully. I began with non-threatening items such as age height, weight, likes, dislikes, staff preferences, etc and then began a line of questions about her family.

Her answers became more and more abrupt and tinged with anger, so I continued along that path. Starting with her mother, I asked her to describe first what she liked about her, followed by what she disliked. Some fairly heavy feelings encountered in the latter and she stated that mother would not really listen to what she had to say. In many cases mother would not believe what was told to her. And her mother would not stand up to her stepfather.

I then shifted to stepfather and BINGO! I think the second thing I asked her was whether he ever messed around or made a run on her in the past. There was not much need for any further questions! Leanne is quite fearful of her stepfather and according to her story, this fear might be well-founded.

I reserve the right to accept as fact what follows until some further delving can be accomplished. So at this time, it is only unconfirmed information. Leanne's family never has any real problem with stepfather while he is sober. When under the influence, quite another situation emerges. There have been beatings and incidents of overt sexual advances.

An older sister left home primarily because of this. Stepfather would come into the girls' bedroom late at night, sit on their bed and attempt to fondle them. He would wait until Leanne was in the bathtub and then walk in on her and ask if she wanted him to scrub her back.

He possessed "Roman Hands" and "Russian Fingers" anytime mother was not around. When Leanne tried to complain to mother about the hanky-panky, mother shut her off and refused to discuss it. She would not even acknowledge the possibility.

Leanne said that she attempted to bring this out while at the other institution but the whole thing was ignored, even though there was family counseling going on. Leanne says that while visiting is going on, stepfather will "mess around" with her legs under the table in the school room. He usually "cops a feel" when goodbyes are being said.

Leanne admitted that this has been on her mind almost continuously ever since it looked like there was a possibility of a furlough. She didn't want to take any action which might jeopardize her going home, since it is the only real place she has to go where little pre-arrangement will be necessary.

Leanne also recognizes that if it reaches the point where the choice is between allowing her stepdad to "do his thing" and running — she is clear that she will run away. This is nothing more than an open invitation to getting "set up" again.

Leanne is really apprehensive about facing her family with this and they will be here to visit on Sunday.

29 December: Care Worker Notes

I talked with Leanne for an hour and a half tonight — after she had gotten over her anger a little. We went back over the entire meeting with parents today, from beginning to end.

First of all it was necessary to discuss with Leanne her overall feelings about today's meeting. She complained that once again she was left there all on her own to do her own talking and felt that I did not give her any support. I laid it on her pretty heavily that it was not my purpose to act as her spokesman — because she was capable of speaking her own mind. She has subsequently proved this to everyone by being able to lay on her parents almost every incident she had told us about previously.

Leanne was disgusted at how it turned out. She at first accused me of being on her parents' side and not believing anything she said. I quickly pointed out how stupid that remark was and told her I wasn't a bit interested in playing patsy for her own shortcomings — if all she wanted to do was project blame, then there were other more important things for me to do.

From then on things went more smoothly. Before we went further, I had some personal impressions I had gathered today on her. She didn't like all she heard, but she did accept it. I told her that I felt that both she and her parents were disappointed in what went on today, but for different reasons. Parents thought this was some minor thing which could be quickly swept away as unimportant, and when this did not occur, they were uncomfortable and anxious to have the visit end.

Leanne felt this was a very important meeting and was disappointed at parents' lack of interest and the way they gave little indication that they appreciated how important it was to Leanne. We ended up with a "Mexican Standoff" and about the only thing accomplished was a better awareness on both sides of where the opposition stood.

I had a lot of trouble convincing Leanne that my major function was as an objective observer and to keep reasonable order in case tempers flared. She gradually came to see that this was in fact true, but she is far from pleased at the outcome — or rather the lack of any definite progress.

Leanne is very fearful that the whole situation will be smoothed over and nothing will be changed at all. She does not even yet want to face them alone and was much relieved when I informed her that either Mr [Social Worker] or myself would be in attendance as long as she felt it was necessary.

We then reviewed the entire meeting and in retrospect, Leanne could see things in a little different light. She finally came to agree that she had received more support from me than her parents had got, and admitted that she had become very angry on two occasions. She seemed surprised when I named both incidents and was really surprised when I told her I fully expected her to get up and stomp out of the room each time.

Leanne admitted that she had wanted to do exactly that, but she "didn't want to give them that satisfaction". There are a lot of bottled-up feelings in this girl still, and they're gonna have to be ventilated before we can hope for any measurable success.

Just before she went to bed, Leanne asked me if I remembered asking her in front of parents if she had anything further that was on her mind which needed to be discussed. I nodded and she told me there were other things but she didn't want to spring anything on parents that she had not told us about previously. Leanne was and is very reluctant to pass this on to us. All she would say was "It would hurt my mother too much!"

She did say "it" had happened while her mother was in hospital and that it involved Leanne and her stepfather. She could not bring herself to spit it out, but said she would try to talk with me about it tomorrow night. Even though she was hung up on this, Leanne was in superb shape at bedtime. I think it's primarily because she realizes that we have not abandoned her – even though she tried awfully hard to put us in that role. She also senses that we plan to be standing by her until this issue is resolved, one way or another.

Now for a few of my own observations picked up during the session today. Stepfather thinks it's all a bunch of bullshit and wonders why in the hell we are sticking our noses into his private affairs. He was quite upset at each of Leanne's accusations, but showed little reaction, except to get a little redder in the face and neck each time. There never was any outright admission from him – he passed each one off as pipedreams or "accidental" or "making the kids behave" or "didn't remember". Personally, I think he's guilty of at least some of Leanne's accusations or else I'm slipping in my old age!

Mother is the "peacemaker" — seldom looks at anyone other than her husband when she is explaining or exclaiming. I heard a lot of platitudes today, but I have a strong feeling that mother also has her own suspicions about her husband. There is no doubt in my mind at all that mother was "discouraged" over today's meeting. I wonder what else might be found under that "rug" that has been "swept under" so many times.

The hell of it is ... everything is too pat, explained away too easily, and too easily excused. Father is too quick to change the subject and mother too busy glossing over everything. Also, both parents were very anxious to get the hell out of here tonight!

31 December

"What I Want in Life" (written between 9:30 and 11:15 pm)

I want to be someone special. By this, I mean that I want to work and keep on building up my life.

I want to be more independent. I'd like to do things for myself like buying my own food, clothes, etc. Work things out for myself. Sure, I know that I can't be all the way independent. I just don't want everyone holding my hand and thinking for me. I find that here, I am getting more responsibilities than a few months ago. When this happens, I feel my age. I feel really great, but at times it is hard. Life isn't peaches and cream.

With this problem I've been having with my parents, I have realized that I'm not doing great here with the people I live with. One staff member told me that my life style shouldn't be affected by my attitude and my moseying around like the world just cracked in half again.

When I talk with the staff, I don't want to just talk about my parents. I want to talk about other important things like my life when I get out and my plans for me, myself, here and after I leave.

I find myself getting closer and closer to the staff. At times it hurts. I've got to admit that I have never before got this close to adults. This is good but I find myself really getting too close. This is really hard to explain.

I want to go home with a few of the staff and see how they live. I would just love to sit and watch Mrs M cooking the food for her family. I don't know why, you probably are trying to figure out what's wrong with me tonight. I want to see how Mrs M lives outside of this place. I can just imagine.

I'm doing a boo boo right now. You see, my light is supposed to be out. I know better but I have an awful urge to write. I know that's no excuse. I don't know what to say about this. I'm embarrassed.

Anyways, you just wait until awhile after I get out. I'm going to be making someone out of myself. I have a lot of things on my mind. One is I want to help people (maybe juveniles that get in hell with society).

I don't want to be one of those old bats that work in an office as a secretary. Right now being someone means so much to me.

I look back and see some of my friends living with their ole man sitting back and doing nothing but getting beat up every other day. I don't want this, can you understand?

This is hard to say but I might as well get it all out. I don't want to go through the open campus trip because I am feeling so good about almost everything. I'm so sure of my success and I know I can make it.

I am able to think things out in a better manner. And most important, I'm more honest with myself. I just don't feel that I need this institution much longer. I want to go out there and meet new people and keep on going from there – not starting off where I left off before I came here.

I look back at when I first got here. I can almost scream at myself for the stupid things I did. I was slick Leanne but not slick enough. Holding all my feelings in almost drove me crazy.

I was trying to play everyone as a fool but I found out that most of them aren't fools. I don't get all paranoid when staff call me to the office door, or down the hall like they used to.

Anyway, these are my feelings at the time and I thought that it would be nice to share them with you. Thank you for reading it.

Leanne

15 January: Summary of the Placement Board Meeting

Leanne has spent the last 7 months in the secure unit. The challenges which Leanne faced at the time of commitment by the Juvenile Court two years ago have remained central to Leanne's progress. These challenges involved family relationships, and in particular, Leanne's relationship with her Native American stepfather which has been especially difficult. Leanne had considerable difficulties at school and was repeatedly kicked out of school for most of her early education. Finally, her drug use became a significant problem as Leanne turned to drugs as a way of coping with feelings of depression, an escape from dealing with her problems.

As far as the family is concerned, Leanne has finally been able to honestly evaluate her relationship with her mother and stepfather. While she feels quite good about her mother, she remains suspicious of her stepfather and has decided that she cannot return there to live. During her institutional stay, Leanne has worked extremely hard in her schooling. She is now at grade level or slightly above, and is functioning as a full time student in the campus school without difficulties.

In so far as her drug use is concerned, Leanne admits that she is probably going to smoke marijuana in the future. The focus of our counseling has been to distinguish between use of drugs and abuse of drugs. So long as Leanne turns to drugs as an escape from her personal problems, then she sets herself up for abuse. It is during these times that Leanne is most likely to act impulsively and do something stupid that may bring her harm or into conflict with the law.

Leanne is a clever girl. She is very perceptive and quickly sizes people up before getting to know them. She is a keen participant in recreation and athletic activities, devoting a lot of energy into being active and competitive. Leanne likes school now and is being successful there. Education is an area that should be a continuing asset for Leanne in the future.

The action of the Review Board was to transfer Leanne to an open campus program that will support her working towards community planning. That program also leaves responsibility for managing daily living routines with Leanne and the other residents.

Leanne has made gains in all areas during the past seven months. She has done a complete turn about face. She is more relaxed. She presents her happy, carefree side most of the time, compared with the "old stone face" image we constantly saw in the past. Future work will be directed towards emancipation as soon as possible.

Addendum

Once Leanne worked out how The System worked, she was clever enough to make the necessary adjustments to the ways in which she engaged her world, the adults who mostly ran that world and the youthful peers who inhabited her world. Leanne worked out that she could do something about her circumstances. She learned that she could "do" education, and could be successful. She left the secure unit as a 17 year-old, determined to achieve emancipation but to maintain some kind of relationship with her mother and her stepfather for as long as they were together. She had grown to experience a much closer relationship with her mother than ever before. The authors have no further knowledge of what happened to Leanne as she carried on her life journey. This young woman was someone who could make things happen if she set her mind to it. We hope Leanne achieved her New Year's Resolution about becoming "*someone special*" because she was someone special!

Aliese's Reflections

In remembering Leanne, fond memories come to mind. And as I started to read the first section and what the Principal said about her being the most disruptive and hard to handle child that his school had ever seen – well ... it just made me laugh. Adults bewildered? Bedazzled? Confounded?

As I recall, Leanne was from a very small backwoods town – and literally, cow tipping was the weekend's entertainment. I am sure the school district did not attract the best of teachers, or principals. What impudence this keeper of education held. Problem with Leanne was she was smart, witty, pretty and a forward thinker – as were many of my closest of friends. She was pretty independent and a lone wolf, like me, and a leader. No doubt she was just as smart as this bewildered principal who was trained to handle adolescent children. Authority and control was A LOT different back then ... and I see what is happening in the world today – with all dysfunction – and so I see the aftermath too, generation upon generation ... THEY were so afraid of thinking outside the box – and everyone wanted it "their way", and had "their" textbook ideas of who we were to be.

All the decisions were made for us, that was their thinking in those days – not just with troubled teens or within the confines of the system we lived in ... but that was the political climate in those days. Especially women – did I mention being harassed by the police for not wearing a bra? I mean it was just weird man, cops were pigs generally and wife beaters. There was no accountability, no watchdog groups, like there is today. There was so much hate coming from the system: they hated the Blacks, the Indians, the Hippies, the College-minded, I mean, America was really going through some major overhauls and we were thrown into this direct-hit system of controlling today's youth.

Keep in mind, that this secure unit was totally different and that we grew up with these other types of facilities and policies. This was one-stop shopping and we either gathered all the tools together here and learned to cope within a hurting world, and survived – or we simply did not. It is very interesting to look back on it now, with an adult perspective.

Note where she talks about her having lots of places to go on the outs and how she is not manipulating her situation so she could go home, etc ... with her parents ... and she talks about handling her mouth and actions – sometimes when we learned to control ourselves, as young ladies and what was perceived – we were then labelled manipulative –

maybe we were, but maybe we weren't ... sort of a damned if you do and same, if'n ya don't.

We were kids, young ladies, trying to grow up in a world that WAS CHANGING BIG TIME, MAN! And we really were trying to find an adult we could trust, we could talk to, we could get a few answers from. And hey, bonus plan, if we were lucky enough to find someone who really gave a shit about us versus someone who just wanted to beat us, scream at us, or sexually abuse us. Leanne and I were close because of our awareness, our experiences, our ideals, and ALWAYS our taste in music. Music defined us and it connected us all. We all related to music, our one therapy, our one happy home in our mind, they could not take away from us. It was true for everyone – Carole King-Tapestry was right on with "You Got A Friend". Leanne was my friend and totally my sister. Friendships and bonds were made quickly and it was for life and for blood. She was a hippie like me and our paths held common threads. I remember meeting her brother once, on a family visit that was an open visit in the cottage. We did not have those very often, but she was sooooo excited to introduce me to her brother, who I thought was a hunk! I believe we corresponded for some time. How I dreamed of a simple farm life.

I think the political climate has so much more to do with foster care and the social systems – a lot more than has ever been recognized. What does policy say? How involved can you become with the child with this revolving door policy and NOW trying something new within the system? Humans are not computers designed like a flow chart, with yes or no decisions or statements.

The lack of staff training was also a huge factor, just as was residing in one institution and then moving to another one. Staff were just people with a great heart and wanting to help families and children in need, and some who simply wanted or needed to give back to society. Basically people are people and the same holds true today. In those days many did not have the luxury of experience or education prior to working at one of these facilities.

One thing that is so different in Indian country, is that our goal is always to reunite the family and get to the root of the problems as a family and tribal unit. That is the court's approach now (ICWA-Indian Child Welfare Act) which is a huge difference from the traditional court system and incarceration processes of our youth even today. We believe (Native Americans) that in order to understand the child, you have to understand their environment.

I mention political climate, and the societal differences of this generation, because some of the off-the-cuff comments about how Leanne dressed – partly style differences and self-expression – whereas in today's political climate, such a thought would never cross your mind. We were of course issued clothing from donations collected over the years….. and it was a real challenge to come up with something decent. I say all of this fondly. Leanne was a country girl and being dressed for her would easily be a pair of jean cut-offs or even bib-overalls and a man's tee shirt. We simply didn't care and didn't want to conform. She wore long hippie skirts and tie-dye and no make-up, those sorts of things. I miss her and I am sure if we met we would still be great friends today.

It is wonderful to see the pride coming through with her scholarly progress. So often, we either struggled or were totally bored with education – none of it seemed very relevant to what our worlds were all about. And the notes of her improvement, her devotion to self and self-care – and then BLAM, out of nowhere, she is involved with a riot. God only knows I may have been the instigator behind that, or not. I'm very curious as to what the demands were – as I am certain, there had to be some grand scheme for such a planned event. Like I said earlier, the letting go is a process that takes time and we have to decipher so much information, emotions, duty and loyalty, and then the big picture – what do we want to do with the rest of our lives?

There is the battle going on inside, churning forever. We were trying to hold onto some identity of ourselves and brave on, in our new world. The sensitive or artistic person took criticism and the basic undoing of our overall personality into a deeper contemplation and we had an awareness of the change that needs to come from within. The letting go process is a valuable lesson and works through all of our lives no matter how well adjusted one is to society. As the example later showed, "Due to Leanne's recent involvement in helping to organize a riot in the secure unit"… , the letting go, the fighting of the establishment for our basic belief systems, it takes time to break those old instincts, as that is what they had become. Fight or flight, all throughout our lives. It must have been an important issue of concern for her to "backslide" like this. You finally realize that it is best to join them, at least temporarily. Maybe you can find some common ground that would be beneficial. To concentrate on our own problems and not to worry about the day-to-day issues and bickering of your roommates is a difficult task indeed. You live with these people. It is a huge task and I commend her wisdom and efforts.

I still see the progress in my own life as time marches on, and the valuable tools I learned. I did not learn them from the system, I learned them from friends who nurtured and loved me. It is great to read these notes, and to value Leanne as a person, and also to know how precious she is, as my sister of pain. To read and understand the phases of self-awareness and finding her own strength brings me much joy. All children, all people must learn to stretch their wings and fly.

In reading through, I felt a little envious of her having a family. I mean, I had a family – but they took my family away from me. Even now, as a grown adult – a little pang of regretting not having those sorts of visits, letters, phone calls, presents even…. presents like new clothes or a new brush or barrette for your hair. And then, of course, the father is a pervert. I mean, really? It just pisses me off, and we wonder why the kids are runaways, or on dope? Dope to cope, baby! How were we provided with these caretakers? A God-given task is parenting. And yet our only chance at success – as Sisters of Pain – is to understand and forgive, gain useful knowledge and skills, constantly reminding ourselves that we would NEVER raise our children this way.

I think some of the labels today numb people. So when you really start talking about the nitty-gritty of life, these youths were growing up with incest, sodomy, gang-rapes, brutal beatings, the sharing of daughters with drunken friends, just to name but a few of the wilder life experiences. Then you have the women in the homes, the schools, the community, and in the churches aware of what their children were going through but with no real outlet to tell and deal with the consequences. I mean, people – even today we have difficulty saying the words, talking about the abuse and the abusers. The silence binds us to this day and age, locking part of us up mentally and spiritually.

We had come to this new place with different rules and now we had to learn to talk, examine, focus, re-language, all sorts of things and then of course to talk about the sexual abuse – horrific! It is so hard for a child, and especially when you're confined, where there is nowhere to run away and hide your shame. Every move and emotion is being watched and recorded and noted and examined.... and then some of them all start looking at you differently too, or worse – that is ALL they want to talk about. Good Lord! This poor child, my poor friend – my heart wrenches for her. Again, this is why my sisters and my co-inhabitants didn't often discuss these things with one another. Society teaches us shame and guilt as part of their controlling factors.

I love when the social worker says about not playing patsy with her and has other things to do. There was always that close connection with the social worker – and a gift that most staff did not possess. He could grab our attention. I feel like any successes I have had, have grown from the hinged relationship on an intellectual level, versus the parental – more of a friendship – that is vital. Forming those inter-relationships and strengthening those bonds were our saving grace.

Dear Leanne recognized she was special, and wanted to become someone special. In my heart of hearts, I believe that she is out in this great big world continuing to be someone special – I know she was (and still is) special to me. She loved to laugh and when she laughed there was a twinkle in her eye.

Noticing: 'Out There' and 'In Here'

Quality out-of-home care begins with social workers, youth workers and carers noticing more closely what may be going on with each young person in their care. Garfat (2003) claimed that there are moments when a youth worker notices the need or an opportunity for intervention. This may involve having to stop something happening, perhaps helping a child understand her own internal dialogues (Fewster, 1990) or helping her make connections with different influences which impact on her life (Garfat, 1993; Garfat, Fulcher & Digney, 2012). Quality out-of-home care may also involve opportunities to intervene in a young person's cycles of maladaptive acting or being with others (Krueger, 1988). At such moments, whilst deciding whether or not to intervene, the worker needs to be actively alert to what is going on – out there and in here – noticing what may be important about this point of intervention.

While this may seem like a simple statement and one that could 'go without saying', it is our nature to not always notice or experience all the things which happen around us. We filter out some things that are clearly available. Without this ability, we may become overwhelmed at times with different experiences of our world (Guttman, 1991). A youth worker or social worker needs to pay special attention to the environment and actions-in-the-environment in which she operates, so as to notice what is occurring, as it is occurring. 'Noticing' happens when the immediate stream of events is disrupted (Eisikovits, Beker & Guttman, 1991), and also when our attention is drawn to a particular event in the stream of events, perhaps for other reasons. While awareness is an on-going process – like meaning making – noticing occurs when a worker's attention and awareness are focused on specific events in the daily life space with a young person, whether consciously or unconsciously.

When noticing daily life events in out-of-home care, youth workers, social workers and carers need to be concerned with how this specific event is connected to the situational, the global, and the personal context of this young person's life history. Thus, when focusing on an event, we must isolate and locate that event within its context. That way we can understand the full extent of what such an opportunity this could mean. We must consider how this event may be connected to the multiple streams of events which shape functioning in this young person's daily life space. It is only through seeing the connectedness of the event to its context that we are able to determine how to intervene through our relationship with that young person.

Noticing starts with us – each carer, youth worker or social worker. It requires that a youth worker or social worker frees herself from preconceived notions about what is, and is not relevant. Sometimes we don't notice, because we don't know about it. Other times we don't notice because we don't want to know about it. Maybe we choose not to know about something. And at other times, we are too busy focusing on something else to notice what is right in front of us! Noticing is like examining the weave and threads of a hand-woven carpet. One thread leads to another and connects to a third and so on, until all the threads weave back to the original one. Noticing depends on the threads that are picked up from the start and also how the carpet weave is looking as a whole. As a carer or youth worker reflects systematically on what's "out there" and what's "in here" before leaping into some intervention(s), so it is that we mirror what Freado called "the outside kid" and "the inside kid", referred to earlier (Freado, Bussell & McCombie, 2005). Youth workers and carers need also to ask what is going on "out there" for a young person like Leanne, and what's going on "inside"?

We introduce the following material because it draws upon research with more than three million young people to assist social workers and youth workers in their practice with those in out-of-home care. The US Search Institute identified forty developmental assets as *"concrete, common sense, positive experiences and qualities essential to raising successful young people"* http://http://www.search-institute.org/research/developmental-assets *Twenty external assets (*out there*) and twenty internal assets (*in here*) were shown to influence young people's future life chances as they transition through childhood and adolescence towards young adulthood and beyond. This strengths-based orientation – what Benson, et al* (2006) called positive youth development – directs attention towards personal strengths and resilience (Gilligan, 2009), reinforcing competencies, bolstering capacities, celebrating achievements and reinforcing aspirations.

The Search Institute identified twenty *External Assets* clustered around four developmental themes – *Support; Empowerment; Boundaries & Expectations;* and *Constructive Use of Time* – which customarily wrap around children, young people and families in culturally defined ways (Fulcher, 2003). External assets involve family members and extended family members, other adults, participation in community life, school, within neighbourhood and peer group boundaries, along with purposeful use of time at school, home and in the community. Twenty *Internal Assets* that help shape daily living and social relations are grouped around four other developmental themes: *Commitment to Learning; Positive Values; Social Competencies;* and *Positive Identity.* These highlight achievements, learning and the nurturing of values – caring about others, equality and social justice, integrity, honesty, responsibility and restraint. Competencies associated with planning and decision-making, interpersonal and cultural skills, resistance skills and peaceful conflict resolution are important, along with personal power, self-esteem, a sense of purpose, and hope for the future.

As shown in the graph below, Search Institute research (2001) found that roughly 1 in 7 young people reported 10 or fewer developmental assets while 2 in 5 reported having more than 10 but fewer than 20 of the developmental assets surveyed. Boys on the whole, reported having 3 fewer developmental assets (17.3 out of 40) than did young females (20.7 out of 40).

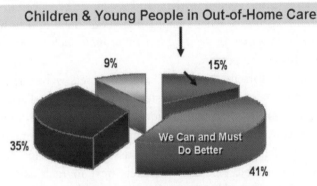

Children & Young People in Out-of-Home Care

9%   15%

35%   We Can and Must Do Better

41%

Reported Developmental Outcomes

Females 20.7/40 Population Means   Males 17.3/40

■ 0-10 Assets ■ 11-20 Assets ■ 21-30 Assets □ 31-40 Assets

From Speaking of Developmental Assets: Presentation Resources & Strategies, (2001), Search Institute, Minneapolis, MN . 55413 (USA)
www.search-institute.org

Other SI research shows that those young people who reported they had 10 or fewer developmental assets were the ones who faced particular challenges. Starkman (2002) found that 9 out of 10 of the young people reporting 10 or fewer assets were not achieving in school; 2 out of 5 were experimenting with drugs; whilst 3 out of 5 had been involved in 3 or more acts of fighting, hitting, injuring a person, carrying a weapon, or threatening physical harm in the previous 12 months. Such statistics profile the histories of most young people in out-of-home care in the Western World.

Noticing what is "outside" and "inside" a young person builds from a practice imperative adopted by the Scottish Government – *We Can and Must Do Better* – to nurture developmental achievements that matter for each child or young person in out-of-home care in Scotland. A major challenge is to find ways of assisting young people – in the 'low assets' population – to achieve developmental outcomes that 'move them towards the population mean'. Or, put another way, why should children and young people in out-of-home care not be given the same opportunities available to any other young person in Scotland, or anywhere else? Carers, youth workers and social workers need to assist young people "to notice what's happening – out there and in here – whilst *working together in relationship* to *promote achievements that matter*" for this young person.

With these factors in mind, ten External Assets were targeted as Outcomes that Matter for use by foster carers, youth workers, social workers and others in fulfilling their duty of care obligations to monitor and report on developmental achievements made by the young people in their care (Fulcher, 2002). Ten external assets and ten internal assets are shown in the table below. In brackets next to each asset is the percentage of young people who reported having these assets through the *Search Institute Profiles of Student Life: Attitudes and Behaviors* survey administered to nearly 150,000 young people in their final year of primary school through the end of secondary school (roughly ages 12-18) in 202 communities across the US in 2003 –
http://www.search-institute.org/what-we-study/developmental-assets
The table also identifies which of the 40 developmental assets were excluded in our revised list of 20 Outcomes that Matter.

206

Noticing Outcomes that Matter

'Out There' Around This Young Person

Support   Carer Support (68% of the SI research sample)
                   Positive Communication (28%)
                   Caring Relationships (43%)
                   Supportive Environments (29%)
                   Carer's Involvement in Learning (29%)

Excluded though Important:
Caring Neighbourhood (37%)

Empowerment   Safety (51%)
                   Service to Others (48%)

Excluded though Important:
Community Values Children & Young
    People (22%)
Children & Young People as
    Resources (26%)

Boundaries &   Boundaries for Daily Living (46%)
Expectations   High Expectations (48%)

Excluded though Important:
Neighbourhood Boundaries (47%)
Child Care, School or Work Experience
    Boundaries (52%)
Adult Role Models (27%) – Positive
    Peer Influence (63%)

**Constructive
Use of Time**   Activity Programmes

Excluded though Important:
Creative Activities (21%)
Religious Community (58%) –
    Time at Home (51%)

'In Here' – Inside This Young Person

Commitment   Motivation to Achieve (65%)
to Learning   Engaging in Learning (55%)
Making Use of Learning Opportunities & Homework (47%)

Excluded though Important:
Bonding to School (52%)
Reading for Pleasure (22%)

Positive Values   Responsibility (63%)
Caring (50%)
Honesty (66%)

Excluded though Important:
Equality and Social Justice (52%)
Integrity (68%) – Restraint (45%)

Social
Competencies   Planning and Decision-Making (29%)
Peaceful Conflict Resolution (40%)

Excluded though Important:
Interpersonal Competence (45%)
Cultural Competence (43%) –
Resistance Skills (41%)

Positive Identity   Personal Power (42%)
Positive View of Personal Future (72%)

Excluded though Important:
Self Esteem (48%)
Sense of Purpose (57%)

Because no moment can exist in isolation from the context within which it occurs (Garfat, 1992), any understanding of a moment, event or opportunity requires some understanding of what's "*out there*" around this young person and what's "*inside*" where the pain lives for this particular young person in out-of-home care. Guttman (1991) suggested that child and youth care operates in the *flow of immediacies*, a stream of ever occurring events which pass so quickly that each tends to flow and overlap with the previous and the events which follow. In deciding whether or not to intervene, a youth worker must notice particular opportunities and identify themes from what's going on in the moment. At the same time, they are connecting that event with contextual elements that are important to understanding and analysing it. Noticing what's going on with a young person's achievement of developmental assets is helpful. Zeroing in on 10 External (*Out There*) and 10 Internal (*In Here*) Outcomes that Matter can assist everyone – young person, carers, youth workers and family members – to stay focused and make real achievements during their involvement with out-of-home care services (Garfat & Fulcher, 2012).

Questions for Small Group Discussion or Guided Reflection

1. How does noticing enhance the quality of relational care with young people in out-of-home care?
2. Throughout all the family counselling, why do you think nobody noticed Leanne's unspoken messages about her father's sexual abuse?
3. Why is it important to notice what is going in here, inside me the youth worker, at the same time that I am noticing what's going on out there around this young person and me?
4. According to information supplied in her narrative, what external and internal assets shown in the table might Leanne's have reported?
5. What may have been left un-noticed about Leanne's daily living activities and school performance that may have resulted in her participation in the attempted riot?

Room 9
Lexie – *Pause, Think and Reflect*

27 November

Thinking

Thinking of the past,
Of how it couldn't last.
The time, it went so fast.
And wondering what the future holds.

Smoking one cigarette after another;
So much time on my hands,
Nothing to do
but think.

The days slip by one by one.
The hours drag on,
Never knowing what's going to happen –
But always wondering.

Sometimes I wish I could see my future,
But if I could see the future,
I still couldn't stop
what was going to happen.

Lexie

They hold the power!
They can tell you what to do!
Don't slip out of line,
Or honey, you're through!

So you try to B.S. them.
And you get it right back.
It's different then,
It's something you can't hack!

I wish for once people could come on straight
and tell it how it is.
Instead, everyone plays little games
with each others' heads.

I know how it is.
I've played a few myself.
There are so many things
I have going through my head.

But there's no one to talk to
And tell how I feel.
So I go out
and get myself into a lot of trouble.

Lexie

8 January: Summary of the Initial Planning Board Meeting

Lexie is a 16 year-old young woman, committed two years ago for incorrigibility, being out of the control of her parents, poor school attendance and performance, and using drugs. After a stay at the Assessment Center, Lexie was transferred to the institution for younger teenagers but she ran away from there several times. She was paroled to her parents in March last year. While on parole, Lexie became involved in drug use again, particularly barbiturates. She ran away from home on numerous occasions, the last time stealing a car with another girl.

Lexie has never voluntarily kept her parole counsellor informed of her activities, plans or daytime whereabouts. She has kept all of her appointments and telephoned when that was requested. A condition of her parole was that Lexie attend junior high school but, without discussion, she quit school and told them she wouldn't be returning for Autumn Semester. Lexie was to have no contact with friends who use drugs but her mother says that all of Lexie's old friends have been telephoning and visiting. A recent agreement was that Lexie have no contact with LM but apparently she has been in continuous contact with LM since her return from detention. Lexie consistently broke curfew hours. In October, she became pregnant but miscarried.

Fantasies

My fantasies are
here and there.

My fantasies take me
anywhere.

I sit alone and stare
but I'm not really there.

I'm far away on Cloud Nine
My fantasies are really fine.

But then it hits me

REALITY!

Then I'm depressed
and want to be free.
Reality is hard and cold.
With its four brick walls, I feel so old.

Time stretches on….
People are gone.
But my fantasies are never done…

Lexie

The door shuts.
The key turns the lock.
And here I sit again ... alone.
In my little room, with no way of escape.

My only escape
is thru my dreams,
And hopes
for a better future.

I've never been able to see the light at the end of my travels.
It's always obstructed by clouds.
But I can dream!
They can't take that away.

Lexie

---

8 January: **Summary of the Initial Planning Board Meeting**
(continued)

Lexie feels angry, anxious and depressed. She feels far too powerless to express her feelings directly to adults. She feels angry towards and fearful of her parents, and this seems to be generalized to all adult authority figures. Because of her feelings of powerlessness, Lexie has a tendency to withdraw from interactions in her environment and to rely on fantasy as motivation for her behavior. She hopes that things will somehow magically work out to her advantage.

Lexie feels that if she does conform, she will give up what little sense of self she has.

This fear of being overwhelmed by her parents and their Mormon religion has generalized to her whole environment, to the extent that she is extremely resistive to environmental pressures and demands.

Underneath her defenses, however, Lexie feels considerable guilt and responsibility for her misbehaviour. When confronted with her misbehaviour, she feels guilt and remorse, and although she has good intentions for improving her behaviour, there is too much anger and her emotional controls too limited to follow through on these good intentions. Lexie feels trapped. There are no viable avenues for the direct expression of her emotions. There is thus likely to be a lot of passive-aggressive behaviour.

Why are there places like institutions?
With laws and rules and people to boost them

Why are there people like you and me?
All we want is to be happy and free.

We have to conform to their way of thinking.
Then they leave here at night to go drinking.

We walk around, follow the rules.
Like a bunch of robots, or just plain fools.

But someday ... someday,
when our ties break away
And our minds are half rotten
with brainwash decay,
Then what will the fuckin' establishment say?

Our children, our children –
look what they do
But establishment, establishment – who did it?
Was it us or was it you?

Lexie

25 April: Summary of the Planning Board Meeting

After a brief period during which Lexie gained ground, she slid into a depression just before an anticipated visit from her parents. This deepened after they had come to see her. As Lexie gains a more realistic picture of her family situation, it hurts. She still yearns for what she lost out on as a young child. Whatever relationship they have in the future will be as adult child and parents.

In school, Lexie presents good written work but doesn't participate in class unless asked. Good skills in PE. In Biology she looks busy, acts busy, but very little actual progress. Avoids adults and has "hush-hush" peer relationships. Does good work in World History but refuses to take Typing.

Overall, she is still an "underground girl". Draw her out into the open. Balance confrontation with praise. Set firm and consistent limits. She may take part in Recreation activities at the gym.

Prison

There's a place where I am, no one's been there before.
It doesn't have a wall and it doesn't have a door.

It's a deep dark secret and very hard to find.
I'll tell you now it's the prison in my mind.

It's the place that now holds me
I may never be free.
It's the prison that holds me
from just being me.

It's the worst kind of place anyone could be
Cuz it's a place where you'll never be free.
It could just hold you,
For all eternity.

When I hear the key rattle
I know it's my time
Once again, I'm locked in my mind.
Any way out – impossible to find.

My prison was built with help from my past.
I was young, I lived hard and I took it too fast.
My prison may fall at last when I die – I'm still not quite sure
And don't ask me why.

Lexie

Fuck authorities
Race minorities
Voting majorities
What's coming down?

Homemade abortions,
Drugs in large portions
Media distortions
When will it end?

Hate and killing
War and drilling
Hunger and filling
Where will it end?

Elections
Rejections
Connections
What is the end?

Lexie

27 June: Summary of the Planning Board Meeting

Lexie was seen for routine evaluation following a change of social workers. She seemed remarkably hesitant about expressing herself. It is significant to note that throughout Lexie's experiences in institutional programs during the past 2-3 years, she has never worked consistently with any one person for more than 3-4 months. Lexie was thus insulated from having to establish working relationships with staff, or learning what trust in a relationship means.

It is also worth noting how Lexie seems to have incorporated a set of institutionalized patterns of behaviour which may, in fact, be more problematic for her now than the pre-commitment behaviors which led to institutional placements. These institutionalized behaviours include things such as getting other residents to speak for her in contacts with adults or influencing other girls to act out and hence, create a stir in the cottage. Such behaviour has the effect of keeping staff away from the matters that are most important to Lexie.

Finally, Lexie's parents have experienced an ongoing frustration with the way institutions have handled their daughter, largely due to the transient character of those who would normally have communicated professionally with the parents about significant aspects of Lexie's program. They claimed that nobody communicated with them.

Dreams

Dreams are like smoke rings.
They drift along peacefully
Until shattered by unknown winds.

Lexie

Clinically, Lexie presents herself as a reasonably self-sufficient teenage girl who reacts to underlying depression with flight or avoidance behaviours while at other times she internalizes such feelings. The result is that mood swings may vary from intense hyperactivity to withdrawing into quiet conversation with her closest peers.

The underlying depression seems rooted in Lexie's confused feelings about her place in the family, although there is indication that these strong anti-authoritarian feelings – common to adolescence – have been reinforced by a series of shallow institutional relationships which Lexie perceived as controlling and non-caring in nature.

Lexie remains constantly on guard and is unable to examine the uncertainty about what the future holds with anyone other than her peers. The result is a façade of conformity with adults where any confrontation about personal behaviour is perceived by Lexie as persecution yet again.

The hunger in me's arisin'
I can feel it getting' strong.
All I know is what I see
And I know I can't hold on.

People come to watch me die
Time and time again
I'm in the crowd but all alone
I wish I had a friend.

I'm falling in darkness
I stumble to my feet
Only to hear a voice so clear
Saying' "Girl, you know you're beat".

They'll push you down
And while you're there, they'll kick dirt in your face
When they're sure they've got you there
You're erased without a trace.

Lexie

Why do people live?
Why do people die?
What makes them laugh?
What makes them cry?

When I see people with their head in the sand
I want to lend a friendly hand.
So many questions with no answers there
Tell me how to find an answer, and where!

There're things in my head that I keep deep inside.
I'd rather help others and let myself glide.
I'd rather see others happy and free
I really am lonely but I guess that's just me.

Lexie

12 September: Summary of the Planning Board Meeting

The period since Lexie's last Planning Board has been one of sporadic growth. On the one hand, we have seen Lexie very much involved and working through feelings in her relationship with her parents and on the other hand we have seen Lexie gravitate to a sullen, covertly hostile, anti-authoritarian stance in the peer group. A fairly consistent pattern is beginning to present itself in which downhill spirals in Lexie's overall performance seems to be directly related to feedback given to her on performance by various staff members. Overall, we see a profile of marginal growth, this coming mostly in the areas of school and personal self confidence, although at the same time we see an increase in general depression and feelings of hopelessness and despair concerning her present circumstances.

Dear [Mr Governor]

I am an American citizen of this State. I was just wondering if you've taken a good look at the institutions here in your State. As a matter of fact, I live in one. And believe me they leave a lot to be desired.

I am in a lock-up cottage at the senior girls' institution. In my lock-up cottage I don't have the right type of program. Some girls have been sitting here for over a year. Listen, these kids could be tomorrow's criminals. They need the right kind of help now! And they are not getting it.

We need more programs out in the community. That's where the problems are ...not here. And you can't work things out if you can't even get to them. It's not right!

This is the second institution I've been through and your State people haven't got the point yet. I really wish you would take a look at this, because it's a big problem for the State.

Over 1000 kids are sent up every year. A lot of useless time is lost. Think about it.

Lexie

Addendum

Lexie did whatever she needed to do to get out of the institutional system. We caught up with her one afternoon, a few years later in a city park with another old friend. They were both young mothers with pre-school children. It was with sadness that we learned some months later that Lexie had died of an overdose. Her pain was foreshadowed in her teenage poetry reproduced here.

Aliese's Reflections

Lexie was my best friend ever. Nicki and I were close, as were Jenette and I, but we did not have that much time growing up together. Lexie and I lived in the same city. She died of a heroin overdose when I was about 22 years old. I found out when her parents tracked me down. I don't know how or why they tracked me down, but they did. I had moved out of state about a year before, so perhaps Lexie had my telephone number written down. Now I wish I had never moved away. I am surprised they called me at all. Naturally I was not well liked by them and was a devil child according to them. Lexie's parents were Mormon and very strict, which is of course why Lexie rebelled so much. They were just so out of tune with the times. And when I met them, they just seemed mean and hard. But who really knows? I was just a kid.

It chills the bone reading these letters and the poetry of my sister of pain. When I read Lexie's poems again, at first, it was like, "*hey, I remember that, I wrote that*". But, I am not the author, just a mere pedestrian on her sidewalk of life. I saw myself in her, I was a part of her and she a part of me. After forty years or more, the deep connection is still there and so is the pain and the anger at a failed society who thought they knew best and who took on the responsibility of this child, my friend, and who failed her miserably. God, how I miss her. She was truly a sister to me. We just allowed each other to exist and accepted each other. We never questioned each other, everything was just understood. It is almost unbearable to type these notes thinking of her. She did not commit suicide, it was an accidental overdose of heroin and they must have gotten hold of some strong stuff. Lexie was not an addict, but rather, an occasional user. I don't know if that will ever matter in the long run. To me it means everything and I am sure it would matter to her surviving children. It should warn anyone about the dangers of the drug.

Lexie's parents blamed her boyfriend and tried to have him convicted of a crime that resulted in her death. It was a simple overdose and I am sure he will never ever outlive the thoughts and the horror of that day. Lexie left behind three children. Prior to her death, she had another baby who died of crib death. At the time of Lexie's death, her eldest son Michael – I will call him – was about six years old, maybe seven. My daughter was only two at the time, I was soon to be married and had moved out of state by that time.

I remember getting the phone call from her dad, I think it was he who called, and he simply said Lexie was dead of a heroin overdose and that was it. All matter of fact. I am sure they were in shock, but I am sure they blamed me in part too, even though I had not been actively involved with Lexie for some time. We were both busy mothers, and I was a single mom at that. We visited each other on occasion, and one of the last visits we had we all went to her home for Thanksgiving. I remember it so well. We were laughing in her small kitchen trying to make mashed potatoes with a blender. Pretty silly I suppose. We were all very poor but we managed and didn't really feel we were the lowest of the classes, or the poorest.

What I remember about her most is that she loved life and loved to laugh. She had the ability to laugh at anything and to make me laugh. We both had a real hate for the System, the establishment and we had a pretty good understanding of the world around us. We understood the greed and corruption, the religious controlling types, the probation officers who were perverts, the men who dated us while cheating on their wives – oh yes, we saw the world through very knowing eyes. As most youth of those days, we were old beyond our years. I don't think the youth of today are nearly as tuned in and there are several reasons for that, but I won't expand on that here.

We had such a great love of music and would sit in her room listening to Led Zepplin and Steppenwolf, The Band, and old Rolling Stones music for hours. We spent a lot of time cruising the streets of our city, hitchhiking everywhere and anywhere we wanted to go. We would pan-handle for money to buy cigarettes and just people watch at one of our famous market squares. Just sit and watch the world go by and discuss politics, our dreams and how we wanted to have a place out in the country raising animals and live off the land.

We went on a few short road trips together and were two lost souls without any family or friends except each other. I was never as close to any one person in my life. I know she felt trapped in her relationship with her boyfriend but mainly it was due to the financial problems and she had wanted so much more out of life. She was encumbered with four children that she had early on and she was very devoted to her children and trying to make a good family life for them all. It is a decision mothers have to make, to be a stay at home mom and forego college, travel, and any career life. And our options in those days were not what they are for women today. It was a decision she was happy with and her boyfriend and her were best friends and had been together for a life time – it was working, why change it.

I know I will miss her for the rest of my life and she was probably the only real family I felt I ever had, except my social worker and my one set of foster parents, all of whom I have kept in touch with all these years. Lexie's story is a real tragedy. She had so much potential, she was smart, pretty, and such a vibrant soul. I have hopes of finding her eldest son one day and hope that if he ever needs me, that I can be a friend to him. I know her family must have such regrets in following the church's strictest of rules and the head trip they laid on Lexie – of guilt, shame, and embarrassment to the family, etc. But I will also say, in their defence, that they were doing the best they knew how to do, and did love their daughter very much. They simply did not understand her, and most American families were going through many of the same issues within their own families.

Pause, Think and Reflect

Noticing is the first priority but then it must be followed by a time of slowing down to think and reflect on what you noticed, and also remain open to the idea that you haven't noticed a lot of things. It is important to pause and think about some of the nurturing activities of everyday life which contribute to the quality of care and "relations of dependence and independence; of giving and receiving" (Lynch *et al*, 2009: 49).

Being cared for and feeling cared for are prerequisites for personal development. The forms of social engagement that emerge from caring relations "are frequently what brings meaning, warmth and joy to life" (Lynch *et al*, 2009: p.1). Out-of-home care is not offered and received merely between those employed to care and those cared for. Out-of-home care involves a wider matrix of care in which "*care-giving and receiving requires and results from human interdependence, from conceptualizing persons as relational rather than autonomous*" (Emond, 2010: 75).

When we stop to think about it, we see how expressions of care are often manifest in the little things of everyday life (Costa & Walter, 2006; Trieschman *et al*, 1969; Whittaker, 1979), a touch, a gesture, the laundered bed sheets, the flowers on the kitchen table. Redl (1966) with Wineman spoke about the need for "*a home that smiles, props which invite, space which allows*" (1957: 6). Conversely, the institutional 'Fire Exit' and 'No Smoking' signs, or the ubiquitous Visitor Book – all features of many care homes – speak of very different life space experiences. Care is not the primarily technical/rational task it has become in dominant professional and political thinking. Care is, in essence, a moral and practical endeavour (Moss & Petrie, 2002; Petrie *et al*, 2006). It is not easily measured and its outcomes are far from certain or predictable. Caring relationships ... "*are predicated on an expressive rather than instrumental relationship to others (based on) trust, commitment over time and a degree of predictability*" (Brannan & Moss, 2003: 202).

In order for care to become an expressive rather than simply an instrumental activity, physical care needs to be transformed into caring care. To illustrate this point we might think about how we get children up in the morning. We could stand outside their room and knock on their door, shouting at them to get up or we could go into their room open their curtains and ruffle their hair. The former approach might achieve its aim of ensuring that a child or young person gets up, the latter might speak of this transformation of physical care into caring care. Some children may only need and/or prefer a less personalised wake-up call and it is important to pause and reflect on such matters before barging in. The true expression of personalized care is a carer's ability to tune into what is right for particular young people.

Care ethics build from the work of Carol Gilligan (1993) and Holland (2009), reinforced by Steckley & Smith (2011) who reaffirmed that men and women adopt different approaches to moral reasoning. A male voice speaks more often of rules and principles thereby foregrounding a justice orientation. By contrast, the female voice reinforces qualities of compassion and intuition, what Gilligan termed a care voice (1993). For this reason, care ethics are often thought of as feminist ethics. Care ethics would suggest that the dominant approach to public care is a justice one, based around rights and principles. It is helpful to be reminded that care ethics, on the other hand, emphasise responsibilities and relationships instead of rules and rights. Pausing to think and reflect on care ethics highlights the ways in which ethics are bound to concrete situations with specific young people, not just pondering abstract principles (Sevenhuijsen, 1998). Likewise Tronto, identifies care as "*a practice, rather than a set of rules or principles.... It involves both particular acts of caring and a "general habit of mind" to care* (1994: 126-7). Anyone who has spent much time in out-of-home care or with young people who have grown up in such settings will identify workers who demonstrated a general habit of mind to care and those who didn't.

According to Held, "*a caring person not only has the appropriate motivations in responding to others or in providing care but also participates adeptly in effective practices of care*" (2006: 4). Participation in caring practices goes some way towards distinguishing between the respective roles of direct care workers and social workers. It is useful to pause and reflect on the differences between '*caring about*' and '*caring for*' Noddings (1984; 2002). 'Caring about' involves having a view or taking a stance on an issue; it does not require the provision of direct care but reflects a general predisposition to see that all children are well treated. But 'caring about' isn't enough on its own. One can profess to care about something without getting one's hands dirty in the messy business of 'caring for'. In this respect, Noddings (1984) argued that '*caring about*' can involve a certain benign neglect. 'Caring about' it is empty if it does not result in '*caring relations*'. ' Caring about' isn't enough on its own.

You pause and reflect – if only in seconds – before intervening with a young person, remember that you are not reacting to this young person!

You are about to respond pro-actively after careful thought and reflection! Tronto and Fisher (1990) and Tronto (1994) argued that care giving on its own is not enough. It must give conscious thought to care receiving and the many ways in which care is a two-way process involving reciprocal relationships. Current policy tends to enlist social workers and carers to dispense care and protection services, thereby reinforcing a view of young people as largely passive recipients of care. It denies the active involvement of youths in caring relationships and the many ways in which agency management shaping their experiences of care. An appreciation of care as reciprocal brings with it an awareness of the complex psychodynamic processes that emerge within out-of-home care relationships. It requires that all in the team parenting team consider that what might work best in one situation between a particular child and a particular worker might not work in another. Practice needs to be grounded in this particular out-of-home care placement and the particular relationships that are operating between a young person and her or his Carers.

PAUSE. THINK ABOUT, AND REFLECT ON
10 EXTERNAL OUTCOMES THAT MATTER

Support
Carer Support
Positive Communication
Caring Relationships
Supportive Environments
Carer's Involvement in Learning

Empowerment
Safety
Service to Others

Boundaries and Expectations
Boundaries for Daily Living
High Expectations
Constructive Use of Time
Activity Programmes

AND

10 INTERNAL OUTCOMES THAT MATTER

Commitment to Learning
Motivation to Achieve
Engaging in Learning
Learning Opportunities and Homework

Positive Values
Responsibility
Caring
Honesty

Social Competencies
Planning and Decision-Making
Peaceful Conflict Resolution

Positive Identity
Personal Power
Positive View of Personal Future

Questions for Small Group Discussion or Guided Reflection

1. Why is it important that social workers and youth workers pause and take time (if only a few seconds) to reflect on and analyze what may be going on before rushing in to intervene in a crisis with a young person in out-of-home care?
2. What was important in the Lexie narratives about her letter written to the State Governor?
3. When reviewing the Lexie narratives alongside the other Sisters of Pain narratives, what might it mean that so many of these young women were friends or comrades-in-arms at other institutions and those relationships continued into their later secure care placement?
4. What theory helps you better understand what may have been

happening in Lexie's life, the conflicts with members of her strict Mormon family, and the warning signals that foreshadowed risk-taking behaviour, such as that which resulted in her tragic death from an overdose?

5. Which of the 20 Outcomes that Matter does the evidence in the narratives show that Lexie was achieving, and what was that evidence?

Room 10
Lisa – *Preparation*

13 June: Two Statements that Lisa made during her Intake Interview

1. *I don't have problems with people.*
2. *I don't have no problems. You're making them all up.*

---

13 June: Placement Board Meeting Notes

1. Security Risk – Fear of New Situations
2. Needs structure and a predictable environment to develop social skills, self concept and self-awareness, and boundaries for daily living.
3. Moves in quickly with relationships.
4. Has trouble accepting responsibilities for difficulties. Feels destined to be rejected and have failures but doesn't see her power to influence what happens.
5. Can control anger. Lisa is quite a weak young woman who presents as a deprived child with limited social skills who withdraws into fantasy.
6. Expects rejection – needs success experiences.
7. Comes on initially with hostile or "don't understand" responses, largely as defensiveness to her own confusion
8. Not a short-term girl in all likelihood.

Lisa can make you angry folks, but watch that we don't jump on her too hard at first. She'll need a lot of support and tender loving care but a firm line. She's a high security risk along with about 5 or 6 other young women in the secure unit right now. Seek Lisa out! Good luck!

---

16 July: Summary of the Initial Planning Board Meeting

Lisa is a 15 year-old Caucasian girl committed by the Juvenile Court because of incorrigibility which included running away from home, truancies, and more recently prostitution during the months leading up to her commitment. As a thirteen year-old, Lisa left school following a disagreement with classmates, went home with a friend and refused to return to her mother's home. After placement back home with her mother, Lisa ran away again and located a licensed foster home for herself with a teacher in a local junior high school. A year later Lisa was picked up for loitering in the inner city, and subsequently returned to her mother's home. Placement was sought in a voluntary children's home but Lisa returned home immediately. Earlier this year, Lisa was sent to live in another town with her paternal aunt and uncle, but she was returned home within two months – reasons unspecified. Referral to the child and adolescent psychiatric inpatient service but Lisa was not accepted for care in that service.

Lisa is the second child born to her parents. Her older sister is said to have had more problems than Lisa and is currently living in a group home located near the city. Lisa was an unwanted child. Her mother has made it clear that she has never liked Lisa, did not want to have her and wants no contact with her at the present time. A year ago, Lisa's father committed suicide by carbon monoxide poisoning sitting in the car he parked in the garage of the family home just after Lisa's mother and he separated. A half-brother was struck by a car and killed 7 years ago when he was 6. The two of them had been out for a walk when he was hit by a car as they ran across a road outside their house. Family members blamed Lisa for her brother's death. She is described as having been the family scapegoat since birth.

In talking about her family, Lisa communicates hostile and depressed feelings. Lisa is clearly aware of her mother's feelings towards her and feels angry about it saying *"she should never have had a child she couldn't love"*. Lisa also cries when talking about the death of her younger brother. She blames herself and is said to have cried for days on end at school following her brother's death. Lisa indicates that she felt more affection from her father than from her mother, even though father is described as having been an abusive, unstable alcoholic by Lisa's mother.

Lisa was described as an alienated and deprived girl whose running away, incorrigibility and involvement in prostitution were a reflection of her alienation. Her loss of parent figures – whether through suicide or complete rejection – have left Lisa with a totally negative view of herself and the expectations which she carries into all new situations and relationships. Lisa expects to be rejected and hurt in some way or another. She has not had the usual childhood opportunities to help her learn basic ways of handling herself independently. Lisa views herself as having been hurt unfairly and feels little hope of regaining control of her life.

In summary, Lisa is an immature young woman who has experienced extensive emotional and social deprivation, with long-established feelings of rejection from her mother. She will need considerable support and tender loving care from female staff and we should encourage any kind of interpersonal contact Lisa can have with women. Female staff should seek Lisa out at any opportunity they have to help form relationships upon which further work can progress. They should be available but not become too involved in counseling until further notice. It is likely that a death theme will prevail in counseling efforts due to Lisa's witness to her brother's death and the crisis of her father's suicide. Physical and somatic complaint may be prevalent and these should be handled by women staff giving personal attention.

But try giving attention and TLC when physical complaints are not present, in hopes that Lisa will not have to use somatic complaints as a means of gaining attention. It's not that her physical complaints are "made up". This has become her only way of getting attention.

Lisa's school history has been marked with erratic attendance and multiple truancies. She was placed in mentally retarded classes at the start of primary school, and continues in 'slow learning' classes. Lisa lacks reading skills and finds difficulties with concentrating. She apparently learns through class discussion with teachers and peers. Lisa is achieving at 4th Grade level at present, and requires much of the teacher's time. She is usually quiet in class and works well, accepted by both peers and staff, and she presents no disciplinary problems. Lisa responds well on a one-on-one basis.

4 August: Social Worker Notes

We need to be working with Lisa on looking at how her mother brings her down and how Lisa can learn new ways of handling her mother in a way that doesn't ruin everything. This can come from talking with her about how she handled mother butting in before, and together work out possible new ways of handling such encounters in the future so as to not fall down. This is tough when mother is such a holy challenge! The question is: "What can you do differently when you know that Mom can mess you up better than anyone?"

1 September: Social Worker Notes

Lisa was laying out her "nobody understands me", "nobody talks to me" and "this place isn't helping me" stories with me today with limited success. I succeeded in making her angry with me! Somebody ought to pick up on this with Lisa and keep the ball rolling. Lisa says she is learning "bad" things here!

5 September: Letter from Grandmother

Dear Supervisor

Will you please order the pants and shoes that Lisa wants and send me the bill? If you tell me where you will be sending them, I can send you a check.

I am working now and can't get away to come over there again like I did last month.

If you would rather, you could send me her waist and hip measurements, and I can get them here and send them to Lisa.

I wrote and asked Lisa to send me her measurements but I guess she didn't understand what I wanted.

Thank you,

[Paternal Grandmother]

25 September: Summary of the Planning Board Meeting

Lisa has made a very slow and sporadic adjustment to life in the secure unit. She is quickly angered in the daily living program while seemingly making gains at school. She is very guarded in talking about her past, and almost refuses to discuss her past with staff. One incident occurred where there was confusion around a letter received from her grandmother when the social worker mistakenly said the letter was from her mother. Upon hearing that she had received "a letter from her mother", Lisa immediately came unglued and her behaviour deteriorated to the point where she had to be placed in her room to regain control of herself. Lisa explained that her social worker was making her go home to her mother and she would fight this under all circumstances. Her social worker had not even considered her going home to her mother! Later, when the confusion was settled, Lisa was invited to consider that a girl who expressed that much emotion and strong feelings around an incident such as this needs to resolve some of those issues "lying under the surface" or there could be ongoing problems like that in her future. Weekly sessions with the social worker were agreed.

6 October: Social Worker Notes

Today we had the best talk we've ever had. Each session opens up with Lisa having a go at me, and me having a go back at her. The primary theme that permeates everything else for Lisa is the undying hatred for her mother. She can now admit that her mother can tie her into knots by simply coming into Lisa's thoughts. This woman is like an octopus which tightens its tentacles around Lisa.

Added fuel for this hatred is her father's suicide and mother's endless list of boyfriends. Lisa's older sister and mother tried to blame father's suicide on Lisa. Our talks will be focusing on how Lisa can break away from her mother's "black-widow spider's web" that has trapped her. We'll also be exploring ways in which Lisa might manage her anger in different ways so that her mother can't say "I told you so!" This was a positive talk. Nothing about future plans but we are building a much stronger relationship and I'm gaining a better idea of what this kid has been through.

15 October: Social Worker Notes

We have continued to explore how her mother controls Lisa by getting her so angry that Lisa loses control. I'm trying to build on the idea that Lisa wants to be in control but must learn how to avoid getting trapped by the ways that her mother goes about throwing things at her, name calling, etc. Lisa seems to be slowly catching on to this idea that her mother is in control and seems to want to change this. We've even talked about how her mother controlled her father, right to the very end with his suicide in the garage, sitting in the family car. We agreed that Lisa would make a list of things that her mother does to make her angry. We may use that list to role play ways in which Lisa might "handle" her mother differently. I suggested that Mrs McG might help her with drawing up the list, and I later confirmed this arrangement with Mrs McG. Lisa isn't pushing to move fast, but is wondering if she might have escorted walks. I encouraged her to keep working on this thing with her mother and that in the long run, Lisa could be stronger and more in control than ever before. I support the escorted walks idea as it may give more opportunities for walking and talking in less formal circumstances. We are in no hurry for Lisa to leave the secure unit though!

16 October: Summary of the Planning Board Meeting

Since her last Board, Lisa has opened up in her relationships with staff in the cottage but she has also let down in her school performance. She is still letting her anger control her performance, both in daily living activities and in school. It is important that she gradually work towards stabilizing this. The focus of counseling that has been working quite well is getting Lisa to see that so long as her anger controls her behavior – especially anger aroused or triggered by her mother – then Lisa is not in control of her life. Instead, her life is controlled by her mother! This makes Lisa very angry and is also providing some added motivation for dealing with this anger. In daily living activities, remain watchful that Lisa doesn't get set up by her older and more sophisticated peers. At school, Lisa has good and bad days. She is very weak academically and could use a full-time tutor. She sometimes irritates her peers deliberately, when bored or wishing to avoid school work.

27 October

Dear [Social Worker]

Say – What's Happening?
Not much with me my way.
I'm still doing the same thing. I'm writing to know if Donnell can call me, or if I can call him. I just want to talk to him for awhile please.
Mr [Social Worker] I have been trying my best. But I don't think you know it, or see it.
I'm about ready to say fuck the whole thing.
The staff here tell me to be myself. And I am myself. So what now?
I tried to talk to the staff but they didn't have time for me. I have talked to one of the male staff.
Well, I have to go now because I have to eat my lunch, okay.

Love, Lisa

8 December: Social Worker Notes

Lisa was down in the dumps today, projecting blame on everyone and basically snarling at the whole world. She made a veiled suicide threat to which I responded by saying that I saw that as her copping out. She didn't seem to want to open up and start getting down to some "nitty-gritty" problem-solving so I excused her saying I would see her Tuesday morning before the Board. One thing that is really holding her back is the fact that she has very little or maybe nothing to work towards in the form of a goal. Without something, what's the use? We may want to try and find a volunteer who could come see Lisa and do some activity on a weekly basis. What do you all think?

8 December: Care Worker Notes

Lisa's jaw was on her shoe tops tonight. As low as I have ever seen her to be. Threatening suicide to me also, but this was in no way veiled! I too, called it the "Grand Cop-out" gesture which did not set too well with Lisa.

She claimed, "this place is driving me crazy and I can't take much more of it!"

Lisa barely maintained composure throughout our talk and finally was able to cry. I merely sat and talked quietly reassuring to her as much as I could. She got herself back in hand after about 15 minutes. Even though Lisa knows she was an unwanted and unexpected child, she claimed that the reminder today had really started her on the skids.

She was able to unload some pent-up emotions and was in pretty good condition by bedtime. I completely agree with that idea about finding a volunteer! We have gotta come up with some sort of a goal that is attractive to Lisa and that she sees as attainable. Repeatedly in our conversations with Lisa, she says she has "nothing to look forward to". Without some incentive, this kid is not gonna move very much.

11 December: Summary of the Planning Board Meeting

Lisa has come a long way since her last Board although she still seems to be having some bad dreams about her father and some questions about her real mother. She is asking to obtain her birth certificate so as to help her resolve some of these questions. Basically, Lisa is dealing with the issues of her past that have been of great concern to her. She has begun using relationships with staff to begin to deal with these matters. It is possible that in looking at placement options for the future, Lisa is looking to her mother's sister as a possible placement. When asked if this would cause difficulties between Lisa's mother and aunt, Lisa felt that it would not because Lisa's aunt has nothing to do with Lisa's mother. Overall we see much less of Lisa's snippy bitchiness and less smoke screening than before. She is much more able to approach adults directly and let them know what she wants to talk about. One last area of significant improvement has been the way Lisa has handled herself during the weekly group meetings. She is able to speak up in group now and is no longer the wall hanger as before. Lisa has been granted escorted walks and off-campus privileges with approved adults. At school, Lisa is making progress and normally handles herself well in class. She has off and on days. She's now feeling very comfortable, protected and cared for in the secure unit and she doesn't want to leave. When Lisa gets cranky, it's usually a "smoke screen" that something is bugging her, so give her support in working out what is bugging her.

23 December: Care Worker Notes

I've been playing social worker and hope I'm not intruding onto your "air space" — even if I did! Lisa showed me that Hospital Record of Birth you had given her and was giving the impression that she was sure she had some "secret" mother floating around the countryside since there was no parent identification other than Mr and Mrs [name of her parents]. Right away, Lisa had deduced that this Mrs was not her real mother after all, and the suspicions she held for a long time were at last confirmed. She was busily developing a fantasy wherein her "real" mother would come swooping down to the rescue.

On Friday, I went to the Bureau of Vital Statistics at the capital and obtained a copy of Lisa's birth certificate. I discussed this with my supervisor tonight and felt that Lisa should know the facts and get this situation settled, at least in her own mind. I gave Lisa her Birth Certificate and she now knows the situation as near to true as it can be ascertained.

She took it well and did not appear to be at all disturbed. We chatted briefly afterwards and she had pretty well accepted that her mother is her mother by the time we had finished.

27 January

Mr [Social Worker]

Say, what's been happening with your crazy self?

Well, ain't too much happening here, just that I still want to come back to [the secure unit] NOW!!!!!

Well Mr [Social Worker] I wanted to know if you would come to my new cottage to eat lunch with me please, on Wednesday January the 29th?

Will you be at work that day or not. If you are, please come. And don't forget, I said "please".

Sorry my writing is so sloppy. I'm busy so far, but not too busy to be writing you. We have to finish talking as much as I can.

Because I guess you know. Don't get me wrong, I'm trying my hardest to talk to staff here. But it's easier for me to talk to you (if you know what I mean).

I have to split because the staff here want to talk with me now. I'll see you later or at least I hope so.

Bye for now,
Lisa

Addendum

Lisa made steady progress and then went to live with her aunt back in the region of the State where she had lived previously. Nothing further is known about Lisa or her life after the institution. If Lisa is still alive today she would be celebrating her mid-fifties! We hope she flourished!

Aliese's Reflections

Wow. I don't remember Lisa, although many thoughts and images are floating in and out of my memory. Tragedy is my first thought. To know you are an unwanted child is the worst – the absolute worst. And obviously the mom was wound a little too tight. Jez! Lisa's life was surrounded by so much death and heartache – so close to home, and so young. Realize this kid was only 15 at this point and look at what life had brought to her so far. I would like to think she is a warrior today, just having survived all the events, placements, the tragedy of her father's suicide – it can take adults years to get through counselling on the suicide issues alone.

From notes on July 16th: "adolescent psychiatric inpatient service – but Lisa was not accepted for care in that service". In my opinion she was spared. God only knows what would have, could have happened to her there. Probably given high doses of Thorazine or shock treatment. Really? Like all of this was Lisa's fault? Poor little girl. She really had a tough start at life and she was very lucky indeed to have landed here.

Although the notes do not go into detail, I hope that she got that 'volunteer', that friend, during her stay, but also, later in her life as well. We all need a mentor, a hero, a confidante, and she needed someone who could make her feel useful, loved and wanted, even in a small way. I am sure that she did experience healthier relationships later in life, and it has always been my experience that people move in and out of lives for reasons beyond our understanding at that time. In the functional family, every member has a role to play. And we all needed to be needed, and to have a sense of belonging. That was a very common thread that ran through all my sisters' stories: we never felt we never felt like we belonged or that were we accepted. No one really engaged us, except to confront us, condemn us, or control us.

That basic foundation in your family unit is vital. You must be secure in knowing you are a part of the family, that you are valued, you have a voice, and that you are loved. Feeling unwanted, unloved, abandoned – those are very difficult emotions for anyone to process, let alone a scared little girl – it just breaks my heart. Sad thing is, the mom was just as much a scared little girl as her daughter, with her own issues, fears and heartbreaks. I am sure it took Lisa a long time to wrestle with these facts of her life and to tuck them away someplace safely at a distance. Yet while she needed to do that for her own sanity and growth, how could she do so immediately, and how could she escape mentally for a short time, while this was being absorbed? There was no place she could run to and hide and she felt very trapped in herself, and at the high security unit. It is a tough place to be and your insides are just screaming to get out.

It gives me hope that she was able to form a friendship with her social worker, that is such a great start in overcoming life's many challenges – to recognize them, talk them over or figure them out … she just needed to get 'dialled in', so to speak. You don't form friendships if you are feeling worthless and unwanted – so I know she was dealing with that aspect of her life which was a great feat. Lisa discovered she held value and that she had choices. I am happy that she was able to move on to her aunt's – who "had nothing to do with her mom". It is probably a good thing.

Preparation

Having noticed what's 'out there' as well as 'in there' for each young person, and having also paused and reflected for a few moments about what might be going on for that young person, youth workers and social workers may be less likely to rush in and try to do something or intervene without adequate preparation. Some don't stop to think about what they're going to do next so as not to stop the flow of whatever is going on. However, one cannot drive a car (very well anyway) without some preparation. The same holds for learning to and just having fun playing a guitar, rollerblading, whistling, and so forth. If we are to perform any skill(s) with competence, then a whole lot of preparation is required to perform well, or even perform well enough.

"*Chance favours the prepared mind*" or so argued 19th Century 'germ–fighter' Louis Pasteur. Preparation – of almost any kind – provides opportunities to consider a wider range of potential interventions and "chance" opportunities that may arise. If we have given ourselves even a few seconds – to pause, reflect and prepare for our potential intervention(s) with a young person – then the chances of a successful outcome from such interventions are dramatically enhanced. Good enough parenting is similar in that it requires a lot of thought and preparation if we are to do our best.

Preparation of self, engaging active self-awareness, and preparing one's 'self' are all about getting ready. Breathe deeply, take a second, rehearse in your mind's eye how the next few seconds or minutes might go. Some call this 'cognitive framing', and Olympic sports competitors are taught to use visualizing as part of their mental preparations: to go through such a process once again, seconds before starting their event. Ward argued "*our self is our primary tool of practice – it is the means through which we experience and conduct our practice, including the psychological and emotional demands which practice entails*" (2010: p. 1). This practice scholar went on to explain how the term 'self' is at times used as a shorthand for different personality and identity characteristics, including our personal beliefs, values, anxieties and attitudes. Preparation of self prior to an intervention involves a combination of rational and intuitive views about the way this life-space and the people in it operate, and thus how we can interact

243

with them in a purposefully therapeutic manner. If we notice what is happening out there, we can also quickly notice what is happening inside us. Has our breathing quickened, our pulse rate increased, do our mouths feel dry, or are our palms now sweating? Active self-awareness is about doing a quick mental and emotional "stock-take" in the seconds of preparation available before intervening. Active self-awareness also involves a continuous monitoring of what is going on inside me whilst simultaneously engaging actively with a young person or family members as an intervention unfolds. How do I read what's going on with this young person as I prepare to intervene?

During those brief moments of preparatory reflection, give some thought to what *alternative interventions* – perhaps holding back – might be most tailored to this young person or group of young people at this moment in time. It is useful to remember that what you think of first is not always your best option. Spend at least a couple of seconds questioning "*What else could I do?*" Quickly reflect on "*How might this young person interpret my intervention?*" This lets me speculate anyway about what meaning she or he is making about the events leading up to this moment. I may question myself briefly as to whether this is really the right time for this particular intervention? Timing is a very important. Are my intended interventions likely to wind children up immediately before bedtime? How might snacks just before mealtimes benefit this young person? What about saying "No" to 'hanging out' with peers because you know that homework hasn't been done. Maybe it could become a shared effort with coffee and biscuits? The central questions are "*How available is this young person to engage with me right now*"? And "*What might I need to do in order to help her or him stay connected with me through the particular intervention(s) I propose initiating?*"

Preparation through anticipatory reflection involves scanning through a mental checklist, *noticing – out there and in here*. Simultaneously I am reviewing what knowledge or experiences I might possibly draw upon which could help me to make this a therapeutic intervention or developmental moment of opportunity for this young person and her or his family members. Such an orientation puts 'self' centre stage each time we move from the preparation phase into purposeful intervention(s). Too often we resort to "default behaviour(s)" and do that which has become a habit or that to which we are accustomed. Habitualized behaviour is highlighted whenever we hear someone say *"it's just the way we do things around here"*. Often it's what we do because that's the way we've always done it. Maybe we haven't thought about doing it any other way – whatever "it" may be. When there is a rule that says X and the consequence of breaking the rule is Y, there are likely to be far fewer daily life events that become transformed into developmental opportunities with young people or adult carers and social workers. Social workers and youth workers will often benefit from discarding their first idea about how to intervene and come up with other options. This doesn't mean that one ignores one's 'gut instincts'. It's just that some 'quick intuitive responses' are more influential and overwhelming than others. That is why pausing to reflect and take even seconds to review options will enhance the quality of relational care provided. What other interventions might also work? Anticipatory reflection is central to good preparation for working with children or young people in out-of-home care.

Community youth work and working with families of children or young people in out-of-home care all benefit from relational work with individual young people or family members. As the number of people involved in some intervention activity increases, so it follows that better preparation is required, even at short notice. Noticing – Out There and In Here – involves a process of cognitive scanning. Pausing to reflect is important – if only for a few seconds – realising that there are usually more seconds available anyway. No matter how quickly, it is important to analyze what is going on here, and asking myself what information will assist me to make better sense of what is happening here and to understand the context in which it is happening. What was happening immediately before and what is happening now? It might be of real value to invite the young person or group of youths to share what they think is going on here. Remember, reflective practice is an active process. One may not stop everyone and say, wait a minute, "I'm thinking". However, invitations to share our thinking together – to share in meaning-making about what we think may be going on here – can often be very beneficial to all parties. Preparation for intervention(s) must be time-limited. Praxis – or *theory-into-practice* – involves action, and Caring is an Action Verb!

Questions for Small Group Discussion or Guided Reflection

1. In what ways might anticipatory reflection assist youth workers or social workers to intervene more purposefully and effectively with young people living in out-of-home care?

2. How might you prepare for initial social work or youth work intervention(s) with Lisa after reading her opening statement: *"I don't have no problems. You're making them all up"*?

3. What preparation might be required to help newly appointed social workers or youth workers engage with a young person like Lisa whose mother never wanted her and whose father committed suicide?

4. 19th Century helper Louis Pasteur asked his professional colleagues *"Did you ever observe to whom the accidents happen? Chance favours the prepared mind!"* How might a prepared mind help social workers and youth workers improve the quality of services they provide to young people in out-of-home care?

5. How is it that noticing "out there" and "in here" can be helpful preparation for intervention(s) with children or young people in out-of-home care?

Room 11
Tanya – Intervention(s)

2 July: Notes on a Sheet of Paper in the File

1.   *My Mouth*
2.   *My Attitude*
3.   *My Temper*

Tanya

24 July: Notes on Another Sheet of Paper in the File

Don't trust people

Tanya

---

25 July: Summary of the Initial Planning Board Meeting

Tanya is a sixteen and a half year old young woman of mixed Afro-American and German heritage. She was born in Germany and has been a "military brat" for most of her life. Tanya is said to have run away from home at least five times in Germany before the family moved to the USA, and then turned herself in to authorities as a runaway here in the State. She was committed by the juvenile court for running away, shoplifting and attempted suicide.

Tanya comes from a rather confusing family background where her father is Black and spent 20 years in the Army before entering civilian life back home in the States. Her mother is a German Caucasian who had a difficult time adjusting to a new culture and dealing with an aggressively acting out daughter. Since coming to the US, mother has felt very much an isolate in the community and may have displaced her depression and frustration about the family situation onto Tanya.

Tanya's mother was described by a former social worker as "a pathetic, non-likeable, self-centered woman who regards her daughter as being responsible for making her experience a bad marriage and for having a difficult time in America". Tanya's father has been out of the home for long periods on tour, leaving his immigrant German wife with sole responsibilities for parenting Tanya and helping her make the transitions from Germany to the US.

Both parents claim that they had no real problems with Tanya until they moved to the US where she was suddenly confronted with the conflicts of her mixed parentage and became very confused about her own identity. Tanya readily identifies herself with Black American culture rather than her mother's German background. This is the only child in the family.

Tanya's father is said to be the more sensitive, cooperative parent who seemed, at interview, to be more in tune with his daughter's feelings and frustrations than the mother. However, father tended to vest Tanya with a lot of power and then sit back and watch the fights between Tanya and her mother. Father often appeared impatient with his wife and indicated his disagreement with her on several occasions through facial gestures. Mother tended to be more emotionally uninvolved with her daughter. Mother presents as basically a very angry person who is frequently burdened with depression.

27 August: Social Worker Notes

Tanya's fighting attitude seems to be cooling a bit and the result looks to be bringing the underlying depression to the surface. We must all be watchful of how Tanya is handling this depression! She has definite suicide potential and we should move in to help her identify what feelings are present and what may account for these feelings.

7 September: Social Worker Notes

We drained off considerable emotion today in my session with Tanya. I'm pleased at how she is progressing thus far and particularly how staff are working to hold her to expectations, challenging Tanya, supporting her and chewing her out when needed. The most notable factor was how Tanya is pushing and prodding herself with expectations of her own creation.

We explored Tanya's need to always have something happening around her in order to feel alive and real. The only times where Tanya has felt content in the past were brief periods with either Mother or Father. Beyond these brief periods, there has been continual tension in Tanya's interactions with others.

It is worth noting that this is the longest that Tanya has ever been in one place with the same people. There are times when Tanya feels that she is going to explode and this frightens her. In past occasions when such feelings have come, Tanya would try to run away or attempt suicide. She appears to be holding herself in fairly tight control which is okay at this point but we could see a deterioration and loss of control, and then potential growth beyond that before we are finished.

Please Note: Be alert to the suicidal risks for Tanya in the event that things begin to fall apart. I don't foresee this at the present time but it is good to remain alert.

Finally, I indicated that it will take some time to lay the foundations for better communications between Tanya and her parents. The months and years which led to the present breakdown in communication could not be realigned in a few weeks time. Some sort of beginning on that task will need to be made before Tanya could realistically move to open campus. Tanya accepted this with resignation but agreed that it was a realistic proposal. This may take awhile!

Undated:

Don't Try to Remember

Momma
Don't try to remember me for what I was.
But try to remember me for the good I've done
And for the good times we've had.

One day I hope
That I'll be home once again.
And things will be good.
Because as I sit here, I see my faults.

And although it will take some time.
I'll change.
And you'll see
A brand new me.

So please don't try to remember me for what I was.
Try to remember me for the good things I did and the good memories
we've had.
For one day soon I hope to be home
And we'll have good times once again.

Tanya

9 September: Notes from Family Meeting

Mother was invited to review what she has seen in Tanya's behaviour during the past three years. From what mother says, Tanya has been playing Mom against Dad ever since she moved to the US from Europe. Dad seemed to believe Tanya and take her side of the stories, right up to when she went to Juvenile Court. Finally, when he went to the Court, he began seeing just how much Tanya had been lying to him. Tanya started "hating" her Dad when he finally turned to the Juvenile Court. Mother explained that Tanya has been almost totally "boy crazy" and this carries over into almost all of her relationships with males. It was generally a good visit and we met briefly with Tanya and her mother before she left. I explained that Tanya would do well to be talking with her mother about important issues at home, and not just her preoccupation with boys.

3 October: Summary of the Planning Board Meeting

Tanya seems to have begun to settle although she continues to have difficulties with both peer group and staff relationships. She has a quick temper and a sharp tongue which often gets her into trouble. During this initial period, Tanya has tried to come across as a very conforming, nice and cooperative girl but increasingly she has found it difficult to cover the depression and anger associated with much of her starting to act out in the first place.

Tanya's mother has visited on several occasions and met with the social worker on one occasion thus far. Mother came across as a cooperative woman who was genuinely interested in Tanya's well-being but is fearful lest Tanya be sent home too early. One visit has been held where father and mother were present with Tanya. This visit was initially described by Tanya as being a super visit. But later it was found that the visit was anything but good.

Following this visit with mother and father together, Tanya requested a "room program" as things had begun to mount up and reach the intolerable level for this young woman. Tanya was authorized to remain in her room during all periods other than school and recreation. She would counsel in a one-to-one relationship with one of the care workers, Mr T. Tanya used her time on this room program constructively where she sought to write about the feelings and thoughts she has had about her life and her family circumstances. Tanya's anger persisted although she was able to avoid peer and daily living expectations while being in this room program.

At school, Tanya participates well in activities. She is very quiet during Health class. In Biology she has mouth problems, is lazy, presents as conceited and her work is mediocre. Tanya is capable in English but lazy, only showing animation during class discussions. In World History, her work is average but she needs constant reminders to settle down. She requires structure to engage in learning. She is progressing slowly in Typing but hates to keep her mind on the subject preferring to stick her nose where it doesn't belong.

28 November: Summary of the Planning Board Meeting

Tanya appears to have come a long way since her last Review Board. She has been able to talk with Mr T at considerable length about significant events in her past and how she felt about them. She has used this one-to-one time quite effectively. However, while she can talk about her problems, knows what the problems are, and how she feels about them – she is still unable to put this learning into practice in her current circumstances. She appears to be handling more effectively the periods of depression to which she was prone in the past. Tanya still remains a very demanding girl who spouts caustic remarks to both staff and peers when she is upset. There have been marginal improvements at school across all subjects. The focus of attention needs now to focus on skills in daily living with others. In coming weeks, Tanya should be encouraged to relate and counsel with all staff. Hold her to expectations in daily living and make Tanya do things for herself. If she is snippy, sarcastic and out of sorts, invite her to use a brief period of room time to regain composure. Then she returns back into daily living activities as soon as possible. Think of how sometimes a young child needs a brief "time out" break from all the frenzy.

3 January: Social Worker Notes

Tanya confronted me about why she didn't get her walks at the Board meeting yesterday, so I took the opportunity to try and clear the air between us. I told her that I thought she had been angry at me since her last Board meeting when I told her that her actions spoke louder than her words.

We reviewed four instances where Tanya had been in disagreement with someone, and I asked if she had done anything about the disagreements. From there on, our talk went well. For the first time I got to see the spontaneous laughter that others have spoken about.

I explained that walks were not granted by the Board because of the ups and downs in her behavior of late. I explained that if I could see her managing herself in a more responsible manner around daily living routines over the next couple of weeks then that would be the evidence. During that time, I didn't want to see or hear about Tanya asking staff about how well she was doing and whether she would get her walks approved by the Board.

We agreed that I would be keeping track of how Tanya was getting on with her newly-found skills for daily living with others. I encouraged her to do the same. It was confirmed that we would talk again in a fortnight's time to see how things were going. That would influence whether I spoke in favor of Tanya getting her walks approved at the next Board meeting.

4 January,

Dear Tamorra[1]

Hi. Well, this wasn't too bad a day. The lights went out and I lost the setting in my ring but I found it.

I got in a hassle with SM cuz I asked to borrow a cigarette and she said no. I said it was pretty funny when I was down to my last 2 packs and I lent her one. Then I end up without cigarettes for another week cus she didn't get her's and my parent's didn't come. So I told her to never ask me for a

---

1   Dated letters written to Tamorra appeared without warning on a daily basis during this period of Tanya's stay in the secure unit. Tamorra was a fictional character to whom Tanya communicated events and her thoughts and feelings about daily living experiences.

smoke again, even if I got 3 cartons full and she ain't got none!

Well, I made last night! Thank goodness. Hope I make it next week.
Well got to go.

Tanya

5 January,

Dear Tamorra

Hi. Well we stripped floors today. I didn't know how so helped L and then she helped me.

My parents didn't come. What a bitch! That means they won't be here for another week. And I'm out of cigarettes. That means it's going to be a bad week, cuz I'm always nervous and mean when I don't have a cigarette.

So I think if I get put in my room, I might stay in Saturday morning cuz I won't have late night and I want to start the week over.

But then I might not. It all depends. I'll go into my room for my comments though. So next week I can have it all clear.

Just have to wait and see. So, till later.

Tanya

6 January: Diary

To Whom It May Concern

I feel like there is no end to this place.

Today BB and some of her pals were talking about me. I know they all dislike me. So I have secluded myself to the Laundry Room for 2 reasons: (a) cuz my room is cold and here beside the dryer that's on, it's quite warm; and (b) because I am on light restrictions in my room till tomorrow night and here I can write with light.

Today was quite an awful day. My parents didn't come so I am without cigarettes and nobody wants to loan me any.

TJ said I owed her a pack and I really didn't. But she continued to say I did. I knew she was lying. She finally found me about 4 cigarettes and that was it. KS and BB swore I did owe TJ a pack of cigarettes. They always say I do things wrong. As it goes everybody believes them so nobody loans me cigarettes.

As far as BB and KS are concerned, I dress wrong, put my make-up on all wrong and anything I do is wrong. So I just stay away from them cuz they're always talking behind my back.

I feel very alone here. It feels like a prison alone in the desert where there is nobody there but me.

Sometimes I wonder if I'll ever see the world again. In my mind I see nothing. It is also empty. I feel as if I'm going insane. Perhaps I am. The world is not different. I am.

The world I seek is of a different nature – a life with love and happiness without end. But on this planet, there is "an end" and I have no way of stopping it. Can it be true that there is happiness somewhere?

I question this, just as I question the love people have for one another. Let's take my parents. How do they show their love for me?

I feel myself in a world of too many hurts, fears and hate to understand the true meaning of love. I know I cannot love. Isn't it strange how one can be lead into one's self by others? What forces they add to your life.

It shall be known one day that it was for the peace within one's own self that I secluded myself. For peace is slow arriving and I can barely find it within my own self.

As of today and maybe tomorrow, it will be for ever gone, or at a new place tomorrow.

Should this diary not get finished, let it be known that I have finally found love and happiness in the world. I have wished for this for so long.

Tanya

7 January

Dear Tamorra

Hi. Well today wasn't such a hot shot day.

The teacher put me in my room from school so there wasn't too much to say. I slept all morning, didn't eat lunch then ate candy all afternoon. I spent the afternoon cleaning out my folders and getting you straight too.

I've been dying for a cigarette all day and I finally got one from BB tonight when I went to the bathroom. I smoked some of it, now I'm just about ready to smoke the other half. I keep telling myself to wait.

I hope I get my cigarettes soon cuz I get tired of asking for shorts. Half the time, everybody says no. When I get my cigarettes, I'll be paying back what I owe and nothing else. I ain't going to give out any to anyone. I'm going to treat them the same way they treat me – "Shitty".

I do hope my parents come this weekend, for sure. Can't keep feeling sorry for myself. Maybe it will be better tomorrow (smile).

Well, I think I'm going to smoke that cigarette. Sometimes I feel like I'm addicted to these things.

Got to go. I'll talk more tomorrow. … Oh, I get my light on again. Love,

Tanya

Dear Tamorra

Hi. Well I got out of my room. School went okay today. But KS tried her hardest to get me in the ass with her. She almost succeed in doing so had it not been for Mr H. KS is not the best thing to waste my time on. I should know better. Guess I'm slowly learning.

There's something strange going on. It seems that every time I ask BB for a cigarette in private, like when I'm in my room or right before I go to bed, it's cool. But when I'm in the open cottage, she always says no. I think she is with all the other girls in the cottage. But it's cool.

I sure wish I was home. I'm going to work my damnedest to get out of this hole. Tomorrow Boards. I wonder if I'll get my walks? Probably not. I'll just have to be consistent for another week although I already blew it once.

Still, I'm going to keep on trying. Maybe I'll still get them.

So much for the day. It was weird but I pulled through. So until tomorrow, be cool, just like me.

Tanya

10 January

Dear Tamorra

Hi. I'm in my room. But I decided to stay in, for a number of reasons.

KS, CS and BB are accusing me of stealing their cigarettes, which I didn't do.

And I'm kind of upset about my parents.

I'm really not sure what my father meant. Whether it was that he wasn't coming up anymore, or whether he is, and he is just trying to help me. I talked to Mr [Social Worker] and he's going to call them.

All I can do is hope for the best. I'm going to come out of my room tomorrow and hope for the best. I have just got to get myself together and get myself Out.

Talk with you tomorrow.

Tanya

13 January

Dear Tamorra

Hi. Well my parents didn't come and it wasn't slick, just a little rain. I don't think I've been so hurt since I was little – well 14 was young – and I tried to kill myself. Don't worry, I'm not going to kill myself. They're not worth it. But I do wonder how much they care about me sometimes.

I think I'm just about ready to tell everyone to go to hell. At least I can still talk to you. Sometimes you aren't much help. Still, writing to you is better than just keeping everything bottled up inside.

The telephone just rang but it was CS's parents. Huh. I wonder if my parents are ever coming. Sometimes I feel like telling them just to fuck off. But that's not going to help matters any. So I'll just hang around, wait and hope for the best.

Until later, I'll finish this.

Tanya

2 February: Care Worker Notes

Mr F and I took Tanya and ED into the school room this evening so they could fire their broadsides at each other concerning the using of peers, threatening behavior and alleged run talk which has been going on.

Surprisingly enough there were few fireworks, with both girls conducting themselves reasonably well. Tanya was more voluble but without anger for a change. ED came across more forcefully – even truculent a couple of times.

As expected, the entire drama was created out of hearsay, misinterpretations, gossip and, in the case of the cigarette deal, some very poor judgment on the part of Tanya. Since there was disparity in the stories each girl told, all three girls involved were invited to spell out their side of the story. Later, all three girls and both staff participated in a free exchange of ideas and the girls expressed some of their personal feelings about each other.

Tanya was allowed to tell her version first. She had loaned a pack of cigarette to VC with the stipulation that she not give any to ED because "I didn't want to see VC get 'used' by ED". Tanya was asked why she singled out ED since at one time or another, almost all peers had "used" one or another. Tanya not really prepared to answer that one. She did, however, admit that others had been guilty of "using" girls and this included herself.

She offered the rather lame reason being that "maybe if Jenette only got to smoke half of the pack herself, she would not pay a full pack back in return". Tanya went on to confess, however, that this was not really a valid reason.

Then Tanya told of a single incident when she interpreted it as ED "demanding" that Jenette get her a cigarette. While she had not personally observed any repetition of similar behaviour on ED's part, other girls had told that they had seen it.

ED was then allowed to rebut. She admitted the incident to which Tanya had referred and she thought it quite likely that there had been similar occurrences. But there had been no intent to "demand" on her part. "That's just the way I come across with people I know and I don't mean anything by it". (Jenette later confirmed this when she came in.) ED could see where others might easily misinterpret her behaviour as bossiness or an attempt to control.

I thought it would be a good idea to invite Jenette to tell her side of the story again. She handled it very well indeed. There was no sign of fear or uneasiness, although Jenette did show some anger a time or two.

Once the cigarette thing had been cleared up, Jenette commented on her relationship with ED. They understood each other very well and she is thoroughly accustomed to ED's mannerisms, so much so that she doesn't even consider them consciously anymore. ED never "demands" things or "orders me around" said Jenette, "I know where she's coming from and she knows where I'm at".

About this time Tanya was looking as though she wished the entire incident would disappear and that she had kept her big mouth shut. Jenette then stated rather angrily that she knew there was some animosity coming towards her from the group and she felt it was because she was White and ED was Black.

There followed a general discussion about the errors in judgment and how each of the three girls had been guilty of drawing the wrong conclusions.

Mr F reminded the three girls that staff were called upon to evaluate girls based on our observations day to day, and this has a lot to do with how decisions get made about their futures. It was obvious that ED (and perhaps the other two) had not ever considered this important aspect of daily life events here.

There is no question in my mind that this session was valuable and therapeutic in a degree. As partial evidence, I offer the fact that all three girls sort of gravitated together during the evening and seemed completely at ease, pleased with each other's company. There was some sharing of worldly goods but to a greater degree, an exchange of thoughts and ideas.

25 March: Summary of the Review Board Meeting

In the time that Tanya has been within the secure unit program we have seen considerable movement from an angry, demanding young child towards a more responsible and controlled young woman. Ongoing work will need to take account of (1) her mixed parentage (mother White and father Black); (2) her considerable challenges in peer relationships; and (3) the apparent instability in her former life as an only child growing up in multiple places overseas and her father's military lifestyle.

Most significantly, Tanya has been able to face how important it is to have people to care about and who will care about her. This, perhaps more than any other factor, has motivated Tanya to begin working out problems with her parents and start learning how to get along with others.

She is recommended for transfer to an open campus program that offers a peer-oriented living environment that offers caring support for Tanya while at the same time holding her to basic expectations for daily group living.

Tanya is managing school classes on campus fairly well. Teachers report that she is capable and for the most part doing well.

In daily group living, Tanya has shown gains in all areas. She still has two major problems – the need to get her family situation worked out and her nose/mouth combination. Tanya has a pretty good handle on the family situation and recognizes that this will not be something resolved easily. Neither will it be settled overnight. Tanya claims that her father has informed her that it will be up to others and Tanya to work things out to their mutual satisfaction. This places it directly on Tanya – where it belongs.

Tanya still has nose trouble, but she is less inclined to butt into the affairs of others quite so often. This is not to say her "nose trouble" has disappeared entirely, but Tanya has made some real effort to eliminate this habit. She still has that tendency to make comments when silence would be a better option, but improvement here has also been noted.

Tanya responds best to a combination of warmth and firmness – each in about equal measures. Tanya has learned to listen – probably the major accomplishment she has achieved; and the most difficult! She remains an extremely independent girl in both thinking and actions, and we see this as a plus in her favour. She has been able to fully retain her independent nature while finding herself at the same time.

Tanya has lost a great deal of the animosity and distrust she held upon entry. Rather than holding such strong feelings of "I'll get even" or "I'll show you Bastards", Tanya now appears to be motivated by what is best for Tanya. She now certainly shows a more realistic attitude towards all aspects of her situation.

Those who watched Tanya in House Group last week were greatly impressed – not only by what she said, but how she came across while saying it. Quite a different picture from how we have been accustomed to seeing Tanya interact in the resident group since arriving nine months ago.

A Few Months Later: Board Evaluation of Myself

Being as this is the first evaluation I am making of myself, I am not sure it's very good. That's because I don't really know what to say. I hope you can accept it and understand.

I entered [open campus] cottage on March 26. I was scared to death, of boys, staff and girls. I was afraid they wouldn't accept me the way I am. That way is straightforward and very mature at times, whereas at other times I am very silly and immature.

On the other hand, I was afraid of staff because it has always been hard for me to trust adults, especially new ones. But I tried. I figured I had to do it for my own sake. So I talked and messed around with staff and found it wasn't so bad. I also found that I really liked some of the staff in my new cottage and got close with Mrs A and Mrs G.

But something inside was crying for this overwhelming feeling of loss. At first I didn't want to admit it to myself or staff what the problem was. But really I knew and it was bringing me down. I started doing deodorant and although it was just one day, it was enough to almost kill me. It also brought me into a depression like I have never really experienced before. Not even back in [the secure unit].

That's when I came out with all my hurts. My main one was because I had to leave Mr B and Mrs S, my favorite adults who had helped bring me through the roughest part of my life. These are the people I learned to trust and love, more than my own parents. They just had that special touch I think every kid should have. I've also got worries at home, of not trusting new adults, and of disliking girls.

Gradually I got out of it and started getting my head together again. I started accepting people for what they are – People. I'm starting to trust people here and am dealing positively with my problems. I'm also starting my furloughs home which I think is just great. I feel things are going to work out as long as I keep an open and positive mind – which I plan to do.

Tanya

Addendum

Tanya carried on with furloughs home and these continued into post-institutional placement back home. She had come a long way since the day she arrived as a snarling, angry young woman transforming into a thoughtful – if at times self-doubting – young woman of mixed-race ancestry. Tanya was bright. We hope she was able to keep things together emotionally and learned to manage her "nose problem". If so, it wouldn't surprise us to learn of Tanya having achieved a lifetime of successes during the past forty years.

Aliese's Reflections

Tanya speaks of forces in her life, and how people hold the power over us. It is so today….and we have to surround ourselves with that which is good, peaceful, calming, like-minded, uplifting and so on. We do not function at a proper level as human beings, with the constant bombardment of negative people, people's problems, the constant hammering of every hateful or hurtful word that your heart absorbed and your mind remembered. Your head could explode with all the negative input, or for that matter, I find, too much of any input. Indeed! I need my down time, and we all do. It is a learned survival skill, a sabbatical, even a meditative or religious experience. It can be. So there is wisdom in removing one's self from the wolf pack on occasion. Referring to one point, where she pulled herself away from the group to focus on herself after she found a little piece of herself in her environment. Tanya was paying attention, and she was smart and quick to adjust, if she wanted. Often the influences of the group were a daily battle and challenge that we would have to deal with, in addition to the reason WHY we were incarcerated. It could be a breeding ground for trouble.

Getting close to people is what gives them the power over us – again, that is true today as adults. It still makes us vulnerable. Tanya was obviously a bright young lady to recognize this. It takes time just to get settled into a new place, new people-who control your whole life. Imagine asking whether you could walk down a hallway, or have an escorted walk outside which was an earned privilege. I personally had a

REAL hard time with that type of authority and control. So it sinks in, you are "stuck" with a whole new set of rules, people who are in direct control of your immediate future, and of course, THE girls – with whom you are now forced to reside. This is not some day trip soon to be over and you have no idea how long this place will be your new home. Everything is foreign to you, and everything is about to change.

The whole cigarette saga showed how it didn't take much of a spark in a place like that to unravel all your hard work. It was easy to land yourself back in trouble and involved with the hostilities that could spread like wild fire. Sometimes it took a lot of hard work to keep our own mojo working, or our balance. I am sure this is one of those typical situations where most staff in other facilities would have exasperated and thrown their arms up in the air. While it seemed so trivial, by taking the time and working through this entanglement, there were some exchanges of thoughts and ideas that came to light and represented a huge breakthrough!

Such pivotal moments are when people need to get busy, meaning to get involved, stay the course and not abandon one another – which tragically is frequently the norm. It is where parents, teachers and society have let down children with repercussions rippling through many generations. Through such critical moments we learn to communicate, process conflict, seek to clarify our confusion, review our decision making, learning to trust ourselves and hopefully one day, to trust others. Society is heavily laden with this burden of failure, generation after generation.

With the established American military bases overseas, it may have been that Germany was a lot more "tuned in" to mixed marriages noting that Tanya went through pure hell when her father was transferred back to the States with his new bride and daughter. Besides the uninvolved father and distant husband, and all the various dynamics that Tanya faced, coming back to the States must have surely been an overload for her. Was the father's sitting back and letting the two ladies resolve or not resolve issues simply his training from the military? Was he disengaged or controlling? Or was it simply the times of how marriages worked? It was noted that he was more sensitive and cooperative, etc... but the inter-relationships of marriage were not as open then with regards to women having a voice, an opinion, or much input. I had a step-father who was in the military and it seemed that those types of marriages were really different on so many levels. I don't know if Tanya's father served in a war, but it is highly likely, due to the time frame. When my step-father came back from Vietnam, the tension in the marriage was apparent, even to me as a very young girl. The divorce soon followed, quite typical of all too many marriages and families who lived a military life.

I was shocked by the 'worker's' description of the mother after their first meeting as "*a pathetic, non-likeable, self-centred woman who regards her daughter as being responsible for making her experience a bad marriage and for having a difficult time in America*". Wow, such words! I think they both got off on the wrong foot and there really was never any dialogue. Sounds like her mother suffered from her own demons and dealt with an absent partner for the most of her marriage – in a mixed marriage, travelling from one military base to the next. That is a tough job for any spouse in the military. I am sure she faced much opposition and felt the real hatred towards her because she was married to a Black man. That took a lot of fortitude. It is so sad that the mother and daughter did not have any real closeness or relationship and Tanya felt driven for some reasons to run away. They could have helped each other in so many ways, had they been close to one another.

Seems like Tanya had no one in her life to share her problems with and was not accepted by her peers. She was locked up emotionally and running away was her way of escaping her problems. Running away is not usually because the child is incorrigible or has some personal deviant problem, but rather, caused by the environment and the situation. Unfortunately, the child then gets involved with some authoritative person or system with grand ideas about how to shuffle you through a series of processes with the aim of fixing and reforming you. It really was (and still is) all hit or miss. Tanya was fortunate to have landed here with the rest of us.

It was later noted that Tanya's mother had visited on several occasions and came across as a cooperative woman who was genuinely interested in Tanya's wellbeing. This is a far cry from what the earlier worker had said: "pathetic, non-likeable, etc". Since so little time was ever invested in meetings and sessions with the family members and considering the work load of the workers and others, the chart notes often left much to be desired. There was certainly a red flag in this case. One wonders if the child actually ever received help in the first six months at any institution, as the social workers had to wade through an enormous amount of written evaluations, not written by co-workers or colleagues, but by total strangers, and the caseloads were very heavy. I know that I had many encounters where they admittedly told me they were not well versed with my file and were here only acting on behalf of the state.

Her first three statements about herself were interesting: my mouth, my attitude, my temper – pretty direct! And then on another note: don't trust people. Those are all very powerful and precise. The initial planning board meeting noted that she was committed for running away, shoplifting and attempted suicide. Runaway and shoplifting are pretty common and a different set of problems in comparison to the tragic attempt at suicide at her young age. It is mind boggling that the parents said they had no problems with Tanya prior to moving to the States, although she had a history of running away at least five times while still living in Germany. The reading of her poem, "Don't Try to Remember" is so full of emotion, it is heart crushing – she just wanted to be loved. This offers proof that the marriage was strained and the imbalance is apparent, with disconnectedness in the family unit as a whole.

It is nice to read that at some point Tanya discovered herself. She was learning the skills she needed to survive in this world. Those became important to her. She started to realize this and makes strides in that direction; "motivated by what is best for Tanya". That was noted, in the chart notes nine months later. That is a long time for breakthrough in some senses, but the main thing is they were steps in the right direction and skills she will have gained for life, a very positive thing. That, coupled with her very independent spirit, leads me to believe she will have made a success of her life. I believe Tanya learned to love herself and what greater gift can any one person offer to a wounded child?

Intervention(s)

Like other young people in out-of-home care, the blues sung by Tanya and other *Sisters of Pain* were being heard well before they left the place they called home and started moving around the care system (Anglin,

2003; Fulcher, 2005). The *formal imposition of care, supervision, or custody* – whether by place of safety or care and protection order, court sentencing or indefinite detention – all out-of-home care placements have an important social history (Scarr & Eisenberg, 1993; Scull, 1977; Seed, 1973). The voices of young people themselves, family and extended family members, neighbours, teachers, health or welfare professionals, and others may not have been heard clearly amid the *noise* of emotional turmoil. If diverted initially into alternative community placements, a boarding school or kinship care, those interventions broke down for whatever reasons and a care or supervision order was issued. The evidence from what few longitudinal studies are available about interventions with children and young people in out-of-home care deserve brief attention (Andersson, 2005; Patton, Goldfeld, Pieris-Caldwell, Bryant, & Vimpani, 2005; Poland & Legge, 2005; Viner & Taylor, 2005; Courtnay & Iwaniec, 2009).

Viner and Taylor (2005) followed a British cohort of more than 13,000 young people from the age of 5 as part of a wider child developmental study. This study collected follow-up data for these young people at age 10, 16, and again at 30 years. A total of 343 young people or 3.6% of that sample population had spent time in public care, with children of colour more likely to have experienced out-of-home care placements than others. Viner and Taylor concluded that public care of children was associated with adverse adult socio-economic, educational, legal and health outcomes in excess of that associated with childhood or adult disadvantage (2005, p. 895). Patton *et al* (2005) reported that the number of Australian children on care and protection orders rose almost 50% between 1997 and 2004, with the rates six times higher for indigenous children. The proportion of Australian children placed in out-of-home care also rose from 3 per 1,000 children in 1997 to 5 per 1,000 in 2004 (Patton *et al*, 2005, p. 437). Ainsworth and Hansen (2012) reported that "*in 2010-2011, the number of children admitted to out-of-home care in Australia was 11,613, while a total of 37,648 children were living in out-of-home care during that period*" (2012: p. 146).

Andersson (2005) reported on a small study that followed 26 children placed when younger than 4 years of age in one Swedish children's home during the early 1980s. This research assessed outcomes at 3 and 9 months after leaving care, and with follow-up data collected after 5, 10, 15, and 20 years. The children's family relations was a prominent theme highlighted over the course of this longitudinal study – early attachments, later parental relationships, and the perception of who was their family. Three distinctive outcome clusters were identified: one cluster involving 10 children who were assessed as having had a "good" adjustment; a second cluster of 9 children considered to have had a "moderate" social adjustment and personal well-being; and a third cluster of 7 children assessed to have experienced "bad" social adjustment and well-being. This latter cluster of young adults had got involved with drugs, criminal behaviour, and had experienced legal sanctions (Andersson, 2005). Andersson concluded "*there is no doubt that family relations matter, whether a birth family or a foster family or alternate family combination ... and to catch the meaning and significance of family relations, the children's voices are essential – at different points of time during childhood and again as young adults, looking back on childhood experiences*" (p. 54).

Social workers and youth workers are reminded of how frequently they operate at a "crash site" where the pain experienced by a person (and family members) referred for placement in out-of-home care confronts discordant expectations of "The System" (Fulcher, 1988; 1994). Most contemporary health and social services operate in a policy environment that is overtly shaped by fiscal considerations, now operating as business units that manage capital and human resources to produce quality outcomes for young people and their significant others (Knapp, 1984). Maier noted (1979) how care for the caregivers is essential to support quality care guarantees made to children, young people, and their families (Burford, 1990; Fulcher, 1991). The professional identity and personal well-being of every worker or prospective worker influences the collective performance of all involved in team parenting challenges (Burford & Fulcher, 2005).

On arrival at a foster home, residential school, group home, or institution, a young person is initially confronted with challenges to her or his *personal and cultural safety* living amongst strangers (Dominelli, 1988; Fulcher, 1998, 2002a). Cultural safety is highlighted each time a person starts engaging with others in a new care environment. "*Are there any people like me here?*" becomes a recurring emotional question, along with questions like "*Are there people who speak like I do?*"; "*Do they eat the way I do?*"; "*What food?*" and "*Why are these people here?*"

Rituals of group membership begin immediately when one enters the door of an out-of-home care placement (Fulcher, 1996). Responsive carers and social workers seek to establish and maintain positive rituals of encounter that promote membership and inclusion for new members, be they a young person, visitor, respite carers, domestic or catering workers, and so on. New arrivals into out–of-home care need to be assisted through the formal rituals of group membership. A new resident must also establish his or her own personal location within subgroup hierarchies, coalitions, and alliances that operate in any resident group or foster home. At the same time, young people are expected to establish purposeful relationships with staff. *Respect for individuality* connects with a client's personal identity and that sense of who they were before admission to care. This brings up further questions like: "*Who are/were their people?*"; "*Who cared about them and for them?*"; "*What was happening that resulted in their being placed in care?*"; and "*What happens next?*" Personal and cultural safety, managing group membership(s), and reinforcing identity are all interwoven in responsive caring, reinforcing the importance of this aspect of intervention with children and young people in out-of-home care (Maier, 1981).

A further dimension of pain is encountered each time a young person is left *feeling shy, embarrassed, ridiculed, bullied or unsafe* – whether while attending day school or camp, or living in a boarding school or group home. Being made the brunt of jokes or feeling ridicule from other residents are too often recurring themes. Carers and social workers must remain vigilant about anyone in care being made the subject of ridicule or abuse by staff. History has sadly documented an abusive legacy in out-of-home care, a history made prominent since World War II through media disclosures of abusive practices in all parts of the Western world (see Canadian Royal Commission on Aboriginal Peoples, 1997; Commonwealth of Australia, 1992; Moore, 1996; Rangihau, 1986; Webster, 1998). When a young person feels unsafe – whether culturally, spiritually, emotionally, or physically – then her or his voice sings a special refrain of the blues about pain that may or may not be shared. Unless that voice and its special theme of pain is heard by social workers and youth workers prompting a sensitive response, young people in such circumstances are placed at even greater risk. Relational care practices must guarantee that from the moment of first contact, no child or young person placed in out-of-home care will be made to feel unsafe or be left in unsafe situations.

The pain experienced by other youths means that they communicate their pain through *anger and fear, often as survivors of abusive relationships.* Young people frequently bring a lifetime of anger into out-of-home care, and they are usually angry for very good reasons (Durst, 1992). Teachers, parents, stepparents, boyfriends, girlfriends and others have "let them down." Young people experience fear or apprehension (as we all do) about joining a new living or learning group. It is important to hear and respond with sensitivity to any young person voicing anger and fear since these powerful emotions in group living may leave her or him vulnerable to potentially abusive situations, whether as perpetrators, victims, or voyeurs – sometimes with consequences that can last a lifetime. Legal obligations in the duty of care guarantee that no young person shall be harmed nor become the victim of abuse of any kind whilst in receipt of state-mandated care (Fulcher, 2002b). Expectations such as these are reinforced by everyone, regardless of whether these high expectations can and are being met.

Finally, when a young person becomes *isolated* from peers, from their caregivers, from family members, from friends, and from virtually everyone around them, social workers and youth workers must hear very loudly and clearly the message of *risk that requires immediate attention* (Guttmann, 1991). Isolation and feelings of personal alienation should not be confused with times when someone is seeking moments of solitude or time out. Isolation and alienation of the type referred to here are associated with fundamental questions of 'being and non-being', and of suicidal ruminations. Burning preoccupations are sometimes tattooed in prominent places on a young person's hands, arms, chest, or face – tattooing that becomes a symbolic reminder and reaffirmation of painful moments – etched as a *moko*[4] into her or his being for a lifetime. *Cutting* or *bruising* on someone's wrists, limbs, breasts, or genitals must always be a concern. *Body language* such as this must always provoke action on by social workers and youth workers.

Much can be learned in hindsight from the death of a child or young person in care. This is illustrated graphically, yet again, through the Scottish Inquiry into the deaths of two young women who jumped off a suspension bridge together in a suicide pact while on run from a residential school (Carrell, 2009). Instances such as these are salutary reminders to all youth workers and social workers. Might we have intervened differently to save young people such as these through helping to relieve their pain (Anglin, 2003)? The messages from any young person who died whilst in out-of-home care by the State are essential reading for all social workers in child protection and youth justice services. The messages of these young people in pain must never fall on deaf ears, nor cease to weigh heavily on the hearts and minds of those seemingly out of tune with the emotional pain in that young person's life.

Questions for Small Group Discussion or Guided Reflection

1. What emotional pain and pain-based behaviours did you find echoing through Tanya's narratives?

2. In what ways might it be said that "cigarettes" featured prominently in Tanya's narratives, perhaps communicating symbolically about Tanya and her relationships with resident peers?

3. In contemporary youth services where cigarettes are prohibited for health and safety reasons, what symbolic replacements – like money, iPods or xBoxes – now feature in interventions with young people in out-of-home care at your place?

4. What interventions are offered – perhaps need to be offered – to military families that help young people like Tanya moving from military base to military base in different parts of the world?

5. In a world where youth suicide is high, how might we facilitate discussion about the *S-word* (Suicide) with youths known to us, or the *M-word* (Method of suicide being contemplated) and the W-words (What other options have you considered) are heard in their worlds?

Room 12
Jessie – *Belonging to People(s) and Families*

16 October: Social Work Intake Interview Notes

Jessie is a young woman who is two months short of her 18th birthday and the age at which she would be considered for discharge from State child and youth services. She has been re-committed by the Juvenile Court following an incident of resisting arrest and self-destructive behaviour where Jessie stabbed herself in the arm.

Jessie was first committed to State Services at the age of 14 for incorrigibility and running away from her adoptive parents' home. After time at the Assessment Center she was placed at the institution for younger teenagers and then paroled back home. Half a year later, she was placed in a local foster home, and then another foster home before admission as an in-patient at the local mental health facility for two weeks, and then placement in another foster home in the city.

Within a month, Jessie was admitted to a second psychiatric facility for evaluation where she remained for two months before placement at a group home. After two months in the group home, Jessie was admitted to another psychiatric hospital. Because this appeared to be a long-term treatment plan with the mental health sector, Jessie was discharged from youth parole supervision.

> However, shortly after discharge, Jessie was asked to leave the psychiatric hospital because she was continually creating behaviour problems such as smoking marijuana in her room. Application was made to the Juvenile Court to re-commit Jessie to youth justice services and transfer to the secure unit for young women.
>
> At the intake interview on the day of her arrival, it was noted how depression seemed to prevail across virtually all of Jessie's functioning at the present time. This may reflect a pattern of self-inflicted helplessness that Jessie uses to place other people in the rescue role. All indications are that she is not as fragile as she would like people to think. She often uses cutting on herself – arms and breasts – or her talk about homosexuality as a means of putting people off balance, thus leaving her in control of the situation.

Jessie made 15 statements about herself covering the incidents leading up to re-commitment:

1. *The last big blow-up that led to me coming here started about two weeks ago.*
2. *My mother had just come back from being in the hospital.*
3. *Things had gone really well between me and my dad while she was away.*
4. *She had been back a few days and things had really gone well. Then she started back into her nagging about little things I did.*
5. *The next day I took the car and went to find a friend to talk to from the mental health center.*
6. *They took me back home. I finally just told my mother that I was going to end it all, and not be in any more trouble for anyone.*
7. *I took the knife and left.*
8. *I went to the school and hid the knife and then went to a friend's house and listened to the police radio. They were talking about me and driving all around the area looking for me*
9. *Then I went back to the school, got the knife and that's when the police found me.*

10. *All I could think of was run, but they caught me.*
11. *I tried to knife myself in the arm but they stopped me.*
12. *They took me to detention and that night I tried to kill myself by cutting my arm. I scared myself.*
13. *I felt good about the judge sending me to this institution instead of a mental hospital.*
14. *I have really great hopes for the future, but ...*
15. *I am afraid of failing.*

Jessie

30 October: Summary of the Initial Planning Board Meeting

Jessie is a young woman not far from the time when she will "age-out" of State child welfare services. She has been in one form of therapy or another for the past four years. During that time, she appears to have developed a very well established repertoire of behaviours geared towards keeping people off balance and making them control her. Jessie seemingly sets people up to reject her because of her bizarre behavior, and then finds it easy to "cop out" by saying that nobody cares – foster parents, group home carers or teachers.

Jessie is an attractive girl of above average intelligence who can play the guitar beautifully and sings well. She has already found a place for herself in the living unit peer group and is able to teach other girls how to play the guitar. Opportunities to use her musical talent should be encouraged and we should seek out appropriate outlets for Jessie's creative talents. While she is behind in her schooling, it is felt that Jessie does have the capacity to perform in school and this should be encouraged.

We will use a behaviourally-oriented approach with Jessie in the initial stages. The aim will be to contain inappropriate behaviour like cutting on herself and channel Jessie towards using her existing strengths and acquire new ones without having to "act bizarre".

Women staff should engage Jessie and offer as much nurturing as possible while restricting counselling to daily life events and school. It may be that Jessie will relate better with male staff and men should be ready to give encouragement wherever she demonstrates responsible behaviour. All staff should feel free to give as much TLC as possible while holding Jessie to all cottage expectations. It is anticipated that she will have periods of quite adequate functioning followed by periods of seeming disintegration, those times when she tends to hurt on herself.

If and when her parents visit, staff should make a point of participating in the visit to get a feeling for how Jessie and her parents interact. After more than four years of therapeutic encounters across a range of services, Jessie is capable of using what she has learned in therapy now to trap people in interpersonal mind games. Controlling people by using bizarre behaviour like cutting on herself is but one example. If Jessie wishes to talk about homosexuality, encourage her and give her opportunities to explore what this might mean for her and for others.

While Jessie is confused and frightened, she is often depressed, and it is during these times that she feels in a helpless state needing other people to control her. Jessie began her stay in the secure unit as a likeable girl who is clever and devious in obtaining her goals. Her guitar playing and beautiful singing have already given her a lot of special attention from the other residents. Loves to talk about herself and her bizarre behavior or situations she has been in.

20 November: Memo from Community Resource Coordinator

The woman who directs the chapel choir Sunday mornings, has requested that I contact you to ask if Jessie could play the guitar and sing at the church service on Thanksgiving Sunday. She also asked that if it were possible for Jessie to do this, might a [secure unit] staff member be responsible for accompanying her? Please let me know if this would be possible. Thank you.

12 December: Social Worker Notes

I took a direct "cage-rattling" approach with Jessie this morning and the focus was primarily around how she feels about her parents not coming before Christmas, and how she handles disappointments and angry feelings.

Somewhere along the line, her adoptive parents have drummed it into her head that "if you're going to cry, go to your room". Her father was the main one to say this, but also mother. She also has the idea that "when you cry, you're ugly". I said that if what she said was true, I did not like the idea of her telling me I am ugly anytime I cried. To this she could only splutter.

I continued to push Jessie to see how she sets herself up to be lonely and miserable when she keeps it all bottled up inside. She squirmed a lot but I think the message came through clearly. I likened her to a cartoon of a dark cave with two white eyes looking out. She keeps herself in that cave and isn't doing very much to come out, and perhaps get herself more together as an independent person who is less miserable.

I said I thought she ought to try a different approach, and teased that unless she started coming out of her cave more herself then we would just have to come into her cave and pull her out! To this she blurted out "You can't force me!" I reassured her that there would be no force involved. We just didn't think she should keep copping out before actually trying different ways of sharing her feelings other than pulling into herself and then hurting.

I said that I thought that she may well cut on herself in order to feel that she is in control of the hurt rather than being the person who gets hurt by others.

Jessie squirmed during 45 minutes of the more than an hour we talked. I think I was touching some raw nerves the further we talked. Continue to use our current approach with Jessie and feel free to move in and be with her when you feel she's hurting. She will try to push you away but hang in there.

I did suggest to Jessie that we might begin seeking permission through the Court to get information on her natural parents. Would you believe that Jessie is already frightened about the prospect of having to go out on campus? I said we hadn't even begun to think about it.

24 December: Care Worker Notes

Jessie talked today – head hanging down and tears in her eyes – the whole bit.

She finally said "I'm bad, all bad because of what I do in my room, and I've been doing it since I was little".

She couldn't bring herself to say it (masturbating) so I said it for her. And then I said "So what? There is nothing wrong with masturbating. This doesn't change my feelings for you. It is your problem but it isn't really a problem. When you realize that people here care and love you, you won't need to feel so bad about yourself".

Jessie is afraid everyone will find out. It happened before and she hated it.

I hope this was a good enough way to handle this!

8 January: Summary of the Planning Board Meeting

Since arrival, the primary objective in our work with Jessie has been to curtail her inappropriate behaviour in her daily living routines. The second objective has been to help Jessie begin exploring her feelings and thoughts about relationships within her adoptive family. It seems that Jessie has been programmed from an early age to avoid feelings and to avoid expressing her feelings, particularly fear and crying around others.

It was agreed that we need to help Jessie find out information concerning her natural parents as she is asking questions about her origins, her nationality and basic factual information about her past, information that she has apparently never had before.

Jessie's cutting behaviour has subsided considerably and at the time of her Planning Board, it has been approximately two weeks since she has demonstrated bizarre behaviour. Jessie continues to express herself quite openly through her music and we continue to use her musical talent as a resource to keep drawing her out of her shell.

Jessie is able to function quite successfully in weekly cottage group meetings. More and more she is able to speak up and stand up for herself whenever the peer group confronts Jessie about her behaviour. She will begin afternoon classes on campus.

5 March: Summary of Planning Board Meeting

Jessie continues to show definite improvement. There has been little of her bizarre behaviour since arriving in the secure unit. She does overdo it somewhat with her hugs and kisses with staff, particularly women staff. Some have felt that Jessie's displays of affection extend almost to the point of sexual overtones.

She seems to be eagerly learning to play the banjo and seems to be conquering the instrument easily.

Her volunteer from the Community College has been very helpful and the music fests that Jessie attends have been very positive experiences as it allows her to capitalize on her musical talents in the community. The parents have not visited at this point but there are indications that they may be warming.

29 April: Letter from Institution Superintendent to Review Board Supervisor

Dear Sir

Jessie was originally committed at the age of 14 to the Assessment Centre and then placed at the institution for younger teenagers. She was paroled at the age of 16 and discharged from juvenile services at the age of 17 and a half while residing in a psychiatric hospital.

Jessie was recommitted at the age of 17 years and 10 months as a dependent-incorrigible child. She was admitted directly to the secure unit and has resided there until the present time.

Jessie remains a severely disturbed girl but she has shown evidence of stabilized behaviour in our environment. However, since she is beyond 18 years of age and was committed for incorrigibility, we must ask for discharge.

Superintendent

2 May: Notice of Discharge

Destination and Plan: Jessie is going to live with her adoptive parents. To our knowledge she has no other plans for work or school. Departure time by bus: 8:15 am.

Addendum

And just like that, Jessie was gone! Just at the point that she was beginning to make real progress, Jessie reached the magic age of 18 and aged out of care, just as happens in many other parts of the world. While some institutions have some discretionary powers and can make decisions based on the best interests of a child, in Jessie's case her latest stay in the institution had already been extended 6 months beyond her 18th birthday. After that, Jessie was on an early bus heading home where little work had gone into preparing for her return. We hope Jessie's music will have helped carry her through the stormy periods and that she has found some well-deserved happiness.

Aliese's Reflections

I didn't remember Jessie during the initial reading – and yet she seems familiar to me. Like I said earlier, there was a recognizable disposition amongst all of us girls. We all had our own ways of disguising our depression, our pain, our insecurities; and we all had our ways of coping or not coping, depending upon how you look at it.

One of the main differences here though, is Jessie had been taught to bury her feelings, to repress them, that she was ugly when she cried; all of that was very demeaning and very undermining to her processing skills. She had no way to deal with any of these emotions, nowhere to put them, no one to describe or discuss them with and I am sure it was making her into a very angry child.

I believe that is why she started to cut on herself, although I don't really know all the reasons behind her actions. It was a silent way she could accept her feelings and get them out in the open. Cutting on oneself, to feel the pain, to erase the "other" pain you are trying to escape from, or take control of the pain, you feel ugly and horrific and you want to make sure the rest of the world does too – I mean this kid had gone through the wringer.

She felt so much pressure in her adoptive home and not being able to show any emotions, and to feel badly about any feelings she had – that is a huge stranglehold on any child or adult for that matter. Locking all that up for so long. It is very disturbing how much power the system and the rules had over our lives. All it took was one bad decision, based on some knee-jerk assessment, or some fella writing the report to have a bad day, not liking the way she looked or whatever ... and you have ruined a human being for "life", a report that may follow her for the rest of her life.

Being committed to these mental hospitals and growing up in places like that is not a very healthy start to life, to say the least. Most of those places were just about medicating the patient, shock therapy, binding them in straight–jackets, or keeping them in isolation. It is so irritating to read, that here she is, she has finally made it to a place where she can get some real help, learn some valuable lessons to carry her through life, but she was soon to be "aged-out", and her chances were slim to none, that she would be receiving any kind of help at all after leaving this facility. The system was not set up that way and to my knowledge there was no "after-care" available. Here she had a chance, here people cared about her, she was making progress, and learning to care for others, and I can only live with hopes that her resiliency pulled her through in the years that were ahead of her.

She certainly learned enough from all these institutions to survive on the outside. Jessie was a very bright girl, who had learned many lessons and who was blessed with such musical talent. I hope that through her music she learned it was okay to cry, to have feelings of frustration and anger and that in life, it is not what happens to you, but rather, how you handle it. It took me a long time to REALLY understand the meaning of that.

Belonging to People(s) and Families

Most children entering out-of-home care – regardless of age – have had their emotional safety threatened and any sense of belonging feels disrupted. This may result from uncertainties about family care and relationships but it is often compounded by multiple or serial placements. A primary task of out-of-home care is to help children feel safe so that *first encounters* with carers and social workers can be crucial in determining how young people might feel and subsequently respond to the placement.

Attachment theory suggests that from infancy we are all prey to a primitive sense of anxiety. Carers need to help manage this anxiety to prevent it from becoming self-destructive for a child. In babies, this happens when caregivers respond to an infant's distress with physical and emotional comforting. When a social worker or youth worker responds with sensitivity and consistency, then a young person starts to form an attachment bond or relationship with these people. If this bond is what Winnicott (1965) termed 'good enough', it nurtures in children what attachment theorists call an internal working model of the world, in a world that is safe and trustworthy. These children learn to regulate their emotions and explore their worlds, confident of a secure base and relationship to which they can turn. 'Good enough' parenting provides what Winnicott (1965) called a 'facilitating environment' – a stable physical and emotional environment where a child is safe yet allowed sufficient space to grow and to build healthy trusting relationships and a personal sense of belonging.

Ward (1995) identified how children may at times need literal containment, in terms of basic care and the setting of boundaries, as well as metaphoric containment where a worker soaks up a child's uncontainable feelings. Out-of-home care needs to create and maintain cultures that are strong enough to withstand and contain a young person's anxieties whilst giving him or her experiences that help nurture more healthy and intimate relationships. A primary aim of out-of-home care, therefore, should be to nurture and manage 'containing relationships' not simply focusing on legalistic and behavioural control issues. Effective control and a sense of belonging only come about when children feel safe and secure in a place where their anxieties and worries are accepted, understood and contained, and they feel emotional care.

Whilst attachment theory lends much to our understanding of inter-personal relationships, attachment to place is also central to a child's developing resilience with a healthy identity, feelings of security and a sense of belonging (Jack, 2010). Belonging involves "*a sense of ease with oneself and one's surroundings*" and involves "*identification with one's social, relational and material surroundings*" (May, 2011: 368). Belonging thus includes a sense of place and a connected attachment with others. Belonging grows alongside feelings of being valued by and attached to others. It frequently involves connections with other young people with whom a young person lives, with peers in a neighbourhood, community or church group, as a player in a football team, a band member, a participant in a theatre group or involvement with a particular cultural group through religious activities, gatherings, performances or celebrations. Belonging is fundamental to developing self worth (Laursen, 2008) and in out-of-home care it is nurtured through the everyday habits, practices and experiences of care (Fulcher & Garfat, 2008).

Belonging provides a secure physical and emotional base from which children and young people comfortably venture into their world, try new things, and successfully engage in new experiences. Belonging with others develops through a sense of identification with those particular others, and evolves as people do things together. Thus, *doing things with young people* is an important part of their development. Belonging is one of the most basic of human needs and without a sense of belonging, a young person feels detached, disconnected and alone, prone to seeking connections exclusively through peers, perhaps through involvement in gang subcultures (Centre for Social Justice, 2009). A focus on belonging might encourage carers and social workers to consider how memories are celebrated and given meaning with children and young people in out-of-home care. The introduction of memory boxes helps children store mementoes and keepsakes from various times in their lives in out-of-home care.

As a means of providing carers, youth workers and social workers with some practical tools to assist in their practice, the following framework is offered as a possible 'gadget' to be included in your toolbox. The *Outcomes that Matter*® Recording framework (OTMR) has been developed to provide a simple and yet more systematic approach to out-of-home care recording. We offer here only a brief introduction; readers who are interested in following this up in more detail should seek further information at www.transformaction.com

The weekly recording template is structured around the developmental needs for *Belonging, Mastery, Independence* and *Generosity* (Brendtro, Brokenleg & Van Bockern, 1990; Fulcher & Garfat, 2012). Young people need to feel *Belonging* – in relationships and place – before they can move towards *Mastery* and *Independence*, or demonstrate *Generosity* of Spirit with others. Outcomes that Matter®

build upon the research carried out by the Minneapolis-based, Search Institute, discussed earlier. 20 of the Search Institute assets were translated with permission into Developmental Outcome statements for use with children and young people in out-of-home care (Fulcher, McGladdery & Vicary, 2011), then extended further to include Achievement Outcomes for young people living in community settings (Fulcher & Garfat, 2012). Outcomes that Matter® are derived from longitudinal research with children and young people where half the research population reported fewer than 20 of the 40 developmental assets identified. Our working hypothesis thus holds that children and young people in State-supervised out-of-home are located in the 'Low Assets Group' – almost universally – so that youth workers, social workers and others should actively attend to and nurture weekly developmental achievements around these targeted outcomes.

The Belonging Outcomes involve "External Assets" that are located around a young person as she or he enters out-of-home care. As a young person moves into their new shared living environment, some sense of Belonging grows amongst those in that shared life space – greeting, connecting with and engaging others to form relationships involving give and take, or 'reciprocity' which is important to all the parties involved. Belonging starts with influences that are external to a young person before gradually, over time, it becomes an internalised experience.

BELONGING OUTCOMES THAT MATTER

Empowerment
Safety

Support
Carer Support
Positive Communication
Caring Relationships

Boundaries and Expectations
Boundaries for Daily Living

These outcome statements are clustered around the developmental theme of Belonging to fashion a recording template such as that illustrated in the Carer Support example shown below, and used in the OTM Recording template with all the Belonging Outcomes.

(E) Carer Support: *(Young person's name)* received personal time, physical care, encouragement and demonstrated a sense of belonging with others in their living environment.

A 2-3 line Word Picture generated through a short narrative about specific developmental achievements this young person has made – this past week – during the course of their daily life events in out-of-home care which are kept for safe storage in his/her personal Memory Box.

For example:

K was sick and throwing up. She couldn't travel around in the car when picking up my girls from school so I made a decision to organize M's niece to look after K at home while I picked up the girls.

Achieving		Mostly Achieving	X	Some Achieving		A little Achieving		Not Achieving		Not Recorded	

(E) Safety: _____ has been safe in a variety of ways where s/he lives, at school and in the local neighbourhood.

(E) Positive Communication: _____ listened to and talked with his/her carers, sought help, advice, guidance and/or representation as appropriate.

(E) Caring Relationships: _____ was offered, received and accepted support from birth family members, personal carers and other significant adults.

(E) Boundaries for Daily Living: _____ received consistent supervision and his/her whereabouts were monitored according to reasonable behaviour guidelines.

Carer(s) and youth worker(s) are invited (with or without direct participation by the child or young person involved) to reflect back over the past seven days to identify daily life episodes when a young person in their care demonstrated achievement(s) around each developmental outcome. Those completing a recording are invited to draw upon a distinctive "CCTV (closed circuit television) capability" that most carers, youth workers (and parents, especially mothers) demonstrate, enabling them to focus on specific relational episodes associated with when the child or young person for whom they care has made achievements around each Outcome. First, the carer records a 2-3 line narrative *word picture* of an episode identified through this CCTV capability. After recording 20 '*word picture accounts*', carers or youth workers then review each entry using the Achieving Scale to arrive at a reflective judgement about 'how often' achievements were happening with each developmental *outcome* during the past seven days. A 5-point Likert Scale draws attention to a particular young person's developmental achievements during the past 7 days.

Questions for Small Group Discussion or Guided Reflection

1. What does belonging mean to you and how do you experience belonging?
2. How might her status as an adopted daughter have shaped Jessie's feelings about belonging?
3. How might one explain the ways in which Jessie functioned quite well when she was with one adopted parent or the other, but less well with both parents together?
4. What meaning might be made of Jessie's inclination to cut on her breasts when her emotional pain became unbearable?
5. What evidence was available that demonstrated Jessie's achieving developmental outcomes that matter around Belonging during her stay in the secure unit?

Room 13
Ali – *Zoning In on Mastery*

To tell you my thoughts is to locate myself in a category.
To tell you about my feelings is to tell you about me.

29 August: Care Worker Notes

Ali has always had to make it on her own so she comes on with a tough act, because people expect it. This tough exterior can be broken through by staff asking her to sit down with them in order to learn to know one another. This girl is really very lonesome and alone, and desperately needs someone to love and care about her. We could get to her pretty fast if we start now. Or we may never do it, if we don't start now.

5 September: Summary of Initial Planning Board Meeting

Ali is a 15 year, 10 month old girl of mixed Indian and Caucasian ancestry who was returned to the Assessment Center after parole revocation and then sent to this secure unit after repeated attempts to find a successful placement in the community proved unsuccessful. Ali spent 21 months earlier at an institution for younger teenagers – from the age of 12 – before being paroled a year ago to a foster home.

During parole, Ali was involved in a variety of offenses, wasn't attending school and wasn't abiding by foster home obligations. Ali changed foster homes after 10 weeks and things went reasonably well until mid-April when her actions at home steadily deteriorated. It was the conclusion of her Parole Counsellor that Ali had reached the point of being unable to control her impulses and idealistic pursuits which was leading to increased exposure to and activity in illegal acts. It appeared that if Ali was not immediately brought under some stronger controls, she would become increasingly self-destructive.

Life is just a matter of survival;
Mixing it with the law is not a means of survival.

5 September: Summary of Initial Planning Board Meeting (continued)

Very little detail is known about Ali's family. Mother apparently divorced her natural father shortly after Ali was born. She was then adopted by a stepfather who subsequently relinquished her at the time her mother was deprived of parental rights. Ali lived in numerous places and foster homes administered by child welfare services. She seemingly never lived in any one place long enough to form relationships. Ali has been in and out of foster homes and child welfare institutions since the age of 10.

Ali's social worker at the Assessment Center offered the following: "Reviewing Ali's history and discussing it with her leaves the overwhelming impression of a girl who has had to adjust to a phenomenal number of placements. She has been manipulated by authorities she couldn't trust, in a world she couldn't understand. Ali has been very much alone since a young age.

From this we have the girl she is today: hostile and fighting on the outside; scared, alone and unsure on the inside. She very much needs and requires security and stability. This, combined with the fact that a further institutional placement would reinforce Ali's association with delinquent peers, makes institutional care an undesirable choice. However, it remains questionable whether Ali can control herself enough to function in the community at present."

Here is a very needy girl who has turned to a delinquent sub-culture for an identity that she's never had. Ali should be considered a security risk and also a suicide risk. The focus of all work with Ali should be to establish relationships as soon as possible from which long term work in a secure setting can take

Sometimes I thought freedom
Was a non-existent word.

5 September: Summary of Initial Planning Board Meeting (continued)

Ali's school records show that as a primary school pupil she was exasperating as she became very emotional and silly in her attempts to gain attention and be accepted by her peers. The Assessment Center teachers described her as sullen, hostile and manipulative. Records further show that Ali has a good understanding in the areas of reading and math but needs help in the mechanics of writing. She also needs to widen her vocabulary to include elements more suitable than her reliance so heavily on very coarse language. Ali was seen as very bright with good academic capabilities which needed reinforcement.

Ali arrived in the secure unit with the big, bad attitude to match the big, bad reputation that preceded her by some 18 months. She has done very little to quash that reputation, rather standing firm or almost going out of her way to emphasize her position. Ali has feelings that she is worthless and that others feel the same about her. She has made a commitment to try to relate to staff.

Hopeless

Hopeless is the feeling I get
Often when I'm all alone.

Perhaps I shouldn't fret
Even though it feels like forever.

Let time fly it away
Even if it's not the happiest day.

Shine it on, minds are to be free
Sunny days – you shall see.

Ali
10 September

17 September: Social Worker Notes

I spoke with Ali for almost an hour this morning. I reinforced the message that I would not be rescuing her. Instead, I was part of the "they" who were allegedly responsible for putting Ali in her room. Ali has not received any correspondence from anyone and is contemplating just "hanging it all up" as regards the letter writing.

I encouraged Ali to stand on her own two feet instead of juggling for leadership of this or that faction in the group. Ali said she can't turn to staff because they want to "change" her and she's not sure about what the "change" will mean. Her fear right now of being "changed into something" is more frightening than being who she is.

I feel good about leaving it up to Ali to get herself out of her room.

Peace of Mind?

Just another key
Behind another locked door.

Just another kid
Who don't wanna live no more.

Sometimes wishing she could go home

Then the hard cold facts
They all seem to come back.

My friends call him hell
The authorities call him reality.

He tiptoes up your spine
And whispers in your ear.

You don't have a home
And you're alone.

Have you seen him lately?

Ali
11 October

21 October: Care Worker Notes

Ali had her first visit with her former foster parents today.

Visions

I wish I could go outside
And feel the cool breeze of
This foggy autumn morn.

To be able to see birds,
Gliding through the morning mist
So full of song.

It would be so nice
To take off my slippers
And wiggle my toes in the dew.

To wait for the morning's sun,
Shine down upon me
And warm my grateful body.

To have no obligations nor burdens,
To clear my mind of all the things
That the new day will bring.

Sitting upon a log waiting for someone to find me,
To search for myself
Preparing for the new day, with glee!

Wishes, desires and hopes – oh, realities so mean.
Come with me to this place,
In my visions and my dreams.

Ali
24 October

26 November

Mr [Social Worker]

My former foster parents have been asking me since their first visit "When can we meet him?" All I could say is that I'll ask you.

Since I'm not in the cottage to sneak up on you and ask if you could spare me a moment or two, I have to write.

Once, you came on the weekend to "meet" and talk with our parents or whatever. Are you planning on doing that in the near future? If so, or if not, please pass the word along to some worthy staff who will deliver the message to me.

Be careful in your choosing. Some aren't strong enough to come down to the cursed Room 13 for fear I'll cast my evil spells upon them, or strike them down with sickness.

Ali

Ali needs encouragement in learning to express herself openly without so much sarcasm and critical tongue. She should be held to all expectations and corrected when behaving inappropriately. When corrected, Ali should be faced with a particular area of irresponsibility and asked to come up with alternatives. These should be noted before Ali returns to the daily living group to try them out. Don't be overwhelmed by the tough exterior. That exterior façade covers a frightened and insecure 16 year old girl who needs considerable nurturing. Encourage and support Ali in all areas where responsibility is demonstrated.

3 January

Dear Mr [Social Worker]

Hello. We were disappointed that we couldn't make it to see Ali the weekend you were there. Ali doesn't have too many friends about whom she's proud enough to want us to meet. But she insisted that we should meet you. That's a good recommendation.

Perhaps you could clue us into the establishment side of Ali's institutional story. We had a pleasant and informative chat with Mrs F on our first visit there a few months ago, but since have just had Ali's perceptions to go on. I can certainly see from her many letters the kinds of changes she's going through, and they've been really great!

Ali thinks that she won't need to stay there for more than 2-3 months. When the time of her release comes, we are going to have to be prepared – physically I mean. We're living in a tiny one-bedroom house near the university and, as cramped as it is, another person means another house.

Finding something for rent which meets our needs is some task – especially with gas prices rising, not to mention creative, mess-making people and two poorly mannered, huge dogs. So advance warning about when Ali might arrive at our foster home would be greatly appreciated.

Another idea... I was shocked at the lack of creative, purposeful activity provided for girls at the institution. Ali can write – but I'm sure that's not true of all the girls. One of the reasons I want to teach art in the public schools is to provide an opportunity for kids to be successful at creating something. It's great for building self esteem!! It seems to me that this is especially applicable for the girls in your secure unit.

Ali expressed interest in some simple weaving techniques I know. They're simple, create beautiful products and offer good therapy through creating a rhythm for meditation. I'd be glad to demonstrate how to do these thing for the girls if you are interested. I was planning on showing Ali anyhow. I also know how to do lots of other safe crafts, too. If there's interest, I'd be happy to play volunteer art teacher on a couple of visits.

I'd be glad to hear from you in answer to my questions and or anything else you'd like to say. Thanks for being a friend to Ali.

Love and peace,
[Foster Mother]

7 January, Feeling good

Dear Mrs M

I feel like writing because I got a few things to say that I probably couldn't say face to face.

People like you give me a lot of hope in these trying times. So many of us are confused about ourselves and love, with the world sometimes looking like its ready to fall apart. It is truly a wonder how so many survive.

At last I have found one answer to a question in my mind, like "How and what makes me want to go on?"

You, are my answer. I see the good, the honesty and the beautiful things that you are forever trying to accomplish. I have not only seen them but I feel it, because you have affected me.

At first, I saw you as a 'staff' who was trying to teach and show me conformity. Then I saw you as a friend helping me while I am growing.

I also saw you as a loving mother, trying to protect me, treating me as I think a mother would one of her own. That's how I hope to treat my children. You didn't treat me like so many have done. Rejecting, giving up, "you're only messed up, mixed up crazy criminals".

For all these reasons, I respect you, admire you and love you. Is it possible to see a person in so many neat ways? I don't know, but it sure is a good feeling.

296

I remember one of the first times we ever spoke and I said "But they gave up on me". A lot of people have. Maybe even myself. I probably deserved it but not you. I don't think your head will ever be in that place. I don't think you will ever give up on people.

I recognize this, and I ask – but why? Maybe it's an urge, an instinct in you, or a love of people? But whatever it is, it's beautiful and it's you. That's partly how I made it so far, wanting to prove to you I could do it, I could make you right.

Perhaps I wouldn't have been able to handle going on hurting others and myself. But now, I can't say I am trying just for myself or you – I think it's both!

Please don't think I'll forget you – because I know I won't. I will forget many ugly things of this place, but not the beautiful things.

Love you's
Ali

9 January: Summary of the Planning Meeting

Ali struggles along. She has found for perhaps the first time that adults can be genuine people and that these same adults can find satisfaction through involvement with Ali, if she will allow them. Ali is very impatient with herself, wanting to change the way she is and how she feels about herself but wanting this quickly. Ali is finding that even situations which she feels are hopeless in relationships with others can be faced and resolved successfully. There continue to be periods of despondency but these are probably the result of letting go of the antagonistic and assertive "big bad Ali" behaviors of the past.

Continue to hold Ali to expectations but use humor wherever possible as a means of furthering a relationship with this girl. She would benefit from staff contact each day, if only on a friendly chat level.

Ali is using her intelligence to reason and ponder on some very important philosophical issues which could spiral into depression during low periods. In chats with Ali, explore the broad topic of a "life plan" as Ali will have to rely almost totally on her own resources to make it in the community. Continue to give the message "we know she can make it" and help her learn better ways of handling rough situations.

18 January

I wrote to my aunt and uncle. It's so weird and so heavy. "Please don't reject me again". After awhile, your heart isn't moved when you say "I have no home – no parents". It is just another material fact that goes along with your name, birth date and numbers.

But thinking and talking about it so much? Then going as far as saying "I want a home"! Too much. You know, it's funny. Those are the only people I would really try to impress, even if I had to change my ways. Those are the only people whose judgment I fear.

Sometimes I think – yeah, I've grown up now. I don't need them – and right when you're convincing yourself, the truth flashes in my head showing me my real needs. I don't want to feel sorry for myself – but the things I missed out on are the most important things to me.

Sure, I got them from other means – but second best didn't supply the foundations, or steps that we need to thrive. I have survived. Writing this I've accomplished nothing except to wallow in self pity and be hard on myself again. Or, maybe I'm trying to shove these "feelings" off the surface?

Being me and the things I've done and missed out on – family life and love – makes me feel insecure and sort of 'weird' and out of place, not normal – because I ain't. If only my father would accept me.

Yeah, you know I'm down but you don't know how far down I am. Or am I really not convincing you when I say I'm okay? You know me that well, perhaps more than me.

He tells me I care for other people more than myself and less of myself because I'm not important. But caring for others, to me, is more important than being self-centered.

Well at least I care. That's more than I can say for a lot of people, even if my reasons aren't the best.

Ali

---

30 January: Summary of a Special Planning Board Meeting

A conference was held with Ali's prospective foster parents and her progress in forming relationships and shared living skills were discussed. In addition, the following points were considered by the Board: (1) living arrangements at the foster home; (2) the need for a realistic educational or work experience plan; (3) having Ali's tattoos removed; and (4) what parole supervision would be required were Ali to leave directly from the secure unit to go back into the community.

Ali was told by the Board that she must now demonstrate her ability to "adapt" to group living in the secure unit, using relationships with staff to learn group living skills. This does not mean conformity as Ali is so quick to describe it. Don't let her "cop out" with "*I can't because of the awful life I've had*".

We accept that her past has been pretty grim and full of pain, but she has the ability to make something of her life in spite of these problems. It will require patient yet firm efforts on the part of all staff to encourage Ali to further develop the basic social skills of communication without always being right.

I must not fear. Fear is the mind killer. Fear is the little death that brings total obliteration. I will face my fear. I will permit it to pass over me and through me. And when it has gone past, I will turn the inner eye to see its path. Where the fear has gone, there will be nothing. Only I will remain.

Ali's Quote from "Dune"

6 March: Summary of the Planning Meeting

Ali has responded to the encouragement of Board to learn to cope with the "trials and tribulations" of the secure unit living environment. She has good-naturedly spoken of this as "training" and agrees that such "training" will be beneficial for her participation in future living situations. Slow but consistent growth has been noted in Ali's ability to interact with adults, and particularly staff with whom she feels she has had the greatest difficulties. Ali is now able to talk about how she hopes to have her tattoos removed and is able to use her relationships with staff to talk about her fears and apprehensions about that.

Due to her long involvement in superficial relationships with kids in institutions, it was considered inappropriate to involve Ali in the open campus program as it would only reinforce her pattern of shallow, counter-productive relationships. Application has been made for funding to proceed with the removal of Ali's tattoos. In the meantime, the assistance of a local volunteer has been enlisted to work with Ali around her writing and in being able to take Ali outside the living unit.

26 April: Social Worker Notes

Ali was in good shape when I saw her today. She feels this past week has been nightmarish but in looking back, it's been full of growth. I encouraged Ali to use her room as a safe way of escaping this weekend, when and if she needed to. Her volunteer worker will be here late Sunday afternoon and I said they could go for a walk at that time. This kid has really been affected by all the changes in here recently — both staff and procedures — but is hanging in there now with the best of them.

24 July

Dear Inmates

I would have said "Dear Friends" but most of you aren't real "friends" just acquaintances. Too many people think that they're friends of one another, but I can count all of my real friends on my fingers. To me a friend is a very personal thing, a very personal person. Not just someone to shuck and jive with. But I won't bore you with my definitions of friends.

I wasn't gonna write because even as people I don't know you very well. But maybe I have something to say that would be useful to one of you. (And maybe it will give you a better idea of where I'm coming from). If only one can really hear me and check out what I'm saying, then I have accomplished something worthwhile and it was worth my time to write.

The thing I wanted to say is this – being in here and locked up is a bitch. Unfortunately, that's as far as most people take it. They don't ask why it's that way. Well, I always was a person to ask a lot of questions and I found out being locked-up physically ain't necessarily a bitch. It's just another experience in life.

You can learn something from being locked up; many things. You can conform if that's your trip. You can take a look at things around you, check out your own mind and look at your values about things in life. You can use the time any way you want.

I don't know if you've ever heard of the term "survival training" but it's a very important word to me. That's what this place can give you without them even knowing it. Survival training is learning to cope and deal with everyday hassles, with people you don't necessarily care for. It makes you stronger and wiser. It makes you more aware because you deal with things and not just ignore them.

301

Unfortunately, too many people are too busy fighting and too afraid they'll lose the likeable parts of who they are – they might get brainwashed or god knows whatever else fear plants in your mind. But you can't fight or resist flow – or you don't grow and you don't go anywhere.

You should use your time wisely – learn things, not necessarily meaning through school either. Learn things by talking to people. Open yourself up to new horizons. Just don't do things now because that's what you think you want to do for the rest of your life.

I'm so hungry to learn things and any kinds of things. It may help me now or later. Right now you may feel so sure that all you want to do is be a prostitute (let's be realistic, it's fast money). Or maybe you don't care for material things and you just want to live off the land or travel around. Is it fair to yourself to deprive yourself of things you may want to do later ... but can't because you don't have the certificate or the knowledge? I don't think so.

Some still think "well, I'll just get married and my husband will support me". Good luck Jack. With all this women's rights bull going on? What happens if ya split up? You gotta be independent or at least know how to take care of yourself without getting busted.

I don't know – a lot of the things I'm saying here are things I've thought about a lot and have come to some sort of conclusion. I didn't have much of a family life and I ain't got no rich relatives from whom I'll inherit royalties. So I learned very young how to support myself, and how to be independent (not always through legal means though).

I am the 4th generation in my family who has been raised as a "divorced kid". My kids ain't gonna be the 5th generation. I want to be strong enough to take the responsibility of raising them in a good strong loving home. LEARN, EXPERIENCE, GROW AND SHARE!!!!!!!!!!!!!!!!!!

> *Try to be happy, and hang in there!*
> *Ali*

8 August: Institutional Adjustment Summary

As a young woman nearing 17, Ali has come into conflict with State authorities since the age of 9 when she was deprived of all contacts with her mother following divorce proceedings between her mother and adoptive stepfather. For the next 6 plus years, Ali became a casualty of the State Welfare System as countless community placements and institutional options were used without success.

While committing status offenses such as running away, not attending school and incorrigibility, probably the greatest problem facing this young woman has been her feelings of total alienation from adults, from figures of authority, and from the very legal system which deprived her of her past; her identity as a person and her place as a member of a family.

The State Welfare System has created an "orphan" in virtually every sense of the word. That System created a "new family" in the sense of institutionalized "siblings"; and "parents" who sought to "treat" Ali for the alienation that no one could touch. The cycle of lost hopes, of spiralling despair, and of reactions to an "uncaring world" created behaviour which would keep people away – an identity which was "big, bad and sophisticated", and an expectation that everyone would give up on her when the "treatment" wasn't working. It is in this sense that Ali entered the secure unit program with a reputation for failure that preceded her by at least 18 months.

In specific terms, it is difficult to say what has changed in Ali during the past year in a secure unit. Relationships mattered. Ali learned that she was essentially a good person who reacted to people out of fear. By finding that there were people who would not be pushed aside, Ali began to find confidence in what she could do for herself instead of reacting to what others were doing to her.

Ali is a highly intelligent young woman who can be most congenial and stimulating. She knows what is right and will generally follow what is right. She is inclined to fight for the "underdog" and can be expected to involve herself in "civil rights" activities in the future. Ali does not suffer fools gladly. She is very skilled in arts and crafts and has a keen interest in political affairs. Ali is approaching life in the community now with her eyes wide open rather than running blindly like before from herself and others, searching for something she couldn't find.

The reasons for recommending parole are simple. During her stay in the secure unit, Ali has experienced her first major success in the past 7 years. She has no family other than a few friends and the foster family who offered her a 'room and board' type placement. Ali stayed with these foster parents before and they have stayed involved throughout her stay in the secure unit.

The primary difference between now and when Ali was placed on parole the first time nearly two years ago is that Ali is now more able to accept her past and to look at the future with hope and with a determination to succeed. She should be placed on parole status as soon as possible. Ali's chances for successfully readjusting to the community are considered good.

Addendum

True to her word, Ali went on parole, got herself discharged from parole, and had no further involvement with the State System. She has had her ups and downs but retained a positive, 'can-do' attitude. Ali (aka Aliese) restored contact with her mother and established connections with her Native American roots and people. She remained an "activist", as anticipated. She gave birth to two children, and recently became a grandmother. Ali is in contact with her daughter and hopes to re-establish ties with her son and his new family in the future.

Some Further Reflections

I was a lot younger than many that came through (yet another) set of revolving doors. I was of mixed blood, American Indian and White, but with light olive skin, always "passing for White". This posed a whole new set of problems of their own for me growing up. Besides witnessing racism through these eyes, when people spoke, they did not know an Indian was present, and I was very much so. I went through various homes; once to a young married couple, who were very religious, a home where they had an older teen–aged daughter who disliked me because I wasn't as hip or rich as her, and then there was the one placement with a cop, out in the country, where there was nothing to do in such an isolated place. A cop, really? I can laugh now, but boy did I resist that home and never gave it a chance-I was out of there within 24 hours, you can bet. You had to wonder where these people came from, and what was the selection process to become a foster parent? I think it was all based on square footage of the space available to the youth and that was probably about it.

Conforming was my biggest issue and I simply did not understand why I could not be with my family. In reading the notes about me, it is all very surrealistic. I wonder what is meant by "unable to control impulses" ? Is that what was really going on – or was it that I processed faster, knew the game, had a different set of values and view on life, and had such an adventurer's spirit that preferred to NOT conform?' I laugh at it all now. I had moved so often and really had no roots and enjoyed travelling and road trips. I would hitchhike all across the states and no one would know where I was. Some outdoor concert for a week, off living in an old A-frame with no electricity, or building a house with some hippies out in the country who never questioned who I was. We all were searching for who we were, it was not a question any of us would ask the other.

Early on, I had a clear understanding that the system did not work, and was not to be trusted. I understood these people who worked within that system had control of our lives. I had up to this point seen it all, and had been through various community programs, orphanages, foster homes, group homes and these assessment/diagnostic centers. We were simply cogs in this matrix of a system that was broken, in a world that was changing ever so fast. Survival – my path, and foreseeing or controlling some sense of destiny – was up to me, not another foster home, another place, with rules and new faces analysing us, all too aware of their own failures within this system. We were not to be toyed with, manipulated, or conformed. This was war of sorts, and finally ending with me at my arrival at this secure unit with the rest of the non-conformists. I see it is noted where I spent quite some time in my room discovering how to interact within the social setting of the group. As I read and write, a smile appears on my face. Looks like my room and I got quite well acquainted and I am sure some of my poetry and letters were written during that spell. I am also sure that it was very heart wrenching and I was probably pretty moody too.

Some of the young women had not experienced all the youth care programs. Here you ended up with an assortment of girls co-existing in this controlled environment from all sorts of criminal backgrounds, personal histories and various problems. Many rules did not make sense to us then and in reflection, make all the sense in the world now, considering what the day-to-day living experience was in the unit. Getting used to routine, self-care and self-image, learning to cope with differences in backgrounds and cultures, in some ways, those types of survival skills would later set us apart from the crowd and give us an edge, should we be able to hone in on these new skills and tools. That is certainly NOT what it felt like then and some of those group sessions could get very heated, as I now recall. Some of these girls had families to go to, or thought they would go back to one of their pimps, or some even had children previously with a boyfriend. So the majority of us were all very different from one another. I wasn't sure, I had a family, but then, I didn't have a family. So, I knew I had to come up with some kind of plan and make a future of my own.

I never found those childhood answers I searched for and I was restless. Instead of answers and justice, I was whisked away like a leaf blowing through their little world landing a short time here and there, and then became a lost child. In my note dated Jan 18 – "steps that we need to survive" – I believe what I was meaning, was to thrive, as I then say, I have survived. That is a key point, as I understood the difference between existing and living; and surviving and thriving. As time went on, I became more and more rebellious and vocal in response to MY treatment but also in the affairs of Indian Country, Vietnam War, Immigration Rights, Women's Rights and the basic oppression of peoples in general. I was always very aware and very sensitive and could not stand oppression of any sorts. Later I learned about passion and what drives me, and I made peace with that restless spirit. My exposure to what was happening in the world came from my own little adventures and travels as I would plan my escape prior to any placement and be back on the road.

I was a runner and spent more time out of these facilities and out of these homes, than in them. I had a warrior spirit and was fighting the wrongs in the world wherever I landed. I fought for these girls too, as independent thinking evolved and we were learning, now, that we could make change – in OUR world. As a leader, I have always been a lone wolf in many ways, but this was a platform in which I could relate to all the girls, regardless of their past. I have only had a couple of very close friends in my during my childhood and those relationships ended tragically with their death. In the notes it mentioned me having some worthless feelings stemmed from not belonging anywhere. I had no standing anywhere except as this leader of the pack role and the girls did look up to me, or feared me and my reputation did proceed me by years and I always thought that was weird. I think it is just like any other social network.

Some of the letters written by the girls to the social worker mention scheduling some time with him, and it is true, we all bombarded the social worker when he came into the den from the "outs". We were pretty shut in at this unit. None of us girls had many visitors and the social worker was hip, cool, with the times, and would go to bat for you, should the cause be in alignment with positive change and effect. Keep in mind, that is what this whole secure unit and facility was all about. People who created and enforced the rules were working alongside the carers and others who operated the secure units and utilized a direct approach and formed relationships between themselves and the youth – that was groundbreaking. We could earn the right to go outside for an escorted walk, or other small reward. Noted earlier, regarding not letting me see the dogs after my visit; I rarely had visitors and I loved those dogs! I am sure there was good reason, but it crushed me. I loved those dogs. You knew who really cared about you – this was a very intense one-on-one program. While you talked to all the staff, you had your scheduled one-on-one weekly time with your "buddies" and there was some leeway in who we had these sessions with. However, we were "expected" to establish some rapport with all the staff. The social worker – again, him being the major player, and the real mover and shaker here – really helped (in my opinion) to spearhead and take initiative, as well as keep the staff on task. Important here, is that he was a risk taker and I knew that.

I could feel the disdain of some of the staff whose views were so alien to mine because I wasn't cooperating, or I wasn't interacting with others as I should. Well I had to put things at ease too, to find my own comfort zone and there was a lot to digest and consider, this being the end of the line. I had always associated with an older crowd, ten years my senior, so my experiences had shown me the end of the line for many people. You know it wasn't easy getting along with a cottage full of hurting girls that were locked up together. Hurting and angry, confused and feeling unloved and unwanted by the entire world. Something came down around 17th September and it probably involved someone trying to set me up. This sort of thing happened all the time and that's why everyone was cautious about getting very close.

Our closest friends, the ones who became our real sisters, and our music were so instrumental in keeping our sanity. We also could cross barriers with music, as the same today. I knew I was a handful and most the time I wasn't really trying to be, but I was never up to taking any one's "handling" me or "giving me lip-service" – ever – in my defence. My wording in my letter cracks me up; "worthy", "careful in your choosing" – etc ... really? I mean, for a fifteen year old kid, that seems pretty wise and deep in thought. Of course, I am looking at myself in the reflecting mirror. We could always sense who genuinely cared about us and could feel condemnation from those who didn't.

In my letter to Mrs. M, my friend, on Jan 7, I am expressing my love and gratitude to her and I think this is really cool and so warming (for me) to remember now forty years later. I have never forgotten her, and we have spoken only a few times throughout the years, but I am very, very glad I wrote her and told her the things I felt about her. When I did leave the secure unit, she walked me down that path – it was like a tradition walking down a long road – and she gave me her wedding band. I still have it today – even though I have lost so many things over the years. I knew she loved me, and I had not had that in my life, up until that point in time. I think this is in part, why I am who I am today. I still don't give up on people and I understand healthy relationships versus enabling co-dependency, and know that hurting people hurt others. People can change, they usually just need the skill set and tools . Love does conqueror all.

When you learn that not all people give up on others, you learn to respond the same way. That's what needs to be taught. We learn to forgive and to love each other, and sometimes that has to be from a healthy distance. I have told people many times throughout the years, that sometimes, if you don't have the strength to do something, and you just can't do it for yourself, TRY to do it for someone else. Believe me, it helps, it works and it is a step in the right direction – a step in a positive change.

To the readers – my mom, children, and colleagues – I know my experience here was a good path for me to have been placed on, though getting there was difficult. I am certain it was through forming healthy and honest relationships that I was able to evolve into a healthy adult and pass along my "wisdom" to those who have suffered. I believe it to be a higher calling, and unless you work within the Youth Care System, have volunteered your time in some fashion, then you can't understand how rewarding it is to be involved directly with re-shaping and re-educating a person who has been beaten down, abused, or brutalized. Never lose your humanness.

Zoning In on Mastery

The therapeutic use of daily life events with young people in out-of-home care is a policy aspiration of most Human Service organizations, often without a clear appreciation of what it really means to live with and influence the lives of challenged and challenging young people during important periods in their lives. The reader here is invited to 'zone-in' on a handful of child and youth care principles (Garfat & Fulcher, 2011) that assist workers to enter *zones of proximal development* in shared life spaces with particular young people in designated out-of-home care placements. Duty of care obligations impact on 'zones' that determine whether daily life events offer therapeutic opportunities for young people that help them to achieve developmental outcomes that matter in out-of-home care.

Participate with Young People as They Live Their Lives

At conference workshops and keynote addresses, Henry Maier used to remind Child and Youth Care Workers, Social Workers, Supervisors and Managers that BEFORE a word is even spoken, the whole *sensori-motor stage* of cognitive development has been re-activated. Maier (1979) further argued that Specialised Behaviour Training with young people is most successful when Bodily Comfort, Differences, Rhythmicity, Predictability, and Dependability components of his Core of Care have been activated (Smith, Fulcher & Doran, 2012). Maier showed how relationships play a significant role in determining whether a young person achieves developmental outcomes that matter to that young person, and to her or his family members and community. Social capabilities and competencies build upon personal attachments. Nurturing self-management and enriching a child or young person's behavioural repertoires are closely linked to quality relationships with carers.

Working in the Now: The child and youth care field has become increasingly aware that learning is a social process rather than just, or even primarily, an individual, deep-brain learning process. Social learning happens in groups, or as Maier noted, at the very least through relationships. While contemporary Western psychological theory focused more and more on individual deep-brain learning processes, the Russian psychologist Vygotsky was arguing that learning and cognitive development take place firstly on a social plane before it is subsequently incorporated into a young person's cognitive schema. Knowledge and meaning are socially constructed by the particular parties involved in the social learning process – teachers or out-of-home carers and learners – rather than information merely transmitted from one person to the other, as more traditional views of teaching and learning might suggest (Stremmel, 1993). Through the assistance of a more capable person, a child is able to learn skills or aspects of a skill that go beyond that child's actual developmental or maturational level, with development following the young person's potential to learn.

Doing 'With', Not 'For' or 'To': From 1926-30, Vygotsky investigated the development of higher cognitive functions of logical memory, selective attention, decision making and language comprehension. This young Russian psychologist studied three different angles: first trying to understand the ways in which humans use objects as aides in memory and reasoning; second, how children acquire higher cognitive functions during learning; and third, ways in which learning trajectories are shaped by different social and cultural patterns of interaction. A central theme in Vygotsky's work related to what he called the '*zone of proximal development*'. Essentially, children or young people grow and can be supported in their personal and social growth towards the next stage of development through the guidance of appropriate adults or more skilled peers. This '*zone of proximal development*' is socially mediated and is shaped through dialogue and relationships in daily life events in their life space. Adults may be accorded a role as 'more knowledgeable others' in working with children, to help these young people to identify and develop personal and social skills. Peers also play a role in mediating personal and cognitive development, and especially social development (Emond, 2000).

Responsively Developmental: Vygotsky's idea of '*zone of proximal development*' lends itself to working with groups of young people because it is fundamentally social, and also broadly educational rather than individual and problem-focused. It reinforces the importance of relationships and thus provides a robust psychological underpinning for the therapeutic use of daily life events in social education or social pedagogy. Tragically, Vygotsky died of tuberculosis in 1934, at the age of 37, in Moscow, with much of his seminal work unpublished until the 1980s. Building later on the '*zone of proximal development*' idea, Eichsteller and Holthoff (2010) concluded that learning takes place when young people actually leave their comfort zone to explore wider dimensions of their environment, thereby extending their learning zone to the extent that young people review capabilities and extend the potential limits of their abilities. Pushed too far, young people enter a panic zone, where lack of knowledge and understanding – along with resultant anxiety – often inhibits their ability to learn. Alongside young people, youth workers and social workers encourage them to step out of their comfort zones and into personal learning zones.

Intentionality of Action: To create opportunities where young people can engage with optimal learning opportunities, she or he needs to experience a degree of safety and trust in their learning moment. The level of challenge each young person faces must offer a manageable fit with how they view their own capabilities. It is here that their '*zone of proximal development*' assumes considerable meaning in practice. Think of how many times, as a youth worker or social worker, one might have heard a young person say '*I'm in the Zone!*' This may have been around a sporting activity such as basketball or football, or an art, sculpturing or photography activity! For that reason, youth workers and social workers must remain attentive to this other 'zone' where opportunities for learning and achievement of developmental outcomes that matter can be nurtured intentionally.

Experiences of achieving developmental outcomes that matter provide a relational platform for continuing success. As Powis *et al* (1989) noted, a young person who lacks confidence in all areas of her or his life may just need achievement in one area from which to gain self-confidence sufficiently to shift personal attitudes about her or himself and experience enhanced performance in other areas of their life. Both *External* and *Internal Outcomes* require achievement if young people are to gain Mastery around survival skills.

MASTERY OUTCOMES THAT MATTER

Empowerment
Safety

Support
Carer Support
Positive Communication
Caring Relationships

Boundaries and Expectations
Boundaries for Daily Living

Connecting with a young person involves carers taking an interest in what sparks learning with each child or young person living in their shared life space. Such interest in learning and learning environments involves External Outcomes. Whether a young person is motivated to achieve and what they are motivated to achieve are different issues. Similarly, whether he or she actively engages in learning and what they achieve are different. Internal Outcomes influence whether he or she takes advantage of learning opportunities. Mastery is nurtured through daily life achievements in relationships with others who matter, over weeks, months and years. The recording format is shown below to review Mastery Outcomes, highlighting one of the internal assets – Actively Engaged in Learning.

(I) Actively Engaged in Learning: *(Young person's name)* got personally involved in learning activities at school, in work experiences or in other activities which further developed her/his life skills.

For example:

K has been busy with her art work for the art expo next week. She has completed 4 pieces of art work that will be displayed.

Achieving	X	Mostly Achieving		Some Achieving		A little Achieving		Not Achieving		Not Recorded	

(E) Supportive Environments: Relationships with teachers, activity leaders and peers offered _____ security, encouragement and nurturing that stimulated his/her learning and achievements.

(E) Carer's Involvement in Learning: Carers actively supported _____ to succeed in school, in work experiences and with other learning opportunities at home or elsewhere.

(I) Motivation to Achieve: _____ did his/her best to learn and to master new life skills or to realise personal goals.

(I) Making Use of Learning Opportunities and Homework: _____ participated in learning activities at home or elsewhere while also completing and submitting school homework on time.

Three of the Mastery Outcomes involve Internal Assets that are nurtured day to day. The other two Mastery Outcomes highlight External Assets associated with school environment and carer's involvement in their learning. Once again, relationships between carer or youth worker and a young person are fundamental to optimal learning and achievement opportunities.

Questions for Small Group Discussion or Guided Reflection

1.   What is meant by entering the Zone of Proximal Development with any young person in out-of-home care?
2.   What did the Russian Psychologist Vygotsky consider were the optimal conditions under which a child or young person will move beyond their personal comfort zone and try out new skills they have not used previously?
3.   In what ways might Ali's journey towards parole have demonstrated Mastery of particular life skills and achievement of developmental outcomes?
4.   In what ways do the Mastery Outcomes feature in Ali's zone of proximal development and her capacity for Mastery of important survival skills?
5.   Why is relationship so important in helping a young person develop Mastery?

Room 14
Tracey – *Survival Skills*

30 October: Summary of the Initial Planning Meeting

Tracey is a 17 year 1 month old Caucasian girl from a rural area of the State. She has been known to the Department for the past two years. After a short stay at the Assessment Center, Tracey entered a treatment program for drug users and was then paroled to the home of her mother. After attempting to forge a check, Tracey was placed in a group home in another town. When she ran away from that group home, she was placed in youth detention where she set fire to some magazines and escaped. Tracey was later apprehended and returned to the Assessment Center before being transferred to an open campus cottage at this institution for older girls. After 10 weeks, Tracey ran away and some weeks later handed herself in to the police back in her home town. While on the run, Tracey overdosed on Seconal, a barbiturate; had ongoing contact with her sister and mother who shielded her from the authorities; began running with an alleged "pimp" and "drug user", contracted gonorrhoea; and entered detention having lost approximately 20 lbs. Upon returning to this institution, Tracey was placed in the secure unit – one of two secure unit programs here – because of her being a high security risk, her skill with manipulation, and her failure to assert any personal responsibility for her actions.

Letter to Tracey from a Male Inmate in an Adult Penitentiary

"Hey Babi"

You really sound "cute" in your letters. Addition to that, I also enjoy the company you bring in each of your letters. I just wish that Claudell had all that cuteness and sweetness in his arms right now!

"Shit Sugar" it's no telling what kind of sex act that I wouldn't implant upon you. (Smile)

Are you positively sure that your caseworker doesn't censor your in-coming mail? Because Claudell sho don't want to say the improper word that will ridicule our correspondenceship! You dig?

Say look here. Send the flick of Suzie and I'll transport it to Lonnie.

And speaking of flicks, I've taken some recent ones. Unfortunately, because of your situation at that time you were unreachable, so I shot them to someone else. (Smile)

Now, the last but not the least, it's possible that I can send you the flicks that you already had. Do you wish for them? If so I'll send it in my next letter okay?

Claudell
Inmate 8373998

---

30 October: Summary of the Initial Planning Meeting (continued)

In summary, Tracey is a skilful manipulator who has conned her way through several programs designed to help her become a more responsible young person. She is a very perceptive girl who can sit and watch people long enough to find their weaknesses and then seeks to use those weaknesses for her own ends.

Tracey is resistive to sharing much about herself unless she feels in control and her energies at the present time are devoted towards keeping people away from her. If she had the option, Tracey would prefer definite sentencing at the adult prison for females so that when she has served her sentence, she could then go about her business. Tracey presents a pattern of dissocial behavior passed down through three generations of women in her family. There is a prevailing helplessness and depression with Tracey which prevents her from doing anything about it. So long as she has been able to manipulate her way around authority figures and people for her own needs, Tracey has had no reason to develop the personal skills to be successful on her own.

Man! Man! Man! Babi!

You do have your letter with a strong fragrant female odor! I love that aroma you send to Claudell.

You know it's so feminine smelling that I caught an erection, and didn't realize it until I was finish censoring your letter. (Smile)

By me being in deep thoughts about you now, I feel like I'm in my mind achieving another …. (Smile) … Yes I need it bad Sugar!

I better bring this to a closure … ha – ha – ha

Take care

Claudell
Inmate 8373998

30 October: Summary of the Initial Planning Meeting (continued)

Tracey is a charming young woman who is easily liked by the people around her. Unfortunately, she tends to use her charms in a self-destructive manner, getting people to do things for her. Tracey is well liked by her peers and while she has the capacity to make friends, it is her choice of friends that often gets her into trouble.

The following goals will guide our engagement with Tracey over the next few weeks.

1. Control manipulative behavior and nurture adequate daily living skills.
2. Help Tracey learn how to deal with direct and honest feedback from adults and authority figures.
3. Develop vocationally-oriented training which can be translated into actual employment situations.
4. Invite Tracey to explore how she might distinguish herself apart from her dissocial web of family and peers.
5. Work towards Tracey setting some goals for herself and beginning to work towards these goals in some sort of consistent fashion.

Her last school reports describe Tracey as an unmotivated, easily frustrated, and in general lazy student who is unwilling to put forth the effort necessary to succeed in school even though her test scores show average potential. Tracey gets along with her peers in the classroom but expects them to cater to her whims and wishes. Teacher-student relationships are poor when confrontation is required. It is felt that Tracey will need a full review of all areas of her educational performance and no attempt should be made to consider the Graduate Equivalency Diploma exam until she brings up her performance with Mathematics.

> The GED option was explored but ruled out because Tracey lacks interest in doing the necessary preparation. Her educational program here will seek to get Tracey motivated in school and to explore those areas in which she shows the most interest and abilities.

Dear [Social Worker]

It has become a great concern of mine, of wanting to know what is happening with Tracey.

As you should already know if you look into your files, you'll find that Tracey and I were given the privilege of corresponding. And for some distance of time, we have been gratefully.

But now it seems sort of funny that I haven't heard from Tracey in several weeks, and I'm complexed behind the fact that you people haven't informed me why this is so.

In due respect, I need some kind of explanation coming from somewhere.

Like I quote above, I am a concerned relative and would appreciate quite highly if you can make it possible that I hear from Tracey soon.

So thank you for reading.

Sincerely,

Claudell
Inmate 8373998

26 November: Care Worker Notes

Tracey contacted me and asked if I would talk with her for awhile in the afternoon. The conversation was very slow getting started and towards the end, it became obvious that Tracey wanted to talk about herself but seemed unable to do so. In following the Board focus, I did little towards taking her off the hook since she is indeed capable of doing things for herself. Nothing of any real significance was discussed but it did sort of set the stage for what transpired about three hours later.

Tracey received a telephone call from her mother when we were about halfway through dinner and she was quite upset by the time the call was finished. Mrs M observed that she was paper-white and under considerable strain, she excused Tracey to her room so she could regain composure. She returned and joined the group about 20 minutes later but was obviously depressed and sort of retreated off by herself.

Tracey asked if I would talk with her again and we got together a little before eight and talked until just before bedtime. First off, I asked her about the telephone call and that opened the door! Generally speaking, Tracey came on in as open a manner as she is probably capable of doing at this time.

Beginning with the phone call, there were some heavy residual feelings even a couple of hours later. At first, Tracey claimed that she was unable to really identify some of her feelings but once she saw that I wouldn't buy that and with a little probing on my part, she was able to sort out these feelings and place a tag on most of them: hate, anger, disgust, betrayal, loss of respect, abandonment — all were there in varying degrees.

There was a lot of ambivalence in Tracey's feelings about her mother. Almost as though she wanted to hold all these bad feelings toward mother, but not willing to totally shut and lock the door between the two of them. She was able to give some examples of the increasing failures in their relationship. Mother has an endless string of boyfriends, is frequently drunk, "interference" in Tracey's life, etc.

When I asked Tracey to describe certain incidents in more detail, it came through very strongly that Tracey at many points in the past kept hoping that her mother would take control of her. Tracey hoped that her mother would stop her from doing some of the things she was involved in. But mother consistently failed to live up to these expectations, much to Tracey's disgust and disappointment. I treaded this area carefully since I was not very sure of my ground.

When I summarized in simple terms what we had just talked about, Tracey offered only token protest and then almost immediately accepted what I'd said and there was little evasion from that point onward. The key points we covered are outlined below:

1. Tracey seems to have an excellent picture of her present situation and has thought realistically about her future, even to the extent of working out some alternate long-range goals, should the primary ones become unattainable for whatever reasons.

2. Tracey claims to hold an intense dislike towards someone "caring" for and about her. Quite staunchly denies that she feels any sense of obligation towards the one or two people thus far in her life who fall into that category. I feel that the exact opposite is true in both cases. Here again, strong ambivalent feelings. She craves desperately to have someone care about her but is afraid to take a chance and/or feels unworthy.

3. Despite her bravado, Tracey is quite fearful of many things, not the least of which is life itself. She vehemently denied at first being afraid of anyone or anything, and in particular: "I'm not afraid to die!" In the end, she admitted that she just "might" harbor some fears but I didn't push it any further because she was becoming quite agitated.

4. Tracey is preoccupied much of the time with thoughts of death and how "great it would be if I didn't have to worry or think about anything anymore". She had thought a number of times that she would have been much better off if she had died the time she overdosed. She smiled when I told her that if that had been the case, I would not have had the experience of meeting her and that certainly would have eliminated a pleasant experience for me.

5. Tracey is both fascinated and repelled by the drug scene. She talks bravely of being able to withstand temptation and claiming if she wanted it bad enough she could get it here in the secure unit with no real risk other than being caught while she was high. So why would anyone believe she was now able to handle it outside? I think she knows damn well at this point that she would not be able to turn drug down if available.

6. Despite her cool and sophisticated exterior, Tracey does not have much confidence in herself. This came out in her continued inability to come up with committed answers — even to the point of yes or no. She would not take a firm stand on anything until I accused her of being a cop-out artist. Even then, she had to be pushed occasionally to settle on something definite.

7. I strongly suspect that Tracey spends most of her time in quite heavy depression, very pessimistic. This came across clearly throughout our entire session. "Nothing really worth living for". She's probably hurting most of the time.

8. One fear Tracey was not at all hesitant to speak about was the State Prison for women or similar places. She said, "If I ever get sent to a place like that I know I'll kill myself, because for sure, my life will end anyway on the day they put me in there. I would soon go crazy if I had to put up with the things that go on in places like that". No further comment needed!!

9. Tracey shared details about her Boards chaired by Mr L and how much she hated him for "threatening me" and generally laying it on the line to her. Tracey went on for quite awhile about what an awful person he was, and how much she detested him. But then she blew the whole thing by saying, "He sure is a good looking guy though! I'd sure like to have him come over and talk to me so I can figure out why it is that I dislike him so much." I asked whether that statement wouldn't be more correct if it went, "I'd sure like to have him come over and talk to me so I can find out why it is that he dislikes me so much!" I only wish everyone could have observed her response to that! The first real color I've ever seen in her face and stunned into absolute silence before finally able to stutter. I couldn't resist kidding with "maybe I'll write this up for Mr L in the Log so maybe he'll come over and talk to you".

That was the end of our conversation. Tracey muttered something about having to go check on her laundry and took off. She even left her cigarettes and ashtray behind. Ten minutes later it was bedtime, so I took these to her room and stood there waiting until she had to go into her room or be late. Tracey had still not recovered her poise and my grin did not help much, nor did my repeating my statement about writing in the Log again. She finally laughed and called me a big mean old dummy, gave me a hug and said "good night" – still grinning.

I was a little surprised by the hug — I thought it would take longer to get the first one. At any rate, I felt our session was quite a success and one hell of a good start for both of us.

Dear [Secretary of Social Worker]

According to your reply explaining the absence of Tracey's social worker, why wasn't I able to further my correspondence with my relative Tracey?

I am still at this present time standing in demand of wanting to know why Tracey hasn't been able to write.

Mrs [Secretary] so far I have had no response from no one.

I want immediately, some sort of reasoning, why Tracey has been cut off from corresponding with her relative.

Shall I take some sort of legal action against all of this? Or just what?

So please do reply. Thank you for reading.

Claudell
Inmate 8373998

2 December: Care Worker Notes

I had another short, but interesting session with Tracey tonight. We talked further about her family — mother, stepfather (in prison), older sister and younger sister. She still holds a lot of feelings towards mother — talked extensively about the many "in and out of the home" moves she made and the circumstances which surrounded each.

I mentioned that from what I had been hearing, it didn't appear that she had made much of an effort towards getting it together with her mother. Tracey replied that she had even gone to a psychiatrist (at the urging of her parole counselor) in an attempt to get something going. Then it came out that she quit going after two half-hour sessions because there were no miracles forthcoming in that time.

Tracey swears that working things out with her mother is impossible and she has given up. So I asked her how come the subject of her mother keeps coming up in our conversations all the time. She had no answer for this, other than to protest that she was not the one to keep bringing it up.

Tracey talked a lot about her depressed feelings and it came out that this occurs quite frequently and almost always is caused by thinking about the things she has done in the past; with no real friends anywhere; and overwhelming feelings of worthlessness and hopelessness come as the result.

When asked how these situations develop, she was unable to describe exactly what happened – "It just comes on – that's all". When I suggested that at times she did this deliberately and even might enjoy being totally down and out, Tracey fell about herself trying to convince me otherwise. She did admit a little later that this was probably true although she had never given it much real thought.

She said nobody around here had ever seen her acting depressed except on rare occasions. I responded by suggesting that it was quite likely that she was depressed most of the time, but seldom was it possible to tell merely by looking at her. Once she got to the privacy of her room, she probably "let it all hang out" and thoroughly wallowed in her depression. This comment also shook her up. She is so caught up in preserving the image of a tough kid who "won't let anybody know she's hurting" that she would literally rather die than let on to any of us how she really feels.

Surprisingly, she agreed to come and let me know the next time she gets so depressed and wishfully conjures up visions of death and "final peace". We will try to talk it out on the spot and attempt to keep it from reaching a point of severity.

I also mentioned that if she ever could break the habit of eagerly reaching out for and embracing her depression, then perhaps it would become only a minor source of irritation instead of a major problem.

By this time, Tracey had quit offering even weak protests. She merely grinned, nodded her head, and departed to get her chores done.

Dear Mr Claudell
Inmate 8373998

I have received your letter upon returning from an overseas trip and regret that I did not inform you earlier of the circumstances around which your correspondence with Tracy was terminated.

When you first wrote me, you explained that you were a relative and this fact was reflected in our decision to permit correspondence.

However, Tracey finally admitted that you are not actually a relative. Her relationship with you has been anything but a relationship of family relatives.

Owing to the pretence around which you originally requested correspondence privileges, these privileges were subsequently denied.

There were clear indications that during the period whilst you were corresponding with Tracey, you did not handle this privilege appropriately.

Sincerely,
[Social Worker]

8 December: Care Worker Notes

I passed on to Tracey the information passed on by the Superintendent to tell her that the recreation supervisor will not be returning to work. Tracey will not be required to make any statement or undergo any interrogation and was quite relieved to learn this. Anyhow, since there were a few disparities in the stories received about Tracey's relationship with Mr J, I flat out asked her what the full story was.

Tracey admitted that she paid for her passage to go AWOL from the open campus cottage by being intimate with Mr. J. I don't know how others feel about his, but I feel that this fact should be included in the official record. I also told her that this would be the last time this subject would be discussed unless she felt some need in the future to talk about it further.

Tracey was in a talkative mood and I allowed her to choose her own course. Nothing of real significance came through, but we did talk about getting to the business at hand concerning mother. We tentatively agreed to begin on this tomorrow afternoon. Tracey is not as unwilling to get started on it as I might have expected.

11 December: Care Worker Notes

We were able to scratch the surface in regards to mother tonight. Initially it didn't go too well since Tracey was pissed at me because she couldn't manoeuvre her way out of doing certain portions of her room cleanup as per expectations.

The anger quickly dissolved when I pointed out that this sort of behavior was part of past patterns which needed to be changed. If she couldn't handle the little and relatively unimportant items of responsibility that were laid on her, how could she hope to make responsible decisions of an important nature in the future? Tracey is still checking us out although she denies this. It's no big deal so long as we realize what is going on.

Tracey was a little reluctant to get into the family situation, but eventually we managed to get under the surface a little bit. There are a lot of bad feelings towards mother and stepfather in regards to the physical mistreatment she received from both. The beatings dated from the time when her mother and stepfather started having marital difficulties.

This took some digging to establish and Tracey apparently hadn't connected those factors until it was pointed out to her. This gave her pause to reflect and she could see where the parents' personal problems must have been a contributing factor towards their abuse of Tracey and her brother. Both parents would apparently grab the first thing within reach and wallop both kids. Tracey had to have stitches in her scalp on at least one occasion and another time stepfather lashed her across the face with an electric appliance cord.

It became easier for Tracey to share information about her family as time went on. She offered the "professional opinion" that her stepfather was possessed of a split personality since he was either in a pleasant frame of mind or else wild and punitive with his behavior – and none of it was predictable.

The indiscriminate beatings began when Tracey was about 14 as she can recall beatings continued for close to three years, whenever she spent more than a half day with her mother at a time.

Tracey finally struck back at mother one time and even though mother still threatens to strike Tracey, she doesn't carry through because Tracey threatens immediate retaliation in kind.

Tracey was never able to dare such self-defence until after stepfather was shipped off to the penitentiary. From the time she was 14, when Tracey told to her mother about an attempt by her stepfather to molest her, her mother has never ceased accusing Tracey of promiscuous sexual relations with all and anybody. Mother flat out accused Tracey of being a liar about the reported molestation attempt, and has never believed her daughter's story to this day.

I get no tangible evidence that Tracey is in any manner racially prejudiced, but she sure as hell believes strongly in racial identity. There are a lot of feelings about mother preferring Black men and the predominant one is that mother has betrayed her own race and demeaned herself by doing so.

Tracey also spoke of her older sister and the problems she experiences, which are minute compared to what her kids have to deal with. Tracey has had boyfriends from both races and there is little doubt as to her own preferences. I had her explain this to me in some detail and friends — the little lady has a handle on the situation to be marvelled at in a person of her age! She spoke of little items like consideration, respect, empathy, compassion (feeling for others were her words), honesty and trust. I was impressed folks! Tracey also talked of racially mixed children and she really holds some strong views on that subject.

Tracey was finally able to admit that she had some good feelings about mother despite the maltreatment at her hands. She has concluded, however, that spending more than an hour or two at a time with her mother is out of the question.

Tracey spoke about a lot of warm and affectionate memories from her childhood prior to age ten when things were really neat and her mother was a loving person towards her. Since her stepfather appeared on the scene there had been zero physical contact between members of the family except on the business end of some sort of weapon.

I kidded her about being a softie at heart and she flared up with "I'm not afraid of anything – I'm not even afraid of dying!" (This is the second time I've heard this same statement in the past couple of weeks.) I didn't pursue this opening tonight because we were out of time, but I did blow her mind by saying, "You know, for a tough hard kid, you sure do think a lot of soft thoughts!" This one really staggered her, but I'm not sure why. From her expression, I knew I had struck a chord.

23 December: Care Worker Notes

We covered some further ground about Tracey's problems with mother. It about blew me away when it finally came out that her mother is a Jehovah's Witness (part-time) and when she is in the religious mode, everyone also had to participate. Tracey and her mother have had many a go-around concerning this topic and much of it orbits around Tracey's younger sister whom mother forces to attend the JW meetings three times a week.

Tracey meanwhile had rebelled and flat refused to have anything further to do with them, and how hypocritical her mother was. Tracey had attended some Pentecostal services with a friend and enjoyed it.

They didn't try to cram religion down anyone's throat and had quite a widely developed young peoples' program with all sorts of activities. One day she took her younger sister with her and she really turned on to this church group.

Mother was absolutely furious and this has continued to be a major source of conflict between Tracey and her mother. I'm sure Tracey provides considerable irritation because there is a lot of competition between mother and herself where her younger sister is concerned.

Mother screams at Tracey to keep her nose out of it, "You're not her mother!" Tracey responds with "Well I might as well be. I practically raised her myself!"

Of all the things I suspected may eventually surface, religion was probably the last thing in the world I would have expected.

Tracey's conversation then wandered before she confessed that there was something nagging on her conscience for the past week. Before going to that, she talked quite extensively about Claudell and her feelings for him. Tracey trying to convince herself that continuing their relationship would be the best course of action. However, all she accomplished was the opposite. She concluded that her only positive course of action was to chop it off, and the sooner the better! I asked what factors were she weighing up about which I was unaware?

Tracey finally blurted out that Claudell is a pimp as are all the members of his family. It weighed heavily on her conscience that she had lied about him and said he was a relative in order to obtain writing privileges with him at the State penitentiary. Tracey is feeling a heavy dose of guilt. Her Social Worker will have heard lies before. The important thing was that her conscience had bothered her and she was able to talk about it in just a few days time.

She is determined that the first thing she will tell [Social Worker] when he returns from leave is about the lie. I said telling you was her own responsibility and she acted a bit affronted that anyone would think it necessary to tell her so. "Hey, I don't need anyone to speak for me! I can do my own talkin'!"

22 January: Social Worker Note

Tracey caught me today for a few moments and apologized for the lie about Claudell. I feel she's doing the very kinds of things we hoped for. Don't feel we have to move too fast.

5 February: Summary of the Planning Board Meeting

The Supreme Court ruling on 18 year-old dependent-incorrigible young people being discharged from State Welfare care has been a real eye-opener for Tracey. She sees that she must prepare herself in six months to go out on her own. Tracey is now looking at future planning and how she can use the rest of her stay at the institution to her benefit. Tracey is initially frightened of making decisions and of taking the initiative on her own, choosing if possible to let staff make decisions for her. However, Tracey needs to learn to make the decisions and we will have to use these opportunities to let her test her new found skills.

5 March: Summary of the Planning Board Meeting

There has been overall improvement in Tracey's total performance in the program since her last Board. She has been enrolled in the GED program in the open campus school and is working hard in this area. She still has trouble with impatience and is easily frustrated. It is during such times that she gets staff to do things for her. She has made strong attachments to at least two staff with whom she has explored a number of childhood experiences.

Tracey needs to be enrolled in full-time campus school. She was given off-campus visits for a night or a weekend – to be evaluated later. The opportunity to work part-time in the Central Kitchen was also mentioned. Tracey still needs to be here and be plugged into people and purposeful activities for awhile. She knows that it will be at least three months before she can take and pass her GED exam, and she accepts this.

Tracey has made more gains in a short period of time than any girl we have had. This is a kid who is well put together, with unlimited potential but she is virtually without resources. Functions okay under stress and can handle disappointments well. Occasional temper problems, but only when pressures are insurmountable. Quickly comes round and is soon able to be the well-adjusted Tracey.

Addendum

No further documents were included in Tracey's file. She stayed on long enough to take and pass her Graduate Equivalence Diploma (GED) and was discharged from the State System at the age of 18 – a looked after kid with qualifications! We hope it went well for Tracey. She deserved it.

Aliese's Reflections

In reading just the first paragraph, you could see this kid had already gone through hell. Forging a check and setting fire to the magazines – well that was pretty ingenious. In the system for say the last two years and all grown up. It is like your life being set before you and you know there is no way of escaping the tragedy. That is how it felt. Although we resisted change, we also knew the inevitable and we all hoped we would not get lost in this new creation.

I find it interesting how so many of the girls that I met throughout all the years, have these similarities in their lives. The older boyfriend, usually someone who has been incarcerated, or is currently serving time – why did we all gravitate towards that which made us comfortable, that with which we were familiar and not necessarily good for us? And are we all so different today? So often, they gravitated back to their pimp and abuser. I never really experienced that so it was hard for me to relate to then and today. Love binds us to people in so many fashions and where we find this so-called love is often at the hands of the abuser.

According to the case notes of the initial meeting, Tracey wanted to be incarcerated and get the whole thing over with. She would have preferred going to a women's prison to serve her time. That is pretty harsh, as prison was no joy ride either. I think that is really how ALL of us felt, because it was more of an adult setting. We resented being treated like children, because we had fought so hard for our independence: independence from our families, our moms, our dads, the schools, the churches, the hood, the string of foster homes and diagnostic centers, and so on. Even if that meant hooking up with a pimp, or a man of our own, who abused us. In prison Tracey could just do the time and move on, and not spend any real time on dealing with any issues concerning her or her family life. All were resistant and it took some time to break through our hard core shells.

Another commonality was these girls had so many issues with their moms and the struggles of the parents, and trying to relate to the parent's failures in their lives, and realizing the mirror image set before them. I guess that goes back to what I wrote earlier and that again, my experience was very different in many ways. My political awareness and passion, my community awareness and activity, moving around so much – I didn't have to sort out all the interpersonal daily relationships with a direct family.

There is mention that Tracey 'tagged' her emotions – and I think it is marvellous to see her perception in this. That is a lot for any PERSON to digest. Let's see, "hate, anger, disgust, betrayal, loss of respect, abandonment" – all were there in varying degrees. I am amazed at Tracey's self-awareness so early on in her life. That leads us to hope that Tracey is a success – somewhere over that rainbow. I can certainly relate to her feeling disconnected and the feeling of not having any real friends. I think many of us only connected to a handful of people at any one given time. I think we could only handle a couple of serious relationships at a time, so if that was our friends or a boyfriend, it was hard to have any real connections with authority figures or alienated parents. Once trust is broken in any relationship it is so hard to restore it.

Sad that the counselling didn't work out for the mom and Tracey – but it is nice to see an attempt was at least being made, IF nothing else, for Tracey to understand – that people are people, and people are not perfect and that is okay. Also to really understand that hurting people hurt others and that so much pain that is caused by our loved ones is not because they want to hurt us, but because, in some cases, they have no control over their actions. It was her goal to step outside of all of that and become her own self, full of her own ideas, opinions and dreams. Tracey was having to learn to step outside of her depressing little comfort zone where she manipulated everything and everyone around her. She was learning lessons of communicating and negotiating in the world around her and was obviously very intelligent.

So astute of the social worker to want Tracey to deal with her problems *now*. One, not reaching out to that familiar space of pain in her life and embracing it; two, "Johnny on the spot" – rather than tunnelling into some deep frenzy of emotion – I MEAN that is what we all needed to learn to do. She gets herself started, getting caught up in this thought process and letting things escalate – and now she is learning to cope.

These feelings of worthlessness, being lost, disconnected, unsure, stemming from her relationship with her mom; could literally choke you to death ... and Tracey lacking any faith or positive experiences from which to draw ... found it quite easy to fall into a very real and dramatic response contemplated through death and suicide. She was very lucky and very blessed to have such an insightful and loving team, at the "end of the road" in that secure unit. Easily enough, all of us could have found a totally different experience here. Keeping the tough exterior holds true today, to some degree, I'm just sayin! Smile.

When you delve deeper into Tracey's story you find all the physical abuse and horrific beatings and physical attacks. It is a wonder that anyone can pull through those types of day-to-day run-ins and stand tall and brave and learn to focus on inter-relationships and coping skills. I mean, WOW! My sweet sister of pain suffered greatly and certainly beyond any trials a young girl should endure – with that being said, I feel certain in my heart Tracey is out there in this world knocking down barriers and finding truth.

Survival Skills

Like other authors of his time, Hungarian Holocaust survivor Eugene Heimler spent a lifetime writing about lessons learned through his experiences as a teenager who survived two concentration camps for political prisoners and two extermination camps, including Auschwitz, where those entering the camp passed under a sign reading *"Work Will Set You Free!"* (Heimler, 1975). As a teenager, Heimler found himself the principal carer of children working in the Camp kitchens supervising the peeling of potatoes and helping with the preparation of food for the guards. Through access to potato peelings and scraps of food, Heimler and some of these children were survivors, and many later re-settled in the West.

Like other survivors, Heimler wrote about psychological experiments involving meaningless work carried out with prisoners. When rubble caused by Allied Forces bombing needed to be cleared, volunteers stepped forward from amongst the prisoners to help clear it. Such activity had a purpose and gave prisoners a form of meaning in life. The Nazi psychologists decided to test the effects of ¨meaningless work¨ requiring prisoners to move rubble from one end of the compound and then move it back again, hour after hour. As exhausted prisoners lost all sense of purpose, time and time again they committed suicide either by throwing themselves upon the electrified fences or were shot while trying to run away.

Based on his professional work with chronically unemployed *workshy* youths, Heimler later highlighted the emotional significance of purposeful activity that facilitates learning and creativity whilst reinforcing personal well-being. For a number of reasons, the central role played by purposeful activity with young people in out-of-home care is often undervalued. One reason may relate to a Poor Law legacy of less eligibility and the lingering assumption that state welfare provision should not be fun but should be about work instead. 'The work' in out-of-home care is often driven through care planning processes that focus primarily on a young person's social, emotional or cognitive deficits. The spectre of less eligibility and the failure to appreciate the central role of play and activities in normal child development can result in activities being used as a privilege that might be withdrawn as a consequence for bad behaviour. An equally valid argument might claim children who misbehave need to engage in more activities.

Another reason that activities do not receive the prominence they should is because the training for social work or child and youth care rarely includes input on the importance of activities. Nor does that training equip carers and social workers with survival training skills that they might use in their daily work. This contrasts with European social pedagogy training where roughly a third of the curriculum teaches practical, cultural and recreational activities that intending workers might use in their work. In the absence of specific training around the purposeful use of activities, most carers and social workers rely on personal interests and skills brought to their work from prior experience.

Most who have worked for any length of time with young people in out-of-home care are likely to reflect that their most memorable or 'breakthrough' moments happened during some activity. Phelan captures this tension between work and play when he speaks about working with children and young people as:

> *"connecting kids with their world … to the universal things they will find in life which are available to us all – fun, games, sea sport,*

mountains, walks … and ideas and knowledge. Is it possibly a sign of our own tendency to expect the worst that we offer all these clich skills to problem children – conflict-resolution, problem-solving, anger-management, self-defence …? I wonder how necessary these would be if we offered them experiences in sailing, vegetable growing, soccer, playing drums or fixing bikes" (2001: 1)?

Play is widely recognised as a powerful vehicle for learning and development, where the rudiments of life skills are trialled and tested. It sparks qualities of imagination and creativity, as well as skills of turn-taking, thus promoting cognitive and social growth that are fundamental to growing independence so that young people are equipped with the survival skills needed to operate autonomously and live interdependently with other people. The nature of play changes with age and stage, and it need not always be formally organised. Seemingly aimless 'mucking about' and horseplay in which teenagers engage can be just as important in helping them gain a sense of their place in the world as a toddler might demonstrate whilst playing with bricks.

Although discouraged within child protection debates, horseplay can be a natural part of growing up, for boys in particular. Biddulph (2003) suggests that in order to get along with boys, one should learn to wrestle. Whilst needing to be aware of the issues that can arise as a result of physical play and different comfort levels associated with in engaging in such activity, it is important not to read pathology into what, for many children, involves normal developmental behaviours. Many concerns have built up within child protection circles that now restrict certain activities like wrestling that involve physical touch.

There are many life skills – and survival skills – to be learned and much enjoyment to be gained through recreation and leisure activities, and also from team sports and competitions. Being active, feeling active, thinking active and living active all reinforce personal health and well-being. There is a growing body of research which shows that participation in activities, hobbies and useful tasks promotes resilience (MacLean, 2003). Steckley (2005) highlighted the resilience promoting possibilities of purposeful activity in her study of team sport in fostering pro-social behaviour and a sense of belonging amongst a residential school football team. VanderVen has written about opportunities that nurture staying power amongst children through an organized family and toddlers' jog (2008).

White argued that sport gives opportunities for children (and adults) to rehearse skills – including survival skills – needed to operate in everyday life, such as *"boundaries, self-expression and training, teamwork, the acceptance of losing and winning, and playing in a defined space and way"* (2008: 170). While not all children or young people are adept at, nor interested in sport, social skills – including survival skills – can also be learned and practised through the purposeful use of activities, whether through role play, theatre, music or art. The survival skill of 'stick-ability', for instance, might be fostered through perseverance in the fine motor skills required in activities such as jewellery making, painting or extended board games, whilst teamwork is as apparent performing in a music group or drama production as in any team sports.

All but one of the five Developmental Outcomes monitored under the theme of *Independence* involve Internal achievements. As a young person moves towards independence, he or she is required more and more to take ownership of, or internalise their own values, beliefs and daily practices so that when they travel, these 'rules for daily living' travel with them, wherever they go. Making good decisions and plans, learning to exercise personal power wisely, behaving responsibly and developing a positive view of the future are all important as young people develop growing independence from their primary carers. Learning to engage in structured activities with others strengthens a young person's resilience around using social skills and competencies learned in one place and time when moving or transitioning to a new place, with new social challenges and opportunities.

The recording format illustrated in the Planning and Decision-Making example shown below is used with all 5 Independence *Outcomes.*

(I) Planning and Decision-Making: *(Young person's name)* exercised positive planning, chose from a number of options and attempted to solve his/her problems.

K is making plans for herself and at the last minute, demanded that I do what she wants. When I refused, she became angry and started swearing around. Maybe because she hasn't spoken to her Mum and she knows that Mum's not answering her calls on purpose.

Achieving		Mostly Achieving		Some Achieving		A little Achieving		Not Achieving	X	Not Recorded	

(I) Personal Power: _____ expressed her/his feelings in a manner that took account of others, and able to have a say over things that happened in her/his life.

(I) Responsibility: _____ demonstrated age appropriate self care, awareness of what constitutes a healthy lifestyle and accepted personal responsibility for his/her actions.

(E) Activity Programmes: _____ participated in two or more structured community activities, hobbies, interest groups or clubs during the past week.

(I) Positive View of Personal Future: _____
demonstrated a positive awareness of his/her culture or spiritual identity, found the world interesting and enjoyable while showing that he/she has a place in it and demonstrated optimism about their future.

Questions for Small Group Discussion or Guided Reflection

1. What survival expertise might you want included in the personal survival bag you might carry when dropped into a wilderness camp, a house in the suburbs, or inner city tenement apartment? What is left out of your survival bag and why?

340

2. What additional survival skills might a young woman like Tracey need if she were dropped into similar locations – a wilderness camp, a suburban group home, or sleeping on the couch in somebody's tenement apartment?

3. What is the emotional significance of purposeful activity amongst children and young people in out-of-home care?

4. What resilience and survival skills did Tracey bring with her from family and extended family experiences and relationships?

5. How does a focus on survival skills in Tracey's story differ from a deficit-focus?

Room 15
Maria – *Generosity of Spirit*

My Story

As early as I can remember from my childhood is that at the age of four I was adopted into a White family. At that time I was the first child in these White parents' family.

Before I became their child, I was beaten and had black and blue marks. I didn't talk with nobody until about 5 or 6 months afterwards. I spent most of my time in my room or by the fireplace.

13 November: Social Worker Notes

Now I know what pulling teeth is all about! By and large, I didn't get much except for the very strong feeling that Maria is very tuned in to what is going on around her and with her at any point in time. She was not relaxed around me. I'm wondering if the female staff might not be able to do a better job in the one to one with Maria.

As an 18 year 5 month old girl, Maria has been at this institution before and lived in one of the open campus programs. She had her extended furlough living in the city cancelled after an incident of attempted assault, brandishing a gun in the office of her parole counselor while high on drugs.

Maria does feel safe here and agreed with me that her life at the present time has very little, if any direction. A "boyfriend" at the neighboring youth justice institution may well be the only real "people" contact Maria has in the world. Please share your thoughts about whether we might want allow this relationship to continue – with monitoring.

I can remember some things like walking on the beach with my White father, or my White mother reading The Three Bears about seven times a day.

My first word I spoke to someone was No. My White mother asked me to set the table and I said No.

Before I used to sing while I was in bed, or talk to myself. I threw up a lot. My folks said I was afraid, then I stopped.

18 December: Social Worker Notes

We have a lead on an Indian foster home. She is an older lady married to a White man and has had foster children before. I think we should go ahead and start checking this possibility out. I have given Maria the name and address so she can write a letter of introduction. We will go slowly and try to check things out at all points. In the meantime, follow through on the issue of anger control and sharp tongue. These behaviors need attention and soon.

Maria's Story (continued)

When I really began talking, I told my White mother that I wanted my real mother and told her that she and her husband took me away from my real mother to be mean.

I said I hated her for it and told her she just wanted to hurt me. I never talked with my White father about it as far as I can remember. Why, I can't say.

My folks took me to Court because I said I wanted my real mother, not my White mother. I was told there was no way I could get into my records.

Maria's Story (continued)

When I was in First Grade, I didn't have too many friends but one who lived 5 houses down from me. Her name was Katie. We were only friends because her mother used to drive Katie and me to school I guess.

I don't know why but I had a hard time in 1st Grade. I didn't read or work very well in school. I got into a lot of fights with the kids because I was called names and put down a lot because I was the only dark skinned person. The rest were White. It hurt me a lot. I used to cry walking home and when I got home never told my mom.

Then one day I asked my folks why I was made out of mud and sand?

344

They said I wasn't. I said "look at my skin and how dark I am from everyone at school". They said it was because I was Indian. I told them that was not so because everyone I knew or saw had real light skin. I threw my dinner on the floor and said I was made out of mud.

---

19 February: Summary of the Initial Planning Board (continued)

Maria is a very intelligent girl who often presents as someone who is dumb. She is very skilful in her ability to perceive what is going on around her and can use this basic survival skill to her advantage if she can establish plans to back them up.

The Supreme Court ruling on 18 year-old youths placed in institutions as dependent-incorrigible status meant that everyone thought Maria would be discharged because of her age. This left Maria up in the air recently but it has since been determined that she will stay at the institution for a short while until new plans can be made out for her future.

Maria's Story (continued)

I hated 1st Grade and my teacher. I remember she had this stick and I used to write with my left hand. Each time I did, she hit me. In reading I daydreamed about things and never read.

I used to throw paper around and outside, I got into fights. I hated the kids because they called me names. And the teacher hit me each time I wrote with my left hand.

2nd Grade was kinda the same. By then I started to steal. I took lunch money and extra things like candy. I took money because I bought candy with it after school or saved it for other days. I didn't get much candy at home so I guess that's why I took it.

Then in 3rd Grade, I took things from the store like candy and toys. One time I got caught. My mom did me in with the dog leash and my grandmother took me up and I had to say I was sorry. I didn't feel bad though.

19 February: Summary of the Initial Planning Board (continued)

Maria is a negative influence in the living unit. She angers easily and holds grudges. Does not accept constructive criticism well, often becoming hostile and refusing to listen. Maria's future plans are rather unrealistic and furthermore, she cares little about finding or accepting work. Her attitude is that the world owes her a living.

Maria's Report:

Since I arrived here, I have done a lot of thinking:

1.   *What did I do to mess up that got me back?*
2.   *What kind of things should I look at to make it, and what should I look at to keep away from what I did to mess up?*
3.   *I've started looking into a job so when I do leave, I would have one waiting for me in at the Indian Community Services Center in the city. I've filled out the application and mailed it off.*

Right now I do realize I have had a hell of a lot of chances and people pulling for me and in many ways doing a lot for me. It is true that I was the one who put myself back into the institution, because I didn't face everything I did while I was on parole.

Now that I am back I've have had some time to think about everything and work out what to do for myself while here. Now that I'm 18, it's all up to me when I walk out of here. I can't be running around like I did, having people find me work and telling them about my blues. It's up to me to keep my job and work out my own downs.

I can't be playing around on drugs and thrashing guns around because it will only hurt me. I am at the point now where I am trying and have made gains to do for myself. Now I have to remember it will be all up to me and no one else.

Maria's Story (continued)

In 3rd Grade my grandfather died. I remember I got up one morning and my grandmother said your grandfather died.

Just like that. I didn't believe her and I asked my dad and he said yes. I didn't talk to no one for a week. Just kept to myself.

He was nice to me and said he loved me. He held me on his lap a lot, and gave me boot rides.

4 April

Dear Mr [Social Worker]

I have some news for you. My sister is in the city and is coming down this Tuesday before 12:00 by bus.

She will arrive in the Capital and I would like to receive an okay to go off with Carole to get her employment on that day.

I feel we need to make some down to earth plans so we know where we stand.

Thanks
Maria

2 May

Request for Discharge

Juvenile Review Boards Supervisor

Dear Sir,

Maria was committed on at the age of 14 as a dependent-incorrigible child. She had been in the custody of a voluntary children's home, but school problems, runaway, and longstanding difficulties with her parents made it impossible for them to help her in the community. She was transferred to the institution for younger teenagers and paroled from that facility three and a half years ago. Less than a year later her parole was revoked and she was transferred to the secure unit.

The Assessment Center recommended intensive treatment in a highly structured program. She was place in a closed cottage for younger teenagers where she remained for nearly twelve months. She then was transferred to an open cottage and then eventually to our Exit cottage. She was placed on extended leave in the summer of that same year but was returned in December and placed in the secure unit for older teenagers.

Maria will soon be 19 years of age. She has been accepted into a vocational rehabilitation program and will be receiving assistance from an agency in the Indian community.

Technically, the commitment order lists Maria as a delinquent-dependent-incorrigible, but the petition to the court was entered as a dependent-incorrigible action and she has been classified dependent-incorrigible through her stay in the system. There are no allegations to support a finding of delinquency.

9 July: Telephone Contact

During a telephone call with her parole counsellor, we received word that Maria is still doing well with her community plan.

Addendum

By the time Maria joined the other girls in this secure unit, she had already survived more than 4 years in the State Welfare System, and before that voluntary children's services. None of the information available about this young woman provided any material about Maria's Native American ancestry. Maria was the person who pursued that journey, and this is where we lost contact with her – working at a Native American community center in the city.

Aliese's Reflections

Well Maria certainly was lucky that she did not get charged as an adult and end up serving hard time after brandishing that gun in her parole officer's office. Are you kidding me? They would have had the SWAT Team there, had it been me, or one of my closest friends! In the beginning, it sounded like she was so out of sorts and not willing to make any efforts on her behalf. Later, it appeared she took interest in herself as a person-that is hopeful. Perhaps she found her identity and womanhood as a Native American.

She had certainly spent the majority of her youth locked up in some facility or home of sorts, and it would have been interesting to know if there had been any real efforts made by anyone, to connect her with her tribe, or some involvement within the Indian community, such as Powwow's and Family Nights when we were taught how to create artwork, tools, clothing, those sorts of things. There was not much thinking along those lines during that time and I think since then, Youth Care in general has made great strides in understanding the value of cultural differences.

There is a difference between children who do not want to conform because the system was broken and those who were simply not making any connection at all. By that I mean, those who did not perceive the problems, the consequences, and the end of the road. I don't think she really understood the whole "end of the road" aspect for some time. I refer to her not being willing to make any efforts. That is certainly problematic because of her age. It takes time for that connection and trust to be founded. She was very lucky indeed to have come to this place in her life, as it appears so many had failed her in the past.

The youth of that day had a lot more backbone in some ways than today – sort of more rooted in their defiance, and though we were all facing hard issues in this nation (USA), it's youth and in Indian Country – that probably helped, in some ways, to keep Maria strong in some ways. As it did with most of us, that old saying about what doesn't kill you makes you stronger. Here she is now, 18.5 years old and lucky enough to be able to stay on for a short period rather than being booted out. It is interesting what it says in the case notes about her playing dumb and that it was not just a game, lack of communication or something deep and dark – just that it was simply a survival skill – that was probably pretty right on. Most of our reactions, actions, the face we put on to show the world came from our trick bag of skills and experiences.

That of course is one of the tragedies, that any one of us could have done something or got involved in something stupid, or without thinking that would have life changing effects, as mentioned with Maria's temper and allowing herself to get out of control. She had access to guns and whatever else she was involved with that no one knew about. It is frightening to think about how any one of these events in our lives could alter our life forever. We all learn that in hindsight, hopefully, and before we experience the devastation. It is not always the case. It sounds like towards the end of her stay that she had finally come to realize this was her life and she better start grabbing it by the reins and get some control.

I am not sure if this was the case with Maria or not, and I am not saying it is a good thing or a bad thing, but I think it is so typical for American Indians to look for work in their own community versus thinking outside of the box, entering college, and experiencing life outside of the reservation. She must have been from a federally recognized tribe to have a community center. While there is not a lot of mention about reservation life, or if she had ever experienced that within the confines of Foster Care, I just thought about that as a side note. Life has offered many changes to the Indian over the years, but forty years ago – we pretty much all stayed together on the reservation or had nothing to do with it at all. It is interesting to note there was no real discussion of furthering her education and I wonder if this was due to her lack of interest, or if the notes simply did not identify her scholastic goals. The system did not recognize the need to push in this area, and Indian life did not offer the same opportunities as the norm. I think they all learned about Indian life and the struggles that are beholden to the Indian community much later.

Either way, a dysfunctioning family life is what it is, regardless of race. It is unknown if this connection to the Indian Community Center was an attempt by her adult support staff or peers trying to get her connected into the Indian community as a means of support. Too bad, as for my reflection, it would be nice to know about her attitudes and goals. I would like to believe the caseworkers and others involved were a good influence upon Maria and that she found herself and her way.

Generosity of Spirit

Contributing is about undertaking positive, caring actions that benefit others. It means doing one's share to help things turn out well. A contributing young person cares about others and their wellbeing. She or he is affected by the feelings and experiences of others. This requires an ability to understand and know about others, their feelings, their culture and the things that they value or believe. Making a positive contribution is not just about doing things for others. It also involves considering how *all* of one's actions might affect other people. There are times when making a positive contribution might involve not doing something that one is tempted to do, for example, when a young person is angry and may want to strike out at someone verbally or even physically. She or he can sometimes make a positive contribution by choosing to calm her or himself, not strike out and engage in positive problem-solving, thereby contributing to the well-being of both self and others. When young people contribute to others' well-being, they demonstrate generosity, or giving of self for the benefit of others. Brendtro and Du Toit (2005) argued that generosity is a fundamental characteristic of healthy individuals.

Generosity grows out of the common things of life, through everyday encounters and daily kindnesses. In helping others, young people develop their own sense of worthiness through making positive contributions to another human life. Generosity is central to one's capacity to care and to be cared for, nurtured and cultivated. When it is, a sense of worth for self and others will ultimately steer young people towards pro-social patterns of behaviour and away from anti-social activities. Young people learn how to contribute to society, not so much through what they are told, but by how they are treated.

Scottish philosopher Hutcheson in the 18th Century argued that humans are imbued with natural feelings of benevolence (Scott, 1900). Such feelings guide their moral acts and instil an innate moral sense that informs their moral judgments, leading them to reach out to others with generosity. Such thinking was replaced by a dominant Enlightenment belief that reason rather than emotion should define and guide human actions. Qualities of reason and dispassion were thus given prominence (Tronto, 1994) and became particularly influential in social work as it developed as a profession. Pre-eminence given to qualities of reason and dispassion have resulted in caring relations understood as duty of care contracts, negligence and contractual obligations. Dominant ideas about what is 'professional' or 'unprofessional' behaviour leave workers vulnerable when trying to reach out to a new child or young person in distress as they enter out-of-home care.

Altruism involves a general predisposition towards concern for the wellbeing of others and for doing good. A growing body of research suggests that powerful benefits are evident in the mental and physical wellbeing of altruistic people (Brendtro & Du Toit, 2005). Altruism may be an abstraction for some. We can be altruistic when, for instance, we give money to charity when it does not involve us directly with the object of our charity. The quality of empathy (called sympathy in some of the literature) takes altruism into the realm of personal feelings for a concrete individual, allowing us to take the perspective of another. Compassion takes empathy or sympathy to the next level again by including the need or desire to take the next step and help alleviate suffering. Children appreciate the opportunity to care for others, to contribute and to be experienced as helpful.

Hoffman described empathy as *"the spark of human concern for others, the glue that makes social life possible"* (2000: 3), a biologically-based disposition for altruistic behaviour that enables us to respond to a variety of cues from another person. This is apparent from infancy through repetitive eye contact. The mirror neurons in our brains are activated by others' actions, expressions and emotions and act to imitate these as though the observer were him or herself sharing the same experience. We are, it seems, hard wired for empathy (Lacoboni, 2008) although any neuro-scientific predisposition towards the other is, not surprisingly, mediated by social conditions, culture and experiences. The empathic development of many young people in out-of-home care is frequently disrupted or distorted by previous experience.

Young people may have had to take care of themselves because others have not taken care of them in the way they should have. Such children learn to mistrust adults and adult expressions of generosity (Smart, 2010) and may come across as selfish, grasping and closed. These young people may respond to previous experiences by resisting or exploiting kindness. They may provoke the unkindness or rejection that characterised previous relationships. At another level, these young people may be burdened by guilt, imagining themselves responsible for things that have gone wrong in their families or with friends. These ways of 'being in the world' – while not necessarily adaptive – may have kept children safe, helped them to feel in control, and give their life meaning.

Empathy can be reinforced through nurturing and interdependent relationships (Perry, 2002). Mirror neurone activity is stimulated in children who grow up in a stable and nurturing emotional environment and through this they develop and learn to demonstrate empathic responses. Children who have experienced neglect or a lack of continuity of care experience less brain activity of this kind. This should not imply any permanent impairment. One of the problems with neuro-scientific perspectives applied to social settings is that information can be interpreted too deterministically. The brain, in fact, demonstrates a remarkable plasticity and resilience – and continues to develop and adapt throughout life.

Children and young people can – in supportive environments – learn how to respond better to others. A sense of empathy can lead to feelings of guilt or conscience pangs when we fail to respond empathically. While carers should try to avoid making children feel guilty, they should nevertheless be concerned about the development of conscience. Within the context of caring relationships and without nagging in any sanctimonious way, parents and carers need to nurture a child or young person's awareness about how behaviour makes others feel. Such experiences are vital to a young person's upbringing, and their development of pro-social behaviours. Within Native American networks such as those available to Maria, generosity of spirit invited her to join them after leaving the secure unit, offering continuing support as she adjusted to life outside of an institution. When we act on feelings of compassion, this behaviour becomes an act of kindness (Long, 2007). To experience kindness as helpful, rather than with suspicion, depends on trust – an emotional bond between people that must be earned and cannot be won or awarded.

The New Zealand Maori concept to *taha wairua* located within *Te Hauora Whare Tapa Wha* framework acknowledges a spiritual dimension of human functioning that pervades the entire being amongst these peoples of the South Pacific. Since Plato, Western readers have found difficulties with this dimension, perhaps through the influential teachings of Kant, Descartes and other philosophers who explored the so-called Mind-Body Problem arguing that in a rational world, the mind controls the body. Indigenous thinkers, including Maori and Lakota elders over generations, have operated from a wider epistemology, or way of knowing the worlds in which they live. We think this spiritual dimension has its place in child and adolescent development, drawing attention to morals, values and purpose in daily living. The five Outcomes that Matter associated with *Generosity* focus on three internal values that are nurtured through relationships with others, and two external outcomes that involve engaging with others and meeting others' expectations.

The five *Generosity* Outcomes – two External (E) and three Internal (I) – are recorded using the same format as shown below with the Service to Others outcome.

(E) Service to Others: *(Young person's name)* engaged in specific opportunities to help others in his/her daily living environment, in his/her neighbourhood or in their wider community.

For example:

K wasn't in the helping mood this week. She made sure that after she finished eating, she hurried into her room or said she will use the toilet so that she's not tidying up. But I always make sure that she does the dishes when it's her turn, to be fair to the girls.

Achieving		Mostly Achieving		Some Achieving	X	A little Achieving		Not Achieving		Not Recorded	

(E) High Expectations: Carer(s) and others encouraged _____ to do her/his best at school, at work or in other activities, and offered her/him recognition for doing so.

(I) Peaceful Conflict Resolution: _____ sought to resolve potential conflicts through compromise without physical aggression or resorting to hurtful action or language.

(I) Caring: _____ demonstrated the extent to which she/he places high value on helping others and considering the needs of others.

(I) Honesty: _____ showed that he/she can tell the truth even when it's not easy.

Questions for Small Group Discussion or Guided Reflection

1. What cultural traditions place high regard on nurturing generosity of spirit among children and young people, and how might those cultures differ from your own personal experience?
2. In what ways might Maria's generosity of spirit have been influenced by being hit by a ruler on the hand every time she was seen writing with her left hand?

3.   What personal, social and cultural challenges do the narratives show Maria had to face as an Indian child adopted as the first child into a White family?
4.   What might cultural safety mean for a young woman like Maria as she reflected back on what got her returned to the secure unit as a parole violator?
5.   What evidence was provided in Maria's narrative that would enable you to complete a short 2-3 line statement for each of that developmental outcomes achieved around Generosity?

Room 16
Irene – *Team Parenting*

8 August: Care Worker Notes at Irene's Intake

Irene started right off telling me what she was going to do. She had about two sentences out before I stopped her. She was told to sit there and be quiet. There were a few short words that she needed to hear: "Grow up" and "Handle yourself", for example, by coming to the office for her own medications.

She should not expect more than her fair share of our time because she won't get it. And if she wants out of here – it's up to her to do it!! She said all she really wanted was a home. I said great, but because you have never functioned very well when living in either father's and mother's home, or in her uncle's home or when living semi-independently in group homes, maybe she should plan on making your own home. She's not the first girl that has had to do this. There are a lot of young women who have made it successfully from here.

21 August: Summary of the Initial Planning Board Meeting

Irene is a 16 year, 7 month old Caucasian girl who came to this institution and the secure unit after having her parole revoked.

She was originally committed by the Juvenile Court for incorrigibility in the community, running away, making suicide threats and one suicide attempt. Prior to her commitment by the Juvenile Court, Irene spent several months at the child and adolescent mental health inpatient facility before transferring to a foster home. When the foster home broke down, Irene was placed in the State Assessment Center and then transferred to an institutional placement in the State institution for younger teenagers. Just over a year ago Irene was paroled to a group home north of the city. In addition to the group home prior to revocation, Irene lived in an interim home and at her uncle's home in another State. Each of these placements was unsuccessful and the primary problems leading to parole revocation involved Irene's behaviours being beyond the control of adults in the community.

On the day Irene arrived at the secure unit, she made the following statements:

1. *I started believing I had problems when I was first at the Assessment Center.*
2. *Places like this cause me more problems.*
3. *I am mad at people in institutions who screw up my life.*
4. *What I need most is a home.*

Since arriving in the secure unit this girl – all 5 foot 9 inches and 180 pounds of her – has spent most of her time being pushy, aggressive and loud-mouthed. Irene has displayed wide mood swings, from being loud, silly and mean, to whining, crying and demanding attention. She has poor grooming and her personal hygiene is poor. Her peer relations are poor. Irene is barely tolerated. She demands attention from adults and behaves like a spoiled, immature child ready to throw tantrums.

Irene has experienced much rejection during her life, and as a result of this rejection has almost insatiable needs for attention and affection from others. Irene is clearly depressed and has a very poor self-image. Unfortunately, however, she has developed a complete repertoire of negative attention-getting behaviours and few positive behaviours or skills for getting her needs met. Time spent in the State mental health and child welfare systems have only reinforced Irene's negative behaviours.

Irene is presently wearing a cast for dislocation and a chip fracture on her left ankle. The doctor felt that there were no further difficulties with her left ankle but as Irene explained that she was still in pain, the doctor felt he had no other alternative than to replace the cast. Irene is also on medication for haemorrhoids.

Irene displayed a "seizure type of behaviour" since she was at the institution for younger teenagers. The group home had Irene tested at the children's hospital and she was diagnosed with a minimal psychomotor seizure disorder. There are still questions about the diagnosis of epilepsy and further tests are scheduled. In the meantime, she is on mild medication for this condition.

Educationally, Irene is said to be a bright girl who has large gaps in her storehouse of knowledge. Preliminary school testing indicates that she is functioning at approximately her grade level. She is lazy, has poor work habits and manipulates her way out of difficulties through the use of weird behavior. During her second stay at the Assessment Center, it was noted that Irene's classroom behavior and overall educational performance had regressed somewhat. Irene's inability to use appropriate behaviors in her interactions with others leave her almost devoid of observable strengths, assets or resources that can be used for enabling her to re-enter the community at a level of marginal functioning. Until the behavioral smoke screens can be modified, it is difficult to say what the future holds for Irene.

The short term goals in working with Irene will be (1) to help her relax in the new situation in which she finds herself; and (2) focus on learning new social skills in her interactions with adults and peers.

22 August: Care Worker Notes

I rang and got hold of Irene's uncle. He told me that he didn't want phone calls from Irene because of the expense and he didn't think she could have got herself together this quickly. He indicated that they were a working family and wouldn't be a resource for Irene until she had sorted herself out.

He mentioned Irene's size and referred to his children as younger and unable to cope with Irene in the state that she was in and the way she was acting, let alone how he and his wife responded to her as adults. Uncle did ask if Mr [Social Worker] would contact him, as Irene's father would be visiting uncle's place in about a week. While father was there, they would probably like to telephone Irene.

I gathered from what I saw her do while talking on the phone and from what she told me later that Irene asked her uncle to send her cigarettes. I think Irene was truthful when she said she was crying for two reasons. First, she had written several times asking for cigarettes and had asked on the telephone. He said, no, that the only interest Irene had in them was to use them. Second, she was crying because she was happy to hear his voice and to talk with them and learn about their news.

Irene immediately wanted to know if she would get to call him and I said "No, for the time being". She then immediately asked to be allowed to call her mother instead of her uncle. I explained that a decision would have to be made by the Planning Board first.

I would suggest that Irene's father be allowed to call, as a resource, if he initiates it and if there is no indication that it may not be beneficial for her. Calls could be evaluated and stopped if there are any problems.

After speaking with Irene's uncle, I feel that Irene will really have to make a lot of changes in order to undo what she has already done in the uncle's home, even if she were to visit there again, let alone go there to live.

Irene's grandmother is old, and was recently in hospital for a short stay. She lives twenty or so miles from Irene's uncle, so he knows there is nothing of a crisis nature as concocted by Irene.

21 September: Care Worker Notes

While D was here visiting another girl Maria, he was allowed to take her picture on the patio. Irene walked over to the patio in her shorts and before I could get to her, D took her picture.

It seems that D is a best friend of SD. That's where Irene and SD got each other's addresses. Neither has seen the other but Irene has admitted writing to SD about her "sexy body"! Now SD is madly in love – Irene read me one of his letters and it was "I love you" etc. He told Irene he was writing to you [Social Worker] for permission to meet this gorgeous girl (Moon Baby is what I believe he calls her!)

20 November: Summary of Planning Board Meeting

Irene is still a massive behaviour problem within the secure unit living environment. She has been on a modified room program for the past 8 weeks and has demonstrated minimal change. She will start attending school in the mornings, attend recreation period and be out in the group in the evenings. Irene needs to tighten up on her school work and start turning in homework, rather than complaining about how nobody gives her a chance.

28 January: Memorandum from Superintendent to Social Worker

You will recall the letter authored by the two visitors from the Juvenile Court to headquarters about the room program used with Irene. I had heard nothing further on this matter until today when an attorney from the Legal Services Section called me. Apparently the two people from the Juvenile Court were reprimanded by their organization for writing such a letter so they passed their concern on to the Legal Services Section.

This fellow now wants to come to the institution to talk with some of us, and to talk with Irene to see if she wants "representation" from them. If she does not, the matter will be dropped. If she does, he will probably want to review her file to ascertain whether or not such "deprivation" is warranted in Irene's case. He will telephone to confirm his visit which may be as early as this Friday.

We should probably take some time to discuss this matter in advance. The attorney was congenial during his call and tried to reassure me that his basic purpose is not to cause trouble, but to assure the protection of the human rights of the confined.

24 February: Letter from Superintendent to Legal Services Attorney

Subject: Your 5 February Visit and Letter of 12 February

Upon receipt of your letter, I asked [Social Worker] to review it, paying particular attention to the "facts" relating to Irene's program. His reply is attached and I think it is complete and to the point.

362

You indicated that your visit was preceded by my invitation. It is important to note also that my invitation was preceded by your phone call indicating that you had received information that a girl was being treated in an abusive manner and I suggested that you come see for yourself.

My reaction to your recall of what we "agreed to" at the conclusion of our meeting coincides with Mr [Social Worker's] recall of that meeting.

1. It was agreed that Irene is a difficult case.
2. It was agreed that other programs were tried prior to the implementation of the room program, but that program was used because we felt it was the best thing we could do under the circumstances.
3. It was not agreed that the staff were at a loss to figure out a successful method of working with Irene, but we did agree to keep an open mind about any suggestions anyone had for a "more successful" method.
4. As Mr [Social Worker] indicates, we wish it had not been necessary for Irene's program to run so long, but in our judgment, there was no acceptable alternative. Any other choice would have been to "give up" on Irene and release her as had been done at previous times in multiple places.
5. Of the conclusions we reached, it was agreed that from a legal standpoint we would have to pay more attention to "constitutional rights" in the future, even though the protection of these rights, may, in fact, influence the length of time a young person remains in the institution.

For what it is worth, I felt the basic conclusion we reached was that you believed we were well intentioned (for a bureaucratic operation), but over-stepping our legal authority.

We believed you were well intentioned, but overstepping your legal role by determining what constitutes "treatment" in a correctional setting. I thought we agreed that we were not "experts" in each other's fields.

I realize it must be frustrating for you to try to deal with "non-legal" people in legal matters since I feel a similar frustration in trying to deal with "non-treatment" people in treatment matters. I did benefit from our meeting, I do know what you are saying, but I don't agree with you on many things.

I do agree that we learned a great deal about each other's concerns. I am a bit puzzled regarding what happened after our visit to lead you to conclude you were "too soft" in your appraisal. In fact, when you left you invited me to refer any further inquiries from people in the community regarding Irene to you for response.

In paragraph 3 of your letter, you classify Irene's behaviour as "undesirable, but not physically harmful". I believe a review of Irene's background and her behaviour prior to and during her time at the institution is quite conclusive in establishing that she does cause physical harm to herself and to others. As a matter of fact, one of the prime purposes of the approach used was to afford protection to the girl and those around her until she could gradually learn to control herself. Without that basic improvement, we foresee nothing but trouble ahead for Irene.

On page 4, your concerns and recommendations regarding the use of isolation should be alleviated in the near future when the official isolation policy is issued in its revised form. We discussed that during our visit on the 5th and I assured you that when it is published we will meet or exceed all of its conditions.

When you left the institution on February 5th, I was of the impression that you were satisfied with the status of Irene at that time but she was left with the impression that you were "representing" her in an effort to secure her release through legal channels. As a result, Irene has slowed down considerably (from what were marginal efforts to begin with) and is marking time until "you get her out".

It appears that you have changed some of your other perceptions since leaving so I am not sure what your current intentions are regarding Irene. She is currently between a rock and a hard place, and I think the uncertainty is causing anguish that if extended could be construed as "cruel and unusual punishment". I would appreciate it if you could let Irene and Mr [Social Worker] know where she stands with you in order to bring about the best result possible for this girl.

7 March: Letter from Superintendent to
Legal Services Attorney

Dear Legal Services Director

Thank you for your letter of February 27th and your comments relative to my letter to you.

As you know, Irene had a one day visit to her home on February 25th and is scheduled for a weekend leave on March 8 and 9. The family living environment will have to receive close evaluation to determine its appropriateness for Irene as a post-institutional placement.

We shall endeavor to keep you informed of progress and/or obstacles encountered in locating an acceptable placement for Irene and we welcome your continued involvement in seeing that her welfare is secured.

Attached is the Isolation Policy that was recently re-drafted for the Department with assistance from your office. While it does not relate specifically to Irene's former situation, I thought you might be interested in seeing it.

If there is anything else we can do to be of assistance to you, don't hesitate to call. Naturally, you are welcome to visit the campus or Irene at your convenience.

Sincerely

The Superintendent

Addendum

Irene was discharged from the institution to the home of her mother and father as soon as possible after the involvement of State Legal Services. The human rights of children and young people in care have since become a significant feature of work across the whole of the child and youth care field with the United Nations Convention on the Rights of the Child. Within a short time after State Legal Services became involved directly into what happened in institutions for young people, it was not long before the status of Dependent-Incorrigible was dropped from the options available through the Juvenile Court. In many respects this heralded a split between child protection services and youth justice services. Amidst all the legal arguments and the determination to protect Irene's human rights, it is impossible to say what actually ever happened to her. We hope she has had a happy life.

Aliese's Reflections

Sounds like this kid had been through the system and finally arrived at the secure unit all in a matter of fact manner according to Irene and her plan. Dysfunctional family life and bad placements where she never really felt at ease or at home lead this child here. Note she says, all she wanted was a home. Putting up with her co-habitants was proving a struggle and she was not getting the full on attention she needed.

I am sure that put her at odds with her peers; in addition to her personal adjustments to another institutional dumping ground. She came with much suspicion, fear, doubt and anger and a total loss of any personal sense of self. It is easy to lose your personal identity as a child, a daughter, sister, mother, student, etc. ... in the system of incarceration. These are the formative years where a child should be honing her life skills, passions, exploring and defining her life.

Incorrigible runaway, I wonder why so many of our youth were running away and when exactly did this phenomenon begin? No one was coping in the family structure and everyone was out of balance. How the heck do you expect kids to cope under those circumstances?

These case notes in particular point out her behaviour pattern and the lack of love and trust in her young family life. All that bouncing around from one facility and housing placement to another simply added to the total disconnect in her life with the outside world. Usually you do not see anyone from the system admitting to any failures on their part or "its" part. It is so refreshing when they do. That in part is what made this new and unchartered one-stop therapeutic community lifestyle a success – taking a good look at what is and is not working in these rehabilitation processes.

It is a never ending process. Most places in the Western World have incorporated such watchdog groups, and open-source communication platforms that help guide and re-shape the child welfare and youth justice systems, as well as foster care networks. Much work still needs to be carried out in all these areas because many of today's youth are still falling through the cracks in the System.

Irene was lucky in the sense that at least she still held the interest of her uncle, who was attempting to make a phone call with her father. That is a good signal and puts a glimmer of hope on this girl's future. Not sure what the stink was about with the attorney's involvement – and the whole "room program" thing – but that would have been interesting to note. I do know that in the past some places used handcuffs when we got out of hand and that was their way of confining us and calming us down, supposedly. Such methods were not in practice at this facility as I recall.

With the changing times at hand, this legal interest in Irene's case was a pivotal point for our generation. We were starting to gain some recognition and some rights. Times were changing. I love the way the social worker responded to the letter to the attorney. As someone who is trained in the legal field, I would have to say that it was very well answered and written. It identified the difference between the two trains of thought and the very different sides of the human issues involved. Here was an example of successful communication and an attempt at clarifying professional therapeutic and human rights issues surrounding Irene's mental health and institutional placement. In struggles such as Irene's case, around the balance of control of incarcerated persons, more often than not, things ended badly for the child. However, with that being said, and considering the times, this situation could have been very explosive. I was pleased with the very detailed account and presentation of the letter that put Irene first and not the "issues".

I always like to feel that these Sisters of Pain came through many hardships and a very challenged lifestyle and that such struggles made them stronger. Hopefully these ladies gained the survival skills needed to recognize the traps that were set on this path of destruction and later to self-awareness.

I am here writing today, knowing full well that all of the positive changes that came about for any of us young women, are due solely to the loving, caring, and outside-the-box thinking caregivers, social workers, superintendents, and many parole officers, foster care providers and others who were in fact searching for answers to life's hard problems. All these people's lives have contributed to any balance, peace, and successes that any of these young women achieved, for this truly was the end of the line. Had these practices been put in place at the beginning of the line, perhaps it might not have taken so much toll on so many lives. Many vulnerable young people have fallen through the cracks, and continue to fall through the cracks!

It is difficult to make any positive effective change in a child's life when you can't control the outside environment. Teaching coping skills is not always an easy task. It takes time for the child to change old ways of thinking and reacting, and it takes a lot of reinforcing as well as love and patience to help heal shattered lives. We all have to learn coping skills. Each child will process and develop at their own pace and seeing us as individuals for the first time in our lives was overwhelming for us. It meant that many of us created *healthy loving relationships*, probably for the first time in our lives. These people did not give up on us, regardless of our differences and they allowed us to develop as human beings with our own identity and sense of being.

Life is just a work in progress and it is an integrated system that works best in dealing with children's lives. It was an unfortunate course of events that led all of us to this place, but perhaps some of us are the better for it.

Team Parenting

It is one thing to talk about integrated services where different adults, professionals and community members exercise purpose around the care and supervision of young people in out-of-home care. It is quite another matter to provide truly integrated services that are directly responsive to the needs of specific young people. This means tailoring services that are woven around each youth in ways that respond in a timely manner to their particular health, education, welfare and supervision needs. It is here that the notion of "corporate parenting" – as used in the British context – helps to better clarify the State's *in loco parentis* role with each child or young person placed in out-of-home care. *Corporate Parenting* refers to the collective responsibility of local and state governments, their elected members and commissioned partners for all children and young people in the care of each local government jurisdiction. Corporate parenting involves the formal and local partnerships negotiated between government departments and non-government agencies providing services. It also includes agencies with contractual responsibilities for working together at some minimum level of partnership to meet the shared care needs of children placed in out-of-home care by the State.

Out-of-home care is provided under the supervision of a designated government-employed[1] social worker who maintains case management

1   In the UK, '*Local Authority*' finds many international public administration and local government comparisons. These range from Municipalities, Counties, Commonwealths, States, Provinces, Federal and National services where duty of care obligations are held for each young person placed in out-of-home care. While the term 'corporate parenting'

responsibilities for a designated caseload of child protection or youth justice cases.

Corporate Parenting[2] of children and young people in out-of-home care is obligated through UK social policy and legislation to administer out-of-home care under State supervision. Corporate parents are required to provide educational and social opportunities that are tailored to the age and developmental capabilities of each child or young person in their jurisdiction. All too often, care and supervision services may appear integrated whilst giving limited opportunities for direct feedback from young people or family members. The use of tagging bracelets with young offenders raises questions about what community returns on the investment are achieved with scarce resources to provide community supervision where relationship receives little priority.

To provide responsive *team parenting*, those working with a young person in out-of-home care need to start with the daily life space – where she or he lives – and start developing shared purpose and a personal care plan that takes account of each young person's identified needs, developmental assets and learning opportunities. Responsive team parenting efforts promote each young person's personal development, as well as accounting for influences in the community that may support that young person in the present and also longer term. Responsive team parenting makes pro-active use of child welfare legislation through asking what _can_ be done not what _can't_ be done? All team parenting partners engaged in the care and supervision of children and young people need to have a shared purpose in their work – promoting the safety, well-being and future of each child or young person placed in their care (Fulcher & Garfat, 2008). Working together with purpose requires a long-term commitment to caring and

does not find extensive use in many parts of the world, the term does provide a useful legal formulation that holds 'The Child Welfare System' accountable for the quality of developmental outcomes achieved by each child or young person placed by the State in out-of-home care.

2   *These Are Our Bairns – A Guide for Community Planning Partnerships on Being a Good Corporate Parent*, Scottish Government, 2008 available at http://www.scotland.gov.uk/Resource/Doc/236882/0064989.pdf

supervision that responds to the needs of a particular young person with whom relationship(s) remain important.

Team parenting involves inviting birth family members or kin group members to become involved as essential members of team parenting TEAM! A child removed for sound reasons from an abusive family situation still requires that some consideration is given to longer term relationships that matter between that child and birth family members. As we have indicated earlier, social workers cannot simply take legal action to remove children without giving ongoing thought to how this child may have continuing contact and involvement with extended family members who are part of a 'team' that surrounds that child and help guard them from identified perpetrators of abuse. The relationships children have with family members are too important to be written off by professionals, acting in the best interests of that child – in the short term. In the months and years to come, future relationships with family and extended family members will remain important – whether any restorative work has been carried out or not. This is why it is important to seek family and extended family participation in all team parenting initiatives.

Working together with purpose to achieve quality out-of-home care means EVERYONE spending time with and actively listening to this child or these young people;

- actively engaging in these young people's lives and building personal relationships with them;
- recognizing that out-of-home care and positive youth development is a whole lot more complicated than basic case management;
- demonstrating readiness to share decision-making powers with this young person and the people who matter to her;
- moving out from behind desks and formal professional roles;
- extending working relationships beyond professional comfort zones as required;
- sharing some personal responsibility for this young person's future; and
- weaving team parenting efforts like an 'invisibility cloak'

around each child whilst maintaining focus on that young person's pain, worries, talents and aspirations.

Care and supervision may appear integrated but all too often, few opportunities are built in to hear what young people or family members are saying about the services they receive. Relationships are given low priority unless services are woven around specific children and young people in ways that respond in a timely manner to their particular health, education, welfare and supervision needs. With team parenting there is little room for professional rivalries in the delivery of responsive out-of-home care and supervision for young people. Team parenting involves entering into relationships and engaging rhythms with particular young people, providing care and supervision in a personalized manner. This also involves monitoring such care and supervision as provided week to week, to ensure children and young people in out-of-home care achieve developmental outcomes and enhanced social well-being during their stay in care. As seen throughout all of the *Sisters of Pain* narratives, without vigilance and intentional use of daily life events to promote developmental achievements in care, young people are extremely vulnerable to becoming yet another out-of-home care statistic with poor prospects.

To the extent possible, the focus of team parenting is to nurture the achievement of 20 evidence-based developmental outcomes: 5 associated with *Belonging*; 5 with *Mastery*; 5 with *Independence*; and 5 with *Generosity*. *Outcomes that Matter Achievement Profiles*™ guide team parenting efforts as illustrated below for one 15 year-old young woman during her first 9 weeks in a foster care placement. Other goals or outcomes may be added to a personal care plan, but these 20 *Outcomes that Matter* represent a minimum guarantee around which ALL members of "the Team" intentionally nurture young people and help them make developmental achievements.

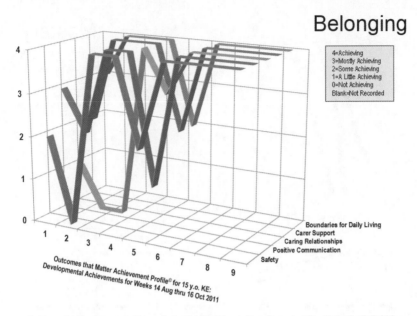

Belonging

4=Achieving
3=Mostly Achieving
2=Some Achieving
1=A Little Achieving
0=Not Achieving
Blank=Not Recorded

4

3

2

1

0

1 2 3 4 5 6 7 8 9

Outcomes that Matter Achievement Profile© for 15 y.o. KE:
Developmental Achievements for Weeks 14 Aug thru 16 Oct 2011

Boundaries for Daily Living
Carer Support
Caring Relationships
Positive Communication
Safety

■ Safety ■ Positive Communication ■ Caring Relationships ■ Carer Support ■ Boundaries for Daily Living

K has had an unsettled two months with great ups and downs. She has shown a reduction in overt sexualized behaviour, but still continues to talk about men and boys in a sexual context. K reluctantly adheres to rules set by adults and is often grumpy and annoyed when boundaries are set. On one occasion K left her course and walked home alone. She manipulates to obtain the things she wants and is constantly asking for permission for another mobile phone. She believes that when she can attend course without supervision she will need a phone for herself. K had an aggressive and abusive outburst aimed at her Carer when told in Week 5 she could not attend a social event one evening. Although Carer was alarmed at the intensity of the outburst, K was later sorry and remorseful, and spoke to the Carers about her behaviour. The relationship between K and the Carer family has been strengthened as a result of resolving this incident.

Team parenting starts where children and young people live – in their daily life space – developing shared purpose according to the identified needs and opportunities required for specific children.

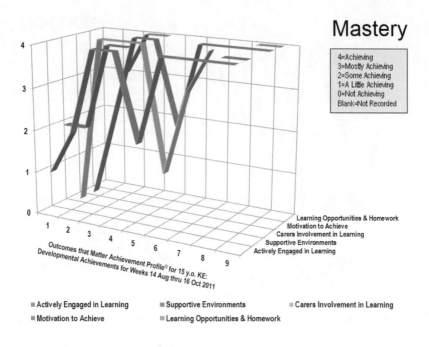

Mastery

4=Achieving
3=Mostly Achieving
2=Some Achieving
1=A Little Achieving
0=Not Achieving
Blank=Not Recorded

Learning Opportunities & Homework
Motivation to Achieve
Carers Involvement in Learning
Supportive Environments
Actively Engaged in Learning

Outcomes that Matter Achievement Profile© for 15 y.o. KE:
Developmental Achievements for Weeks 14 Aug thru 16 Oct 2011

- Actively Engaged in Learning   - Supportive Environments   - Carers Involvement in Learning
- Motivation to Achieve   - Learning Opportunities & Homework

K is settling well into her community educational programme, showing enthusiasm each morning to attend, and generally applying herself to what is happening. K enjoyed her Art Expo day and received compliments on the quality of her work. She is growing in confidence in her own ability to achieve. Although currently achieving at an acceptable level, K shows little ability to stay on task unsupervised and demonstrates little capacity for self-directed learning, requiring constant supervision to stay engaged. She is easily distracted and gets irritable when bored. K's ability to achieve and enjoy is still very much dependent on her mood at any given time. K doesn't really know what she'd like to do in the future. She talks about becoming a nurse but doesn't want to talk about the work she needs to do in Maths and English to be accepted onto a course. K shows little capacity to stick to plans.

Team parenting partners work together with shared purpose to promote the safety, wellbeing and future prospects of each child or young person placed in their care (Fulcher & Garfat, 2008). Team parenting also involves a long-term commitment to caring and supervision that is responsive to the needs of a particular child or young people placed in our care.

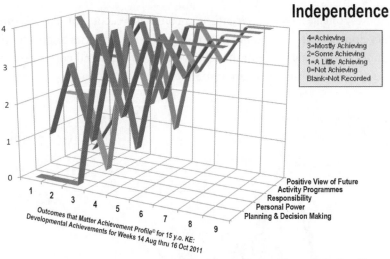

Independence

4=Achieving
3=Mostly Achieving
2=Some Achieving
1=A Little Achieving
0=Not Achieving
Blank=Not Recorded

Positive View of Future
Activity Programmes
Responsibility
Personal Power
Planning & Decision Making

Outcomes that Matter Achievement Profile© for 15 y.o. KE:
Developmental Achievements for Weeks 14 Aug thru 16 Oct 2011

■ Planning & Decision Making   ■ Personal Power   ■ Responsibility   ■ Activity Programmes   ■ Positive View of Future

K is very confident about expressing her feelings. At the beginning of this month K would talk about returning home to her Mum. K had a birthday visit with her Mum and 2 brothers at the office and since then K has not asked about her Mum nor talked about returning home. K is given the opportunity to call her Mum each week but has been declining to call. K was taken out for the day by her Grandma and Uncle. She expected a lavish day of gifts and food and was disappointed with what she actually received. K's mood and behaviour was erratic around her birthday time. She refused to pick up her laundry when asked and would not hang her towel up. She began the month talking about finding a mature man so she can get pregnant and return home to her Mum. After the birthday visit from Mum and she found out that Mum was no longer with her boyfriend, K showed no interest in returning home, saying she did not like her Mum's new boyfriend. K is confused about her future, uncertain if she is staying with her current Carers or will have to move. K constantly changes her mind and ideas in respect to future goals. She rang her social worker who encouraged her and reminded her of what a long way she has come. This lifted K's spirits. She is hoping to have respite with her Nan during the Christmas holidays and is saying that when she turns 17 she is going to live with her Nan.

Responsive team parenting promotes each young person's development. Team members also engage with activities and potential opportunities available in the local neighbourhood and community to nurture developmental achievements.

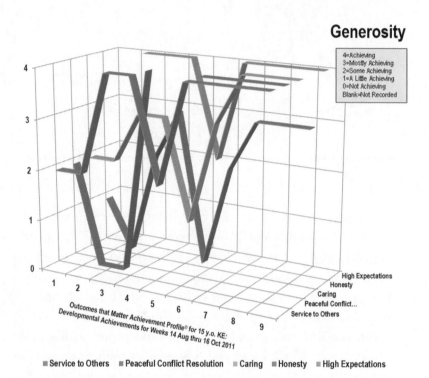

Generosity

4=Achieving
3=Mostly Achieving
2=Some Achieving
1=A Little Achieving
0=Not Achieving
Blank=Not Recorded

Outcomes that Matter Achievement Profile® for 15 y.o. KE: Developmental Achievements for Weeks 14 Aug thru 16 Oct 2011

High Expectations
Honesty
Caring
Peaceful Conflict...
Service to Others

■ Service to Others   ■ Peaceful Conflict Resolution   ■ Caring   ■ Honesty   ■ High Expectations

K can be very helpful at times; picking up dishes, offering to make coffee and willing to help out. She finds it very hard to say sorry, but will express remorse with her helpful actions. She can be very stubborn when told to do something, responding more positively if asked in a quiet tone. She cannot always be trusted. There are still concerns about her general health. On occasions her feet swell up for no apparent reason and K claims this is to do with her dysfunctional kidneys. The Carers have taken K to the doctor several times and this will be ongoing until such time that her health is no longer a concern. K enjoys the company of the Carers' daughters who set a good role model example in respect of working hard at school and having career goals. Overall, good progress is being made during these early weeks of the placement and now careful consideration needs to be given to K's longer term care plan.

Team parenting in out-of-home care involves entering into personal relationships and rhythms with particular children and young people. Working together with shared purpose involves first getting started, then building up personal and professional working relationships and networks. Team parenting involves working out how different contributors participate in decision-making around important care and supervision activities for specific children or young people. This is not about transforming authoritarian, expert-driven teams into inter-disciplinary teamwork with shared decision-making. Nor does it replace expert-driven approaches with more democratic practices. It IS about locating the best possible resources available for each child or young person in OUR care and weaving these resources and capabilities around THIS young person in a manner that supports her or his best interests – both for today and for tomorrow!

As can be seen in K's example shown above, team parenting has to include birth family and kin group members as essential members of THE TEAM! There is no room for professional jealousies. It means providing care and supervision – and monitoring that care and supervision – to help young people achieve developmental outcomes and enhanced social well-being. Everyone needs to contribute towards ensuring that each young person feels special in a positive and strengths-based way! This young person is not special because of some label they may have acquired. They are special because someone gives them daily recognition for what makes them special – nurturing these personal qualities right now, today and tomorrow.

Responsive team parenting makes pro-active use of health, education and welfare legislation to ask what can be done with and for this young person, not to explain what can't be done? Shared purpose requires – to the extent possible – that young people participate in decision-making about their lives and any plans we may be making about their futures. Permanency planning is about how children and young people learn to make life decisions, through participation and interaction with others in decision-making, planning and implementing the transitions! It is especially important that young people participate in decision-making around their present and future circumstances. This is how they learn to engage responsibly and achieve mastery of life skills essential to independent or inter-dependent living. Remember, better care outcomes are achieved by young people in out-of-home care when birth family and other significant community members participated in decision-making about the care they received (Burford & Hudson, 2000).

Questions for Small Group Discussion or Guided Reflection

1. What organisational challenges are associated with achieving quality outcomes with children or young people in out-of-home care?
2. What potential violations of principles in the United Nations Convention on the Rights of a Child are noted in the way Irene was treated by secure unit staff?
3. At what point might a behaviour modification programme used with a young person like Irene become synonymous with torture?
4. What is your critique of the letter written by the Institutional Superintendent in response to the lawyer about claims in Irene's legal case?
5. Under what circumstances might there be justification for locking up a child or young person admitted under child protection legislation when there has been no reference to offences?

Conclusion

Some Parting Words from Marty

MY HOPES AND DREAMS AND WILL THAT I SHALL CONQUER

Yesterday and today I have felt so great. I have been thinking about a lot of things. Like "Who am I?"; "What am I?" and "What am I going to be?"

I have thought about myself and other people. I have found that I have a new outlook on myself and my surroundings. I'll be eighteen soon and have new and different feelings.

I feel I am going to bust wide open. I have such a feeling of self pride. I know I am an individual and have a lot of feelings. I know what I am. I am a Mexican-American. I know who I am. I am nobody but myself and will be nobody but myself. Why try to imitate other people when I can just be me?

I know what I want to be – a person of integrity and a person who has self-respect for myself. I want to further my knowledge of life and enlist in the Army.

If I can't, I'll just try to be a person who has a meaning in life. A job may be like a veterinarian since I love animals. Or work at a transcontinental company where I can use the two languages I love. Either way, my life outlooks are changing.

I really don't know but I'm happy to know people care enough about me to help me get on the right track. I think when I am in the Army, I might volunteer as a Chaplain's assistant.

Either way, I am going to follow the inner voice I have received. And even when I explode, my inner voice says be happy, not sad; be contented, not bad. I cannot change the past. Neither can I change the future. I can only live day by day, not thinking about past or future, but living in the present.

This I shall do and I must – to prove to myself I can do it. And that I have the courage, the ability and the know-how. Otherwise, I shall always be a failure to myself, to my peers and to the world especially. I must try and conquer, and I will.

In Heaven's name I will conquer and be brave.

Marty
22 December

---

9 July: Telephone Call to Social Worker

We received news today that Marty is doing well in her community placement. She has a job and plays first string on the lady's softball team. It looks as though she will be discharged from parole in the next couple of months. Such pleasant news!

The *Sisters of Pain* narratives remind us of how pain-based behaviour all too often resulted in premature placement of young people in long-term institutional care. In contemporary times this population includes more young men than it does young women, although both still contribute to the record numbers of inmates "locked up" in the American penal system, or on death row awaiting legalized execution. In the forty years since these narratives were written, health and youth welfare services available to society's most vulnerable children and young people in American cities and towns have been decimated. Community mental health services for poor and transient families are virtually non-existent. Are we the only people who find it paradoxical that the world's wealthiest and mightiest country in the world should treat its children in out-of-home care with such disdain, as expendable strays?

Americans continue to justify massive expenditure on policing, Homeland Security, body scanning, armed guards at schools, and an ever expanding criminal justice system giving little thought to child and youth care cost-benefit equations that should be a concern to every American taxpayer. Investment in childhood matters! It is cheaper to send a young person through university on full scholarship as a residential student than it is to 'maintain' a youthful inmate in a State or Federal prison. These youths are blamed for the pain that became all motivating in their lives.

The American public simply does not join up the dots, but then neither do government policy makers intent on 'contracting out' penal institutional services to private businesses. In America today, approximately 130,000 people are locked up in private prisons run by 'for-profit companies', and that number is growing very rapidly. The U.S. has approximately 25 percent of the entire global prison population even though it only has 5 percent of the total global population. The United States has the highest incarceration rate on the entire globe by far, and no nation in the history of the world has ever locked up more of its own citizens than we have. (Snyder, March 12, 2013). The baseball metaphor of "three strikes and you're out" at the old ball game (as the baseball song goes) has been applied to 'behaviour that is case managed by the criminal justice system'. It matters not whether the behaviours which led to a life of crime were "pain-based" in origin. It no longer matters to the public and its policy makers. Care cost-benefit equations don't matter to most politicians but more importantly, to interest groups that lobby for tax cuts and votes against gun control.

And after yet another decade of US military deployments in war zones and strategic defense bases, there remains a prevailing 'silence' about the impact of US military training assignments and deployments on the lives and upbringing of the children in military families. The educational and mental health needs of military children represent another cost-benefit equation that American policy makers have been hesitant to calculate. So long as American politicians 'preserve fighting strength' amongst its military workforce of enlisted personnel and officers in their part of the country or supported by strategic international defence alliances, it follows that there is little motivation to examine too closely the social and developmental needs of 'military brats' growing up with parents in the military. The *Sisters of Pain* narratives speak of this issue, as does Aliese, and Aliese's mother in what follows.

Within social work and youth work training during the past twenty years, residential group care has been subject to a persistent ambivalence. There have been many detractors and few lukewarm defenders. At the heart of this ambivalence lies a failure of social work to appreciate the reciprocity inherent in care giving and care receiving. In some quarters, social work has considered itself '*so tainted by its associations with care that the word should be expunged from its lexicon and its rationale*' (Maegher & Parton, 2004: 4). Social work pays lip service to the nature and importance of care. This is manifest in psychological explanations for child care and protection that operate from a problems-focus. The new "forensic social work" contributes little towards promoting a young person's growth, social flourishing and happiness. While psychological theories may offer helpful insights about working with children and young people, such formulations rarely capture the breadth and intricacies involved with therapeutic use of daily life events in their out-of-home care.

Public service administration has raised expectations across the Western World about outcome driven services that can be monitored through organisational practices that are driven by managerial and annual fiscal targets. A consequence of all this has been that, in many minds, care has become a technical task, amenable to short-term performance indicators. Visit any home for the elderly for local confirmation that this statement is true! Care has become a list of tasks, much like ordering from the Drive-Through menu at McDonalds or Burger King.

Care is no longer viewed as the moral, practical and relational dynamics we have been exploring in this volume. We live in a world that speaks of '*risk, rights, protection, best practice, evidence, standards and inspection*'. These voices commonly crowd out a 'care voice' that speaks of love, making connections, building relationships and therapeutic containment. (Steckley & Smith, 2011: 191).

We think out-of-home care needs to be transfused with moral purpose. Social workers and youth workers need to recognise that caring is more than a list of case management tasks carried out the same way with every kid. There is moral purpose in striving to engage in shared decision-making and work in partnership with family members, seeking – wherever possible – the inclusion of extended family solutions that reinforce belonging. Social workers and youth workers need to believe that they can make a difference in the lives of young people and, as corporate parents, they can provide these young people with the same love, supervision and aspirations that any good parent or extended family member would want for their children.

Young people in out-of-home care deserve people who believe in them. If encouraged to think it is possible, family members can and will work in partnership with carers, and participate in shared parenting. We advocate for 'team parenting' of this kind being available to each young person placed in out-of-home care!

A Mother's Reflections after 40 Years

As Aliese became an active participant in the development of this volume, she shared a draft of the work with her mother, with whom she now has a good relationship. This mother – whose relationship was once broken with her daughter – shares her own thoughts about what happened.

It was devastating to read these girls' stories and especially my daughter's story. No matter their actual ages, they were all still children. Most were placed in that institution by circumstances beyond their control, and some were placed beyond their parents' control.

I believe that, with this particular time frame and set of counselors, this was the first place where many of the girls felt safe. Scared, definitely, but safe. Some would go back to their old ways, but hopefully with better survival and coping skills. A few, like my daughter, would go with the knowledge that there was a better life – one that they could control. Perhaps this was their first opportunity to grow and learn to cope with their feelings.

Ali was a happy bubbly child, always active who loved being "mother's helper". She was constantly playing house. She would vacuum with her toy vacuum cleaner, pretend cooking on her toy stove, etc. It doesn't surprise me that "home & family" remain some of the most important things in her life.

Her grandmother – my mother – spent countless hours trying to find out where Ali was, after I was told that I could be arrested if I persisted in calling Social Services seeking information about her. When Ali finally turned 18, her parole officer took her to my mother's house. After spending some time with her grandmother, Ali flew down to California to be with me and my third husband, Chris.

The reunion was highly emotional for both of us. But for me it brought back all the guilt I had buried for years. She told me that she had run away countless time trying to find me.

Guilt, like death and taxes, never ever completely goes away. It overwhelms you and eats away at your soul. It plays with your memories and always asks the question "What If?". The guilt wipes out the good memories and re-plays the bad ones over and over in an endless loop.

It took many years to bury the guilt and live a "normal" life, if there is such a thing as a "normal life". But guilt raises its ugly head from time to time and the guilt replay loop starts again.

Ali and I don't talk about our separation. I think this is an emotional safeguard for us, even though we have a very close relationship and consider ourselves best friends. Now and then she will mention something regarding these times, but it is never elaborated on. She often talks about Lexie with whom she was very close, and kept in contact with long after she was out of the system.

Monetary wise, I came from an upper middle class family. My parents fought often and when they finally split up and divorced, I was fifteen. I had been dating Ali's father who was in the Air Force, for about a month when he suggested we get married. So I married at age fifteen. We were together for about 4 months before we separated due to Gary going for training out of state. I moved back in with my mother and soon to be my stepdad.

At that point I decided I wanted to finish school as I felt I was too young to be married. When Gary finished his training, he came to re-claim me as his wife. We tried to pick up where we had more or less left off, and this is when I became pregnant with Ali. Not knowing that I had become pregnant during this "reunion", I stayed with my mother to finish school and Gary went on to his next duty station. Gary and I discussed getting a divorce, mainly because I felt we were both too young. So I filed for divorce, but had to wait until after Ali's birth for it to be final. So at age seventeen I had Ali, and was on my own.

Ali has deep rooted abandonment issues. When she was a toddler, I left her with my cousin while I was looking for a job and an apartment. This was only for a month, but I'm sure that it is in her subconscious. When Ali was three I married her stepfather, Dave. Dave loved Ali and wanted to adopt her. So her natural father Gary relinquished his rights and Dave adopted her. During this marriage I had two other girls. Dave was in the Navy and deployed often, so there was abandonment there too.

When Ali was to start kindergarten, she and her sister contracted TB from one of our friends. At that time anyone with TB was placed in a sanitarium, since TB is highly contagious. So Ali and her sister were placed in a hospital ninety miles away. Even though visiting was discouraged, I drove every weekend to see them. Being so young, Ali and her sister didn't understand why they were there. They would cry to come home with me. So this was one more abandonment. Ali was released after four months, but couldn't understand why her sister couldn't come home also. Again, abandonment. Her sister was hospitalized for two more months.

When Dave and I divorced, he also relinquished Ali's adoption and his parental rights. So, another abandonment. But the biggest abandonment was being taken into the system. This was the most traumatic one, and it has had a tremendous effect upon her psyche and her life overall.

When Ali came to California to live with me and my third husband Chris, she settled in and her life was pretty much like any other young woman, though much more mature than most. She worked and associated with a good crowd. Since we had a pool table in the garage, we often had her friends at our house. Chris was ex-Navy and an avid pool player, so he really enjoyed having these guys around. They were a tight knit group, and most of them had only been away from home for a short time, so I more or less became "Mom" to them. A few years ago, they held a reunion here in California, and everyone caught up with each others' lives. It was rather bittersweet, as one of the wives was terminally ill and Bob, to whom Ali had been engaged, and was the leader of the group, had died of a heart attack while only in his 40's.

During the past six years, Ali and I have become especially close. We are the best of friends as I've mentioned before. We do have separate residences since I lost my job several years ago, but we communicate daily.

Writing her reflections has been very emotional for her and I'm very proud of how she is handling it and her writing skills. Her insight into the girls she writes about, is to me incredible. It is interesting to note that since she has been co-authoring "Sisters of Pain" she now calls me Mommy rather than Mom.

I have always been very proud of Ali. She is a very intelligent, positive, loving and giving individual. She always thinks of others and is generous to a fault. She will do without, to give to others. She has had a lot adversity and major disappointments in life, yet she always keeps a smile on her face and in her heart.

I know I'm supposed to be writing about my experience as a mother in losing a child to the system. But this is the best I can do.

Losing your child this way is like losing them to death. And that is how I felt. It was the way I coped. There was such a rage inside for the longest time, then that slowly became grieving. It takes pieces of your soul month after month. In some ways I became two or three different persons. The public person, well liked and respected, professional in the workplace, always in the top percentile in performance reviews. Someone who always remembers birthdays and special occasions, who is quick to give an "Atta boy" to someone for their accomplishments. Then there is the private me, who wishes to be left completely alone, preferring the company of my pets, books and movies. Feeling like I never want to interact with any human being again. The other side of that is, while I prefer not to attend social gatherings, I do like to associate with a select few friends.

There is no real ending to this narrative. Life just goes on. Step by step, and day by day, seeking peace and a degree of happiness. Being thankful I have my beautiful and intelligent daughter back in my life.

Some Afterthoughts

We are a throw-away nation. We not only throw away our children, but also our elders. Some are thrown into the various systems and the others just into the wind of invisibility. They are unseen and forgotten.

Thousands of children have been thrown into foster care and the system. Many foster parents only do it for the money the State gives them for the child's necessities. Many have had zero training on how to care for and *handle these children, so they are often passed on to the next set of foster parents and the next. Most of the children are scared, and confused, not really understanding what or why this has happened to them. Some of the children don't conform to the foster parent's ways and others are defiant. Usually, they are scared of the uncertainty of the situation.*

When they max out at age 18, many are still "thrown out" on their own. Very few have the life skills to lead healthy and productive lives. It is very rare that foster families allow their "charge" to continue living with them and help them with the necessary skills they need to be self-supporting. There don't seem to be many programs around that help these kids to adjust to living on their own, or if there are such programs, there aren't enough of them. It means that many young people in "the Youth Justice System" end up in the "adult" system and so the cycle continues – invisible and forgotten.

Chana

Aliese's Final Comment

It has been many years since I have thought about those earlier days in my life. Being re-united with my mother at the age of 18 was phenomenal and unexpected. I think that over the years, I figured I would never see her again. I jumped at the opportunity to meet with her and her husband and stay with them, at least temporarily. I was engaged to be married to an Army man and I had to leave him behind to make this move. He later visited and after some time passed, I moved back east with him and later returned back "home".

As my mom writes, we never really discussed the past and she is probably correct by saying that it was an emotional safeguard for the both of us. I wanted to focus on the here and now and I knew there was no undoing the past and I had to learn to live with the loss of my family, and that was something I was just going to have to live with. I don't believe I ever fully recovered, but that is a different story.

You can train yourself mentally to adjust over time, but the heart – well that is another matter. The move was a huge change and it took me a long time to sort this out mentally. I belonged, but yet, I didn't. At least I was trying, and I wanted to make the best of the situation.

I know that I still have some abandonment issues, and for me, knowing what my strengths and weaknesses are helps me to live a balanced life. I cannot undo my past or make my half-sisters and adoptive family love me or want me to be a part of their lives. I cannot bring back my grandma and grandpa who were alive and wanted me to live with them, but the system thought it knew better. It is hard when you are raised with your family and then pulled away, never to see them again. It made me very angry as a child and I had to learn to accept what I could not control, even though I knew "they" (the system) were totally wrong in what they were doing to me and my family.

It doesn't take much for a youth to fall from grace, when a set-back happens, or a major let down. And it takes a lot for them to get back to that place of balance, when they haven't learned all the coping skills; and finally, that you can't control everything in your life. That is part of "growing up", or becoming mature. We learn to concentrate on doing what we can, and not to concentrate on what we have no control over.

A young person needs to find that they are good at something, that they hold worth and value, and can have their own personal goals and dreams that are attainable. I think it is important to instill those ideals close to the first encounter with the youth, rather than later.

Disturbed and disrupted adolescent growth patterns and social skills – like misaligned stepping stones – can be identified, re-learned and reinforced by you. A child needs to learn a new language that "I am good", "I can do this job", "I have a good life and good friends", and learn to control those thoughts that are demeaning and hurtful.

I have had to learn to make friends quickly due to all the moving around I did as a child with my family, from the East and West coasts; and later through all the youth care programs. It came easily for me and it didn't take long for me to make new friends and leave behind the past that I was very willing to forget. I connect quickly with people, or I don't; and I place a high value on my friends because I learned early in life, that nothing is certain. I kept in touch with only a few of the girls and with the passing of time, we have lost contact. I know I was very fortunate to have survived those earlier years and I often wonder why I was "spared" and not them.

As I look back on all this now, I know that so much of what I experienced has made me into a strong and independent lady. There was so much tragedy and very little hope within the lives of these young women when they arrived at the secure unit – but I would like to think that, like me, they came out stronger because of the close bonds of friendship they made during their stay. Your past does not define who you are as a person. That is a very hard step. Guilt and the shame can devour a person.

Okay social workers and youth workers, if you think your job is going to be tough – just imagine what the young person must be enduring. I can guarantee, nothing will be more rewarding than knowing you have helped a child untangle the mess that others have made in their lives, to see them move forward from the decisions and consequences of their own undoing, and blossom into the person they were meant to be.

Love, and a good heart are the keys to your success. Knowledge on its own is not enough.

Aliese

References

Ainsworth, F. (1997). *Family-centred group care: Model building.* Aldershot, Hants: Ashgate.

Ainsworth, F. (2006). Group care practitioners as family workers. In L. C. Fulcher & F. Ainsworth, (Eds). *Group care practice with children and young people revisited.* New York: The Haworth Press, pp. 75-86.

Ainsworth, F. & Hansen, P. (2012). Doing harm while doing good: The child protection paradox, *Child & youth services.* 33: 146-157.

Andersson, G. (2005). Family relations, adjustment and well-being in a longitudinal study of children in care, *Child & family social work.* 10(1), 43-56.

Anglin, J. (2002). *Pain, Normality and the Struggle for Congruence, Reinterpreting Residential Care for Children & Youth,* New York: The Haworth Press.

Beker, J. & Eisikovits, Z., Eds., (1991). *Knowledge utilization in residential child and youth care practice,* Washington DC: Child Welfare League of America.

Benson, P. L., Scales, P. C., Hamilton, S. F., & Sesma, A. Jr., (2006). Positive youth development: Theory, research and applications. In W. Damon & R. Lerner (Eds.), *Handbook of child psychology* (vol. 1, pp. 894-941), Hoboken, NJ: John Wiley & Sons.

Biddulph, S. (2003). *Raising boys: Why boys are different and how to help them become happy and well-balanced men.* London: Thorsons.

Bion, W.R. (1962). *Learning from experience.* London: Heinemann.

Brannen, J. & Moss, P., Eds., (2003). *Rethinking children's care.* Buckingham: Open University Press.

Brendtro, L. K., Brokenleg, M. & VanBockern, S. (2002). *Reclaiming youth at risk: Our hope for the future.* Bloomington, IN: National Educational Service.

Brendtro, L. & du Toit, L. (2005). *Response ability pathways: Restoring bonds of respect.* Cape Town: PreText Publishers.

Burford, G. (1990). *Assessing teamwork: A comparative study of group home teams in Newfoundland and Labrador.* University of Stirling, Scotland: Unpublished PhD thesis.

Burford, G. & Casson, S. (1989). Including families in residential work: Educational and agency tasks. *British journal of social work.* 19(1): pp. 19-37.

Burford, G. & Hudson, J., Eds., (2000). *Family group conferences: New directions in community-centered child & family practice.* New York: Aldine de Gruyter.

Burford, G. E. & Fulcher, L. C. (2006). Resident group influences on team functioning, *Child & youth services.* 28(1 & 2), 177-208.

Burgheim, T. (2005). The grief of families whose children have been removed: Implications for workers in out-of-home care. *Developing practice,* 13, 57-61.

Cairns, T., Fulcher, L. C., Kereopa, H., Nia Nia, P. & Tait-Rolleston, W. (1998). Nga pari karangaranga o puao-te-ata-tu: Towards a culturally responsive education & training for social workers in New Zealand, *Canadian social work review.* 15(2), 145-167.

Canadian Royal Commission on Aboriginal Peoples (1997). *For seven generations: An information legacy of the royal commission on Aboriginal peoples.* Ottawa: Libraxus Inc.

Carrell, S. (5 October, 2009). Suspected suicide leap by two teenage girls. *The Guardian.* Accessed at http://www.guardian.co.uk/uk/2009/oct/05/suicide-leap-teenage-girls.

Centre for Social Justice (2008). Breakthrough Glasgow: Ending the costs of social breakdown www.centreforsocialjustice.org.uk/client/downloads/BreakthroughGlasgow.pdf (accessed 27th July 2011).

Commonwealth of Australia (1992). *Aboriginal deaths in custody: response by governments to the royal commission, volumes 1-3.* Canberra: Australian Government Printing Services.

Costa, M. & Walter, C. (2006). 'Care: The art of living' in R. Jackson (Ed) *Holistic special education: Camphill principles and practice.* Edinburgh: Floris Books.

Courtney, M. E. & Iwaniec, D. (2009). *Residential care of children: Comparative perspectives.* New York: Oxford University Press.

Davies, P. (2011). The impact of a child protection investigation: A personal reflective account. *Child and family social work,* 15, 201-209.

Department for Children, Schools and Families (2005). The Government's response to the education and skills select committee's ninth report of session 2004-05: Every child matters... Available here: http://www.everychildmatters.gov.uk/.

Digney, J. (2007). Towards a comprehension of the roles of humour in Child and Youth Care. *Relational Child and Youth Care Practice,* 18, 4. pp. 9-18.

Durst, D. (1992). The road to poverty is paved with good intentions: Social interventions & indigenous peoples, *International social work.* 35(2), 191-202.

Eichsteller, G. & Holtoff, S. (2010). Social pedagogy training pack. ThemPra Social Pedagogy Community Interest Company.

Eisikovits, Z., Beker, J. & Guttmann, E. (1991). The known and the used in residential child and youth care work. In J. Beker and Z. Eisikovits, eds *Knowledge utilization in residential child and youth care work.* Washington D C: Child Welfare League of America, pp 3-23.

Emond, R. (2000). *Survival of the skilful: an ethnographic study of two groups of young people in residential care,* Unpublished PhD thesis, University of Stirling.

Emond, R (2010). Caring as a moral, practical and powerful endeavour: Peer care in a Cambodian orphanage, *British journal of social work* 40(1): 63-81.

Fahlberg, V., Ed. (1990). *Residential treatment: A tapestry of many therapies.* Indianapolis, Indiana: Perspective Press.

Fahlberg, V. (1991). *A child's journey through placement.* Indianapolis, Indiana: Perspective Press.

Fanshel, D., Finch, S. J., & Grundy, J. F. (1990). *Foster children in life course perspective.* New York: Colombia University Press.

Fewster, G. (2004). Just between you and me: Personal boundaries in professional relationships, *Relational child and youth care practice. 17(4), 8.*

Fewster, G. (1991). Editorial: The selfless professional. *Journal of child and youth care,* Vol. 6 No. 4 1991. pp 69-72.

Freado, M. D., Bussell, D., & McCombie, J. W. (2005). The inside kid: A little light in a dark, dark night. *Reclaiming children and youth,* 13(4): 196-198.

Fulcher, L. C. (1983). *Who cares for the caregivers? A comparative study of residential and day care teams working with children.* Stirling, Scotland: Unpublished PhD thesis.

Fulcher, L. C. (1988). Putting the baby back in the bathwater: Rethinking the practice curriculum in social work education, *New Zealand Social Work,* 12(3 & 4), 4-9.

Fulcher, L. C. (1991). Teamwork in Residential Care. In J. Beker & Z. Eisikovits, Eds., *Knowledge Utilization in Residential Child and Youth Care Practice,* Washington DC: Child Welfare League of America, pp. 215-235.

Fulcher, L. C. (1994). When you're up to your neck in alligators, it's hard to re-member that the original aim was to drain the swamp!: Some Lessons from New Zealand health sector reform, *Australian Social Work.* 47(2), 47-53.

Fulcher, L C (1996). Changing care in a changing world: The old and new worlds. *Social work review.* VII (1 & 2) pp. 20-26.

Fulcher, L. C. (1998). Acknowledging culture in child and youth care practice, *Social work education.* Vol. 17, No 3, pp. 321-338.

Fulcher, L. C. (2002a). The duty of care in child & youth care practice, *Journal of child and youth care work.* 17, 73-84.

Fulcher, L. C. (2002b). Cultural safety and the duty of care, *Child welfare.* 81(5), pp. 689-708.

Fulcher. L.C. (2003). Rituals of encounter that guarantee cultural safety, *Journal of relational child and youth care practice.* 16(3), 20-27. http://www.cyc-net.org/lz/a-3-2.html). Accessed 14th Sept 2011.

Fulcher, L. C. (2005). The soul, rhythms and blues of responsive child and youth care at home or away from home, *Child & youth care.* 27(1 & 2), 27-50.

Fulcher, L. C. (2006). It's only a matter of time: Cross-cultural reflections, *Relational child & youth care practice.* 18(4), 58-64.

Fulcher, L. C. (2012). Intervention with institutions. In C. A. Glisson, C. N. Dulmus, & K. M. Sowers, (Eds.), *Social work practice with groups, commu-nities, and organizations: Evidence-based assessments and interventions.* New York: John Wiley & Sons, pp. 229-264.

Fulcher, L.C. & Ainsworth, F. (Eds). (2006). *Group care practice with children and young people revisited,* New York: The Haworth Press Inc.

Fulcher, L. C. & Garfat, T. (2008). *Quality care in a family setting: A practical guide for Foster Carers.* Cape Town: Pretext Publishing.

Gannon, B. (2008). *The improbable relationship.* CYC Online, 110 (April). Re-trieved December 31, 2010 from http://www.cyc-net.org/cyc-online/cycol-0408-gannon.html

Garfat, T (1992). Reflections on the journal entries of a residential hunter. *Jour-nal of child and youth care,* 7(3), 59-66.

Garfat, T. (1998). 'The effective child and youth care intervention: A phenomenological inquiry', *Journal of child and youth care,* special edition, vol 12, nos 1-2.

Garfat, T. (1993). 'Developmental stages of child and youth care workers: An interactional perspective', *The international child and youth care network*, issue 24. www.cyc-net.org/cyc-online/cycol-0101-garfat.html (accessed 10th Sept 2011).

Garfat, T. (2003). *Four parts magic: The anatomy of a child and youth care intervention.* Available online from: www.cyc-net.org/cyc-online/cycol-0303-thom.html.

Garfat, T. (2008). The interpersonal in-between: An exploration of relational child and youth care practice. In G. Bellefuelle, & F. Ricks (Eds), *Standing on the precipice: Exploring the creative potential of child and youth care practice.* Edmonton, Alberta, Canada: Grant MacEwan University Press.

Garfat, T. & Fulcher, L. C. (2011). Characteristics of a child and youth care approach, *Journal of relational child and youth care practice*, Vol 24 (1&2), pp. 7-19.

Garfat, T., Fulcher, L. & Digney, J., (Eds). (2012). *The therapeutic use of daily life events.* Cape Town: Pretext Publishing.

Garfat, T. & Fulcher, L. C., (Eds). (2012). *Child and youth care in practice.* Cape Town: Pretext Publishing.

Gharabaghi, K. (2013). Becoming present: The use of daily life events in family work. In T. Garfat, L. C. Fulcher & J. Digney (Eds). Making moments meaningful in child and youth care practice. Cape Town: Pretext, pp. 111-121.

Gilligan, C. (1993). *In a different voice: Psychological theory and women's development.* Cambridge, Massachusetts: Harvard University Press.

Gilligan, R. (2009). *Promoting resilience: A resource guide to working with children in the care system.* London: BAAF.

Guttman, E. (1991). Immediacy in residential child and youth care work: The fusion of experience, self-consciousness, and action. In J. Beker & Z. Eisikovits (Eds)., *Knowledge utilization in residential child and youth care practice,* Washington, DE: Child Welfare League of America, 65-84.

Halverson, A. (1995). The importance of caring and attachment in direct practice with adolescents. *Child and Youth Care Forum.* 24(3), 169.

Heimler, E. (1975). *Survival in Society.* London: Weidenfeld & Nicholson.

Held, V. (2006). *The ethics of care: Personal, political and global.* Oxford: Oxford University Press.

Hewitt, P. (2003). *The looked-after kid: Memoirs from the children's home.* Edinburgh: Mainstream Publishing.

Hoffman, M. L. (2010). *Empathy and moral development: Implications for caring and justice.* Cambridge: Cambridge University Press.

Holland, S. (2009). Looked after children and the ethic of care. *British journal of social work,* 40 (6) 1664-1680.

House of Commons Select Committee (2009). *Children, schools and families, third report: Looked after children.* London: Westminster.

Iacoboni, M. (2008). *Mirroring people: The new science of how we connect with others.* New York: Farrar, Straus and Giroux.

Jack, G. (2010). Place matters: The significance of place attachments for children's well-being, *British journal of social work,* 40(3): 755-71.

Kendrick, A. J. (1999). Residential child care in Scotland: A positive choice? In Barlow, G. (Ed.), *Child care policies and structures: An international perspective* (pp. 3 – 8). Realities & Dreams International Conference on Residential Child Care, 3-6 September 1996, Glasgow: Centre for Residential Child Care.

Kendrick, A. J. (2012). 'What research tells us about residential child care' in M. Davies (Ed) *Social work with children and families.* Basingstoke: MacMillan.

Knapp, M. (2006). The economics of group care practice: A re-appraisal. In L. C. Fulcher & F. Ainsworth, (Eds), *Group care practice with children and young people revisited.* New York: The Haworth Press, pp. 259-284.

Krueger, M. (1988). *Intervention techniques for child-youth care workers.* Washington DC: Child Welfare Leagues of America.

Krueger, M. (2002). (2002). *Moments with youth: Place,* available at http://www.cyc-net.org/cyc-online/cycol-0402-krueger.html.

Laursen, E. K. (2008). Building respectful alliances. *Reclaiming children and youth,* 17(1) 4-9.

Leigh, J. W. (1998). *Communication for cultural competence.* Sydney: Allyn & Bacon.

Long, N. *(2007). The therapeutic power of kindness, available at* www.cyc-net.org/cyc-online/cycol-0307-long.html consulted 24th April 2011.

Lynch, K. Baker, J & Lyons, M. (2009). *Affective equality: Love, care and injustice,* Basingstoke: Palgrave MacMillan.

MacLean, K. (2003). 'Resilience – what it is and how children and young people can be helped to develop it' - In Residence No. 1. Glasgow: Scottish Institute for Residential Child Care.

Maegher, G. & Parton, N. (2004). Modernising social work and the ethics of care. *Social work & society*, 2(1): http://www.socwork.net/sws/article/view/237/412

Maier, H. W. (1975). Learning to learn and living to live in residential treatment, *Child welfare*. 54(6), 406-420.

Maier, H. W. (1978). *Three theories of child development, 3rd Edition*. New York: Harper & Row.

Maier, H. W. (1979). The core of care: Essential ingredients for the development of children at home and away from home, *Child care quarterly*. 8(3):161-173.

Maier, H. W. (1981). Essential components in care and treatment environments for children. In F. Ainsworth & L. C. Fulcher (Eds.) *Group care for children: Concept and issues*. London: Tavistock, pp. 19-70.

Maier, H. W. (1987). *Developmental group care of children and youth: Concepts and practice*. New York: The Haworth Press.

Maier, H. W. (1992). Rhythmicity — A powerful force for experiencing unity and personal connections. *Journal of child and youth care work*. 8, 7-13. Available here: http://www.cyc-net.org/cyc-online/cycol-0704-rhythmicity.html

May, V. (2011). Self, belonging and social change, *Sociology*, 45(3), 363-378.

Mead, M. & Calas, N. (1953). *Primitive heritage*. New York: Ramdom House.

Meagher, G. & Parton, N. (2004). 'Modernising social work and the ethics of care', *Social Work and Society*, accessed 8th Dec 2010.

Milligan, I. (1998). Residential child care is not social work! *Social work education*, Vol. 17, No 3, pp. 275-285.

Moore, C. (1996). *The Kincora scandal: Political cover-up and intrigue in Northern Ireland*. Dublin, Ireland: Marino Press.

Moss, P. & Petrie, P. (2002). *From children's services to children's spaces*. London: Routledge/Falmer.

Munro, E. (2011). *The Munro review of child protection: Final report – A child-centred system*. London, Department of Education.

Noddings, N. (1884). *Caring: A feminine approach to ethics and moral education*, University of California Press, Berkeley.

Noddings, N. (2002). *Starting at home: Caring and social policy*. Berkeley: University of California Press.

Patton, G. C., Goldfeld, S. R., Pieris-Caldwell, I., Bryant, M. & Vimpani, G. V. (2005). A picture of Australia's children, *The medical journal of Australia*. 182(9), 437-438.

Payne, M. (1997). *Modern social work theory, 2nd edition*. London: Macmillan.

Pennell, J. & Burford, G. (1995). *Family group decision making project implementation report, Volume 1*. St John's, Newfoundland: Memorial University of Newfoundland, School of Social Work.

Perry, B. (2002). Childhood experience and the expression of genetic potential: What childhood neglect tells us about nature and nurture. *Brain and mind*, 3, pp.79–100.

Poland, M. & Legge, J. (2005). *Review of New Zealand longitudinal studies*. Wellington: New Zealand Families Commission.

Petrie, P., Boddy, J., Cameron, C., Wigfall, V. & Simon, A. (2006). *Working with children in care: European perspectives*. London: Open University Press.

Phelan, J. (2001). Another look at activities. *Journal of child and youth care*, 14(2), pp 1-7.

Powis, P., Allsopp, M. & Gannon, B. (1989). *So the treatment plan. The child care worker*, 5(5) pp 3-4.

Ramsden, I. (1997). Cultural safety: Implementing the concept. In P. Te Whaiti, M. McCarthy & A. Durie, (Eds.), *Mai i rangiatea: Maori wellbeing and development*. Auckland: Auckland University Press, pp. 113-125.

Ramsden, I. & Spoonley, P. (1993). The cultural safety debate in nursing education in Aotearoa, *New Zealand annual review of education*. (3), 161-174.

Rangihau, J. (1986). *Puao-te-Ata-tu (Daybreak): Report of the ministerial advisory committee on a Maori perspective for the department of social welfare*. Wellington: Department of Social Welfare, Government Printing Office.

Rangihau, J. (1987). "*Beyond crisis*". Keynote address to the first New Zealand conference on social work education, Christchurch: Rehua Marae, University of Canterbury, Department of Social Work.

Ricks, F. (1989). Self-awareness model for training and application in child and youth care. *Journal of child and youth care*, 4(1), 33-42.

Redl, F. (1966). *When we deal with children*. New York: The Free Press.

Redl, F. & Wineman, D. (1957). *The aggressive child*, New York: The Free Press.

Scarr, S. & Eisenberg, M. (1993). Child research: Issues, perspectives and results. *Annual research psychology*, 44, 613-644.

Schofield, G., Moldestad, B., Hojer, I., Ward, E., Skilbred, D., & Young, J. (2010). Managing loss and a threatened identity: Experience of parents of children growing up in foster care, the perspective of their social workers and implications for practice. *British journal of social work*, 40(5), 1-19.

Scott, D., Arney, F., & Vimparni, G. (2010). Think child, think family, think community. In F. Arney & D. Scott (Eds.), *Working with vulnerable families: A partnership approach.* Sydney: Cambridge University Press, 7-28.

Scott, W.R., (1900). *Francis Hutcheson: His life, teaching and position in the history of philosophy*, Cambridge: University Press; p. 234-5.

Scottish Government (2007). *Looked after children and young people: We can and must do better* (www.scotland.gov.uk/Publications/2007/01/15084446/0, accessed 20 February 2008).

Scull, A. (1977). *Decarceration: Community treatment and the deviant – A radical view.* Lexington, Massachusetts: Prentice-Hall.

Seed, P. (1973). Should any child be placed in care? The forgotten great debate 1841-1874. *British journal of social work.* 3(3):321-30.

Sevenhuijsen, S. (1998). *Citizenship and the ethics of care: Feminist considerations on justice, morality, and politics.* London: Routledge.

Sharp, C. (2006). Residential child care and the psychodynamic approach: Is it time to try again? *Scottish journal of residential child care.* 5(1) 46-56.

Shook, E. F. (1985). *Ho'oponopono: Contemporary uses of a Hawaiian problem-solving process.* Honolulu: University of Hawaii Press.

Simon, J. & Smith, L. T. (2001). *A civilising mission? Perceptions and representations of the New Zealand native schools system.* Auckland: Auckland University Press.

Small, R. & Fulcher, L. C. (1985). Teaching Competence in Group Care Practice. In L. C. Fulcher & F. Ainsworth (Eds.) *Group care practice with children.* London: Tavistock Publications, pp. 135-154.

Small, R. W. & Fulcher, L. C. (2005). Developing Social Competencies in Group Care Practice, *Child & Youth Services.* 27(1 & 2), 51-74.

Smart, M. (2010). *Generosity, learning and residential child care*, http://www.goodenoughcaring.com/Journal/Article139.html.

Smith, M. (2009). *Re-thinking residential child care: Positive perspectives.* Bristol: Policy Press.

Smith, M., Fulcher, L. C. & Doran, P. (2013). *Residential child care in practice: Making a difference.* Bristol: Policy Press.

Steckley, L. (2005). Just a game? The therapeutic potential of football. In D. Crimmens & I. Milligan, *Facing the future: Residential child care in the 21st century*. Lyme Regis: Russell House Publishing.

Steckley, L. (2010). Containment and holding environments: Understanding and reducing physical restraint in residential child care. *Children and youth services review*, 32 (1). pp. 120-128.

Steckley, L. & Smith, M. (2011). 'Care ethics in residential child care: A different voice' *Ethics and social welfare 5 (2), pp.181-195*.

Stewart, T. (1997). Historical interfaces between Maori and psychology. In P. Te Whaiti, M. McCarthy & A. Durie (Eds.) *Mai i rangiatea: Maori wellbeing and development*. Auckland: Auckland University Press, pp. 75-95.

Stremmel, A. J. (1993). Introduction: Implications of Vygotsky's sociocultural theory for child and youth care practice. *Child and youth care forum, 22(5) 333–335*.

Stuart, G. (2009). *Principles and practice of psychiatric nursing, 9th ed.* St. Louis, MI: Mosby.

Tait-Rolleston, W., Cairns, T., Fulcher, L. C., Kereopa, H. & Nia Nia, P. (1997). He koha kii – na kui ma, na koro ma: A gift of words from our ancestors, *Social work review*. 9(4), 16-22.

Trieschman, A., Whittaker, J. K. & Brendtro, L. K. (1969). *The other 23 hours: Child-care work with emotionally disturbed children in a therapeutic milieu*, New York: Aldine De Gruiter.

Tronto, J. (1993). *Moral boundaries: A political argument for an ethic of care* London: Routledge.

Tronto, J. & Fisher, B. (1990). Towards a feminist theory of caring, in E. K. Abel & M. Nelson (Eds.) *Circles of care: Work and identity in women's lives*, State University of New York Press, Albany.

VanderVen, K. D. (2008). *Promoting positive development in early childhood: Building blocks for a successful start*. New York: Springer.

VanderVen, K. D. (1985). Activity programming: Its developmental and therapeutic role in group care. In L. C. Fulcher & F. Ainsworth, (Eds) *Group care practice with children*. London: Tavistock Publications, pp. 155-183.

Viner, R. M. & Taylor, B. (2005). Adult health and social outcomes of children who have been in public care: Population-based study, *Pediatrics*. 115(4), 894-899.

Ward, A. (1995). The impact of parental suicide on children and staff in residential care: a case study in the function of containment. *Journal of social work practice.* 9(1) 23-32.

Ward, A. (2010). What is self? The international child and youth care network, accessed here: http://cyc-net.org/cyc-online/cyconline-sep2010-ward.html

Ward, A. & McMahon, L. (1998). *Intuition is not enough: Matching learning with practice in therapeutic child care.* London: Routledge.

Ward, A. (2006). *Working in group care.* (revised second edition) Bristol: Policy Press.

Webster, R. (1998). *The great children's home panic.* Oxford: The Orwell Press.

Whittaker, J. (1979). *Caring for troubled children,* San Fransisco: Jossey-Bass.

White, B. (2009). *Youth justice in practice: Making a difference,* Bristol: Policy Press.

Wilcox, R., Smith, D., Moore, J., Hewitt, A., Allan, G., Walker, H., Ropata, M., Monu, L. & Featherstone, T. (1991). *Family decision making and family group conferences – practitioner's views.* Lower Hutt, New Zealand: Practitioners Publishing.

Winnicott, D. W. (1965). *The family and individual development.* London: Tavistock.